Religious Minorities in Pluralist Societies

Studies in Territorial and Cultural Diversity Governance

VOLUME 19

The titles published in this series are listed at *brill.com/tcdg*

Religious Minorities in Pluralist Societies

Critical Perspectives on the Accommodation of Religious Diversities

Edited by

Roberta Medda-Windischer, Kerstin Wonisch and Alexandra Cosima Budabin

BRILL | NIJHOFF

LEIDEN | BOSTON

Library of Congress Cataloging-in-Publication Data

Names: Medda-Windischer, Roberta, editor. | Wonisch, Kerstin, editor. | Budabin, Alexandra Cosima, editor.
Title: Religious minorities in pluralist societies : critical perspectives on the accommodation of religious diversities / Roberta Medda-Windischer, Kerstin Wonisch and Alexandra Cosima Budabin.
Description: Leiden ; Boston : Brill/Nijhoff, 2024. | Series: Studies in territorial and cultural diversity governance, 2213-2570 ; volume 19 | Includes index.
Identifiers: LCCN 2023040261 (print) | LCCN 2023040262 (ebook) | ISBN 9789004446809 (hardcover) | ISBN 9789004446816 (ebook)
Subjects: LCSH: Religious minorities–Legal status, laws. | Religious pluralism. | Multiculturalism–Law and legislation. | Religion and law. | Pluralism.
Classification: LCC K3242 .R45 2024 (print) | LCC K3242 (ebook) | DDC 344/.096–dc23/eng/20230926
LC record available at https://lccn.loc.gov/2023040261
LC ebook record available at https://lccn.loc.gov/2023040262

Typeface for the Latin, Greek, and Cyrillic scripts: "Brill". See and download: brill.com/brill-typeface.

ISSN 2213-2570
ISBN 978-90-04-44680-9 (hardback)
ISBN 978-90-04-44681-6 (e-book)
DOI 10.1163/9789004446816

This book is printed on acid-free paper and produced in a sustainable manner.

Contents

Notes on Contributors

Francesco Alicino
is Full Professor in Public Law and Religion and Constitutional Law, Constitutional Law, Law of the Third Sector, and Immigration Law at LUM University. He is also a member at the Italian Council for the relationship with Muslim communities at the Italian Minister of the Interior.

Alexandra Cosima Budabin
is Senior Researcher at the Eurac Research Institute for Minority Rights (Bolzano-Bozen – Italy) where she researches transnational advocacy around minority rights, cultural heritage, conflict, and security.

Alessandro Ferrari
is Full Professor at the University of Insubria where he directs the Center for Research "REligione, Diritto ed Economia nello Spazio Mediterraneo" (REDESM). His research looks at religious freedom in Europe and Mediterranean spaces.

Silvio Ferrari
is Distinguished Fellow at the Bruno Kessler Foundation in Trento and has taught law and religion and comparative law of religions for many years at the Universities of Parma, Turin, Milan, Leuven and Strasbourg. He is honorary president of the International Consortium for Law and Religion Studies (ICLARS).

Kiryl Kascian
is a Board Member at the International Centre for Ethnic and Linguistic Diversity Studies, Prague. His primary research areas are constitutional law, minority rights, political representation and electoral behaviour with a focus on Central and Eastern Europe.

Elham Manea
is a *Privatdozentin* at the Political Science Institute, University of Zurich. Her research focuses on countries of the Arabian Peninsula, Gender & Women under Muslim Laws, and Islamism. She has published academic and nonfiction books in English, German, and Arabic.

Roberta Medda-Windischer
is Senior Researcher and Group Leader for *Equality and Diversity in Integrated Societies* at the Eurac Research Institute for Minority Rights (Bolzano/Bozen – Italy) where her research focuses on international law, minority issues, human rights, diversity governance and minority protection.

Anna Parrilli
is Post-doctoral research fellow in comparative public law at the University of Verona. Her research focuses on state secularism, legal pluralism, Muslim and Jewish law, and minority rights.

Kyriaki Topidi
is Senior Researcher and head of the research cluster on "Culture & Diversity" at the European Centre for Minority Issues. Her research interests focus on diversity management, minority protection rights and mechanisms, and human rights law.

Christos Tsevas
is an Adjunct Lecturer in International Human Rights and Refugee Law at the Democritus University of Thrace. He has worked as an asylum expert with UNHCR, ICMC and the Greek Asylum Appeals Committees. His research focuses on public, human rights, refugee and migration law.

Hanna Vasilevich
is Chair of the Board of the International Centre for Ethnic and Linguistic Diversity Studies, Prague. Her research interests include state ideology and propaganda, identity issues, conflict resolution, interethnic relations, national and religious minorities.

Avishalom Westreich
is Associate Professor at the College of Law and Business in Ramat Gan, Israel, and a Research Fellow at the Kogod Research Center for Contemporary Jewish Thought at the Shalom Hartman Institute, Jerusalem. His research focuses on modern family law and the Talmudic laws of tort.

Elimelech (Melech) Westreich
is a professor (Emeritus) of Law at the Tel Aviv University Faculty of Law and was a visiting professor at the University of Chicago Law School. He has written many articles on Jewish law, especially on family topics, commercial instruments, and bioethics.

Kerstin Wonisch
has worked as Researcher at the Eurac Research Institute for Minority Rights (Bolzano-Bozen – Italy) where her research focused on the rights of religious minorities and the governance of religious diversity, Islamic pluralism, gender and human rights.

Introduction: Squaring the Circle: Critical Reflections on Religious Minorities, Diversity Governance and Pluralist Societies

Roberta Medda-Windischer, Kerstin Wonisch, Alexandra Cosima Budabin

1 Introduction

The accommodation of religious diversity in contemporary pluralist societies is undoubtedly amongst the most salient issues on today's political agenda, not least due to the challenges posed by migration. Although economic actors and political decision-makers generally recognize immigrant communities' useful contributions to the labour force and their positive impact on demographic structures amid a steadily ageing population, the presence of large immigrant communities poses manifold challenges regarding religious and cultural differences, protection of individual and group rights, and preservation of social cohesion and unity. A subject of considerable debate is how to reconcile the demands of religious and cultural diversity alongside political unity, that is, how to create a political community that is cohesive, stable, and satisfies the legitimate aspirations of minorities.[1]

These debates capture interactions not only between majority and historical minority religious communities within countries, but also interaction with 'new' religious minorities, namely groups stemming from more recent migration flows. The terms historical, traditional, autochthonous minorities – the so-called 'old minorities' – refer to communities whose members have a distinct language, culture or religion compared to the rest of the population, and became minorities as a consequence of a re-drawing of international borders and their settlement area.[2] This often meant that these minority groups

1 J. Marko, "Ethnopolitics: The Challenge for Human and Minority Rights Protection", in C. Corradetti (ed.), *Philosophical Dimensions of Human Rights: Some Contemporary Views* (Dordrecht, Heidelberg, Springer, 2012); C. Joppke, *The Role of the State in Cultural Integration: Trends, Challenges, and Ways Ahead* (Washington, DC, Migration Policy Institute, 2012).

2 W. Kymlicka, *Multicultural Odysseys: Navigating the New International Politics of Diversity* (Oxford, Oxford University Press, 2009); R. Medda-Windischer, *Old and New Minorities: Reconciling Diversity and Cohesion. A Human Rights Model for Minority Integration* (Nomos, Baden-Baden, 2008).

DOI:10.1163/9789004446816_002

changed from the sovereignty of one country to another or did not achieve, for various reasons, statehood of their own and therefore form part of a larger country or several countries. Instead, the 'new minorities' refer to groups formed by individuals and families, who have left their original homeland and emigrated to another country generally for economic and, sometimes, also for political reasons.[3] The 'new minorities' encompass not only recent migrants, but also the influx that began in Europe a few decades ago.[4] This category includes not only the first generation of migrants, but also their descendants, extending to include second and third generations of individuals with a background of migration.[5] Many of them are born in the country of immigration and thus they cannot objectively or subjectively be subsumed under the category of 'migrants'. The presence of new and old minorities has led to increases in pluralism with effects on state-society relations, particularly where religious minorities are concerned.

State responses to cultural, linguistic, ethnic, and religious diversities as well as the institutional arrangements to accommodate said pluralism can be analyzed from different perspectives. Scholars, mainly from the fields of comparative constitutional law and the social and political sciences, have identified a variety of models for accommodating minority claims and cohesion.[6] This

3 R. Medda-Windischer and K. Crepaz, "Fundamental Rights and Non-EU Minorities: From an Ambiguous Concept to an Integrated Society?", in T. H. Malloy and B. Vizi (eds.), *Research Handbook on Minority Politics in the European Union* (London, Edward Elgar Publ., 2022); R. Medda-Windischer, *Old and New Minorities: Reconciling Diversity and Cohesion. A Human Rights Model for Minority Integration, supra.*

4 J. Marko, "Ethnopolitics: The Challenge for Human and Minority Rights Protection", *supra*; C. Joppke, *The Role of the State in Cultural Integration: Trends, Challenges, and Ways Ahead, supra.*

5 It must be acknowledged that the term 'new minorities' in general is subject to difficulties and criticism not only because it encompasses an enormous variation of situations, but also because it seems to imply that migrants and individuals with a background of migration are in a 'minority' position, such that their status is 'minoritized'. On the contrary, the term underlines the diversity accompanying these individuals and groups, which requires protection and promotion, if desired. The use of the term is intended to refer to 'distinct' groups, and it by no means implies a weakening of their status. Rather, it aims to offer additional legal tools with which to respond to their specific needs for protection.

6 J. Marko, "The Law and Politics of Diversity Management: A Neo-Institutional Approach", (2006) 6 *European Yearbook of Minority Issues* 251–280; R. Bauböck, *Transnational Citizenship* (London, Edward Elgar Publ., 1994); B. Parekh, "Integrating Minorities in a Multicultural Society" in U. K. Preuss and F. Requejo (eds.), *European Citizenship, Multiculturalism, and the State* (Baden-Baden, Nomos, 1998); T.H. Malloy, "Conceptualizing Democratic Diversity Management for Multicultural Societies: Theories of Society and Law", (2008) 6 *European Yearbook of Minority Issues* 281–306; J. Hochschild *et al.* (eds.), *Outsiders no More? Models of Immigrant Political Incorporation* (Oxford, Oxford University Press, 2013); C. Joppke, *The*

has meant combining studies conducted on the accommodation of religious diversities in religious communities stemming from more recent migration flows with analysis of so-called historical long-standing 'old minorities'. State responses to diversity and cohesion can be described as ranging from *exclusionist* and *assimilationist* models to *pluralist* approaches. The two former policies deny minority groups either civic standing or participation in the polity, as well as force minorities to give up their identity in order to be integrated into mainstream society.[7] In contrast, the pluralist model does not condition integration and political belonging on cultural conformity. This model is based on the assumption that, on the one hand, the recognition, protection, and promotion of minorities, in particular religious ones, should constitute an integral component of a State's constitution and appear among its fundamental values. On the other hand, in both the private and public realms, minority and majority communities are expected to share some core universal principles such as human rights, democracy, rule of law, gender equality, and minority rights.[8]

Consequently, any effective mechanism for the governance of religious diversity is based first and foremost on the protection of the right to identity and the principle of equality, and also on the will of States to accept international as well as regional obligations, especially in the field of human and minority rights.[9] However, for traditional religious communities and long-standing religious minorities, there are well-established standards at the national and international level that have been traditionally conceived and applied to long-standing minorities such as the CoE Framework Convention on the Protection of National Minorities and the UN Declaration on the Rights of Persons Belonging to National or Ethnic, Religious and Linguistic Minorities.

Role of the State in Cultural Integration: Trends, Challenges, and Ways Ahead, supra; D. Pero and J. Solomos, "Migrant Politics and Mobilization: Exclusion, Engagements, Incorporation", (2010) 33(1) *Ethnic and Racial Studies*; R. Hasmath, *Managing Ethnic Diversity. Meanings and Practices from an International Perspective* (Toronto, University of Toronto, 2011); D. Rodriguez-Garcìa, "Beyond Assimilation and Multiculturalism: A Critical Review of the Debate on Managing Diversity", (2010) 11 *International Migration and Integration*; F. Barker, *Nationalism, Identity and the Governance of Diversity. Old Politics, New Arrivals* (London, Palgrave Macmillan, 2015); R. Medda-Windischer, "Integration of New and Old Minorities: Beyond a Janus-faced Perspective", (2017) 14 *European Yearbook of Minority Issues*.

7 J. Marko, *Autonomie und Integration* (Vienna, Cologne, Graz, Böhlau, 1995), at 531.

8 R. Medda-Windischer, *Old and New Minorities, supra*; R. Medda-Windischer, "Integration of New and Old Minorities" *supra*; A. Xanthaki, "Multiculturalism and International Law: Discussing Universal Standards", (2010) 32 *Human Rights Quarterly*, 21–48.

9 P. Thornberry, *International Law and the Rights of Minorities* (Oxford, Clarendon Press, 1991), at 392.

Yet, despite positions in favour of an extensive interpretation,[10] it is still open to debate whether these legal provisions are applicable to religious communities stemming from more recent migration flows.

Minority rights, along with human rights, represent important tools for the integration of minorities, particularly the integration of new minority groups, as they create a legal framework in which minorities can see their claims recognized within the limits of the legal provisions enshrined in the texts of relevant international instruments. Moreover, this legal framework is composed of rights and freedoms, but also of limitations and restrictions, thereby providing a guarantee that minority claims will not exceed certain limits. In this way, minority claims for diversity and the more general concern for unity, cohesion, security, and public order can be accommodated in the framework of an 'institutionalized' dialogue in which national and supranational bodies, in cooperation with one another, act as objective and neutral third parties. Clearly, this dialogue can only succeed if all parties involved have an open and receptive attitude and a willingness to reach common solutions.[11]

Therefore, in our diversified times, a critical reflection on both traditional long-standing minorities and new communities stemming from more recent migration flows and the institutional accommodations, legal frameworks and policies conceived by and/or for them is relevant and indispensable. Such policies will be necessary for fostering integrated societies, which are based on the recognition of dignity in the various lifestyle choices and traditions and in the context of equitable access to rights as well as on fair and non-discriminatory sharing of resources, goods, and services. In particular, the circumstances around how new as well as long-standing religious minority communities

---

10 See for example UN Special Rapporteur on Minority Issues, *Effective Promotion of the Declaration on the Rights of Persons Belonging to National or Ethnic, Religious and Linguistic Minorities*, Report to the UN General Assembly, A/74/160, 15 July 2019; R. Medda-Windischer (2017); T. Jacob-Owens, "Immigration and Multicultural Citizenship in Europe: Insights from the Framework Convention for the Protection of National Minorities", (2021) 29(1) *International Journal on Minority and Group Rights*, 167–197; K. Crepaz, *"Old" and "new" minorities – Regional synergies, differences and perspectives*, Project Report: MinMig – Accommodating Linguistic, Religious and Cultural Diversity Through a Comparative Analysis of Minorities' and Migrants' Claims,(Bolzano, Eurac Research, 2021). For a critical perspective, see A. Xanthaki, "Against Integration, for Human Rights", (2016) 20(6) *The International Journal of Human Rights* 815–838. The author argues that the current integration narrative and policies limit human rights and dilute the protection that old and new minorities enjoy under international human rights law.

11 D. L. Eck, "What is Pluralism?", (2006) The Pluralism Project, Harvard University, accessed September 20, 2023, available at: http://pluralism.org/what-is-pluralism/.

make claims for accommodations on grounds of religion raise questions concerning freedom of religion and secularism, the accommodation of religious diversity, social cohesion, integration and citizenship. Consequently, these questions trigger the need for analysis of the place of religion in secular societies, not in the least as growing religious diversity is seeking recognition in the public sphere. This recognition challenges the notion of a radical or 'militant' secular Europe,[12] a notion that to some scholars neglects historical evolution as well as contemporary struggles on the meaning and boundary of religion and politics.

2 The Relationship between Secularism and the Governance of Religious Diversity

In this regard, it has to be acknowledged that discourses on secularism and on related terms and concepts have undergone various changes since the 19th century. During the Enlightenment period, secularism was primarily equated with the arrival of 'civilisation', a progressive alternative to 'religion' that was to be separated from the State. Today, however, secularism as a concept serves a particular political narrative about immigration and the diversification of society as much as it is equated with Western beliefs and practices as opposed to Islam.[13] Nevertheless, in the 19th century, sets of oppositions such as 'political' and 'religious' were deemed to address the nation vs. institutionalized religion. State vs. Church was soon to be followed by the separation of market and politics and of 'public' and 'private'. Such divisions continued well into the 20th century. Yet, since the end of the Cold War and in particular the events surrounding 9/11, the meaning of political and religious has changed to become heavily associated with liberal democracy vs. Islam. A new discourse of secularism emerged that replaced a Soviet communist threat to social order with the threat of Islam.[14] In contrast, one could argue, in many ways Judo-Christianity evolved as a synonym for democracy, and thus, political secularism poses an

12 R. Medda-Windischer, "Militant or Pluralist Secularism? The European Court of Human Rights Facing Religious Diversity", (2017) 45(3–4) *Religion, State and Society.*

13 J. W. Scott, *Sex & Secularism* (New Jersey, Princeton University Press, 2018), at 10–14.

14 K. Wonisch, "Religion, Gender and Law: A Tense Relationship", in J. Marko *et al.* (eds.), *Religious Diversity, State and Law* (Leiden, Brill, 2023); J.W. Scott, *Sex & Secularism supra.*

obstacle to religious pluralism and multicultural equality in a democratic society.[15]

Liberal-democratic States are in general rather hesitant to adopt institutional pluralism. Hence, the legal status of religions range from no special treatment to minimal and even wide and deep legal recognition and regulation. In this regard, scholarship commonly upholds three basic models predominant among European States: the State-Church, separation and cooperation systems. A close constitutional link between a particular church/religion and the government characterizes the State-Church system, whereas in a separation system, based on constitutional provisions, religion has no place in the public sphere of a State. Finally, the cooperation system, based on a constitutional separation of religion and State, emphasizes cooperation between them in the shape of formal or informal pacts between institutions of government and religious organizations.[16] In their chapter, Kiryl Kascian and Hanna Vasilevich show how collaboration between the church and State on migration accommodation policies in Russia offers an example of a dominant religious authority amidst a diverse religious landscape. Meanwhile, Francesco Alicino shows how the bilateralism principle governing Church-State relations that once prevailed in Italy is inadequate in light of religious pluralism.

Regardless of the prevailing model regulating relationships between religious communities and States, most States with liberal-democratic constitutions accommodate religious diversity by referring to the right to freedom of religion. Yet, not all States grant special group-differentiated rights. Accordingly, the individual, being a citizen of the State and member of a religious minority group, is at least able to claim the right to equality as well as the right to freedom of association under the State's law.[17] The claim for an institutionalization of difference, namely for the inclusion of religious minority identities as a public identity in the institutional framework of a State, *per se*, does not contradict the underlying values of democracy, namely justice and

15 T. Modood, "Rethinking political secularism: the multiculturalist challenge", (2021) 55(1) *Patterns of Prejudice*, 115–124; T. Modood, "Moderate Secularism and Multiculturalism", (2009) 29(1) *Politics*, at 71.

16 See N. Doe, *Law and religion in Europe. A comparative introduction*. Ed. 1. (Oxford, Oxford Univ. Press, 2011), at 28; see also G. Robbers, "State and Church in the European Union" in G. Robbers (ed.), *State and Church in the European Union*, 2. ed. (Baden-Baden, Nomos, 2005), at 577; and H. Kalb, Potz, R., and Schinkele, B., *Religionsrecht* (Wien, WUV-Univ.-Verl, 2003), at 15.

17 A. Krishnaswami, *Study of Discrimination in the Matter of Religious Rights and Practices*, E/CN.4/Sub.2/200/Rev. 1 (New York, United Nations, 1960), at 46–50.

equality.[18] The balancing of these claims is demonstrated in the chapters by Alessandro Ferrari, Kyriaki Topidi and Christos Tsevas and, with a critical perspective by Elham Manea, through examples looking at Italy, Greece, and the United Kingdom.

Cultural and religious diversity is widely defended across different liberal theories of multiculturalism as well as in theories of identities. However, a more democratic, universal approach towards institutional pluralism is missing, partially due to a static understanding of secularism deeply influencing laws and policies. Subsequently, religious communities, long-standing and newcomers alike, face considerable pressure to accept the predominant version of secularism and Church-State relationships.[19] Admittedly, States are required to be neutral in relation to *conceptions of the good*,[20] yet organized religion still plays an important role in terms of social well-being, national ceremonies, cultural heritage, and in the formation of a national identity. Therefore, in acknowledging the fact that the public domain is not morally neutral and public order not religiously, ethnically or culturally blind, religious minority groups legitimately demand to have their distinctive identities publicly recognized[21] instead of facing assimilation.[22]

Modernity did not lead to a disappearance of faith, thus it is no longer a secular age – at least in its radical or 'militant' form – but one of religious diversities, marked by the co-existence of traditions, practices and faith, each of which demands visibility and recognition.[23] As the contibutions in this volume reveal here, many diversities are located within religions and there is slow recognition by States to the heterogenous practices and legal claims by minorities within religions. Since democracy does not essentially depend on a strict separation of religion and State relationships – as for instance in cooperation systems – forms of synergies and cooperation are possible and

18 T. Modood and Kastoryano, R., "Secularism and the Accommodation of Muslims in Europe" in T. Modood *et al.*(eds.), *Multiculturalism, Muslims and Citizenship: A European Approach* (New York, Routledge, 2006), at 162.

19 B. S. Turner, *Religion and Modern Society: Citizenship, Secularisation and the State* (Cambridge, Cambridge University Press, 2011).

20 J. Rawls, *A Theory of Justice* (Cambridge, Harvard University Press, 1971) and J. Rawls, *Political Liberalism* (New York, Columbia University Press, 1993).

21 C. Taylor and Gutmann, A., (eds.), *Multiculturalism and "the politics of recognition". An essay* (Princeton, NJ, Princeton University Press, 1992).

22 V. Bader, "The Governance of Islam in Europe: The Perils of Modelling", (2007) 33(6) *Journal of Ethnic and Migration Studies* 871–886.

23 V. Bader, "Post-Secularism or Liberal-Democratic Constitutionalism?", (2012) 5(1) *Erasmus Law Review* 5–26, at 18.

secularism should no longer be understood as an *a priori* category. In an age of religious diversities, secularism should rather be understood as a category through which the phenomenon of politically and legally negotiated roles and places of religion in public is addressed, as underlined by Anna Parrilli and Avishalom and Melichem Westreich in their contributions on Israel.

In this volume, we bring together a set of scholarly contributions that seek to "square the circle", by confronting the question of how to reconcile the demands of religious diversity and political unity, that is, how to create a political community that is cohesive, stable and satisfies the legitimate aspirations of religious minorities. This dilemma has been the subject of considerable discussion ever since the rise of the modern State, and particularly during the past few decades and more recently with greater urgency due to migration flows. The following contributions demonstrate how policies that seek to reconcile social cohesion, unity and diversity are confronted with a veritable minefield of dilemmas. Societies need to evolve their own appropriate legal and institutional frameworks suited to their history, traditions, demographic composition, political requirements, and unique characteristics, but which principles should guide their decisions? Fostering a sense of common belonging, unity and respect for religious diversity are important principles, but to what extent can they be achieved and, at the same time, combined? This is a central challenge in modern societies because seeking to accommodate minority claims implies the need to look for a balance between unity and separation, cohesion and respect for diversity. If one opts solely for unity, the risk is assimilation and the disappearance of minorities as distinct groups; if one chooses only diversity, the result can be the cultural 'ghettoization' of minority communities with their consequent separation and marginalization from society. These are questions authors of this volume seek to address in their contributions, drawing on cases from across Europe to the Middle East.

3 Outline of the Volume

Kyriaki Topidi concentrates her analysis on the Muslim-inhabited region of Western Thrace in Greece as a unique scenario of State-recognized implementation of a plural legal system in Europe. Topidi notes that, in general, plural legal systems have manifold problems ranging from extreme variance within religious legal orders loaded by intense asymmetries of power to the instrumentalization of religion for political or moral purposes, including the recognition of morally intolerable values (e.g. gender inequality). For Topidi, the risk of this fluid norm development track is the erosion of common values and shared forms of citizenship and the fragmentation of the public sphere. Despite the historical interaction with so-called 'Old Islam' – referring to the Muslim minority in Western Thrace – Topidi acknowledges that there is still resistance from the Greek State to providing religious freedoms to the 'New Islam' (i.e. immigrants). Topidi concludes that the 'new normal' emerging in scenarios of overlapping and conflicting legal orders – porous legality or legal porosity as defined by Sousa Santos – requires States to reconfigure their role – from main lawmakers to mediators. And she notes that in the absence of a formalized public engagement framework for all sides concerned, there remain risks of persistent normative conflict and societal disruptions and disorder.

The nexus between historical minority communities, such as the Muslim community in Thrace, legal pluralism, migration and of the general human and minority rights framework informs the chapter of *Christos Tsevas*. Based on the ECtHR judgment *Molla Sali vs Greece,* Tsevas investigates whether the EctHR could set standards in the governance of a religious diversity equation that includes the migrant and refugee communities in the European human rights context. States need to consider the religious identity of refugees and migrants as a fundamental element that shapes society's identity and impacts the role of the State. Tsevas notes that the legal side of refugees' relations, as enshrined in integration or inclusion contexts, is necessary to fulfil their rights, especially in the family law context. In his analysis of *the Molla Sali* judgment, Tsevas draws our attention to the impact that the interaction between State law, the ECHR and other human rights instruments has on the role of Islamic law in a minority context. Muslim communities, like others, have to safeguard an adjustment of constitutional norms with evolving norms on human rights and minority rights. In this regard, a comparative law approach as well as a legal framework that governs the existence and application of Islamic law in a European context is important. However, Tsevas suggests a shift from the focus on State-Church relations towards State neutrality with the need to take "local sensibilities" into account in order to consider the "very essence of freedom of religion or belief". Part of this paradigm shift towards legal pluralism in line with human rights standards could be, according to Tsevas, an interaction between "different normative systems" and national, European or international human rights coupled with a "translation" of religious norms into constitutions and European Human Rights documents.

Elham Manea's main focus of investigation is legal pluralism in the UK – soft legal pluralism as she defines it – through the analysis of Sharia Councils and Muslim Arbitration Councils. Manea discusses the main criticisms against these religious bodies, with a particular focus on family disputes, domestic violence and cases of child abuse. Criticisms range from experiences of sexist and misogynistic discrimination to corruption to petty politics and lack of transparency and accountability resulting in increased distrust towards faith-based organizations as institutions operating for the best interests of women and vulnerable individuals within Muslim communities. Manea notes that the approach of the UK authorities of 'looking the other way', as part of the multicultural maxim of group difference and the collective cultural rights of others, has been based on the fear of interfering in the religious domain of minorities as the issue is considered 'sensitive'. Manea continues by noting that, as the fascination with multiculturalism as a State policy started to wane, the sensitivity shifted to a fear of providing the far right with fuel for xenophobia. Manea concludes by noting that these criticisms must be taken very seriously into account when considering legal pluralism as an instrument for resolving conflicts and drawing a balance between diversity and equality.

In a context in which legal pluralism flourishes, as is the case in Israel, the place, changing relationships, and jurisdiction of religious courts certainly shape society. *Avishalom Westreich & Melech (Elimelech) Westreich* therefore discuss in their contribution the dynamic relationships between rabbinical courts and civil courts, and their influence on Jewish Israeli society. In this regard, the question of jurisdiction is a crucial one that defines the limits of religious courts. However, as the authors demonstrate, the complex Israeli family law system does not provide for the sole application of Jewish laws in rabbinical courts or for civil courts to only apply secular civil law. Rather, both court systems can find themselves in contexts in which they have to apply the laws and norms of their respective counterpart, with religious courts to include liberal aspects in their interpretation of Jewish religious law that originated from the work of secular civil courts. As the authors demonstrate, the impact of rabbinical court decisions ultimately depends not only on the jurisdiction of respective courts, but on the involvement, integration and influence of civil law and civil courts on the religious legal framework. Nonetheless, despite the fact that there is an ongoing process to limit and reduce the jurisdiction and the influence of rabbinical courts on Jewish Israeli society, they are still of great relevance to Israeli society.

The contribution by *Anna Parrilli* examines challenges the non-Orthodox Jewish minority faces in the Israeli *millet* system in matters of personal status and citizenship, not the least as the coexistence of legal pluralism, secular and religious courts and the partial establishment of Orthodox Judaism in State institutions results in citizens finding themselves "trapped in their ethno-religious communities". This communitarian paradigm, as explained by Parrilli, not only constructs citizenship along ethno-religious lines, but ignores the inherent intra-religious pluralism. Given that religious communities enjoy a certain degree of organizational and jurisdictional autonomy in matters of personal status, the application of Orthodox interpretations of Jewish law by religious courts thus triggered the establishment of private religious courts. As Parrilli states, this does not only impact on the already complex relationships and components of the Israeli judicial system and enable "forum shopping" between religious and secular courts, but also impacts the right of citizens to equality before the law and their right to freedom of and from religion.

In the quest to address the challenges of today's pluralism, *Francesco Alicino* investigates the Italian system of Churches-State bilateral legislation with a special focus on atheism and agnosticism as well as Muslim communities. Alicino notes that the system of bilateral legislation is attractive to some confessional organizations, while it creates unfavourable distinctions for others, including non-religious bodies. Indeed, the bilateral principle is based on the discretionary power of a Government that can decide not only whether an organization is defined as representing a religion and is eligible for the benefits of bilateral legislation, but also whether to initiate negotiations with any religious groups as this decision largely depends – as underlined by the Italian Constitutional Court – on the unpredictable reality of national and international political relations. For Alicino, the use of this discretionary power might result in discriminatory distinctions between denominations with a formal agreement with the Italian State (*intese*) and those without such forms of agreement. In conclusion, Alicino notes that the bilateralism principle does not conform with the current Italian society, which, due to immigration and globalization, is no longer a monocultural society. Accordingly, Alicino concludes by saying that the bilateralism principle can be perfectly applied when referring to traditional Judeo-Christian denominations, but this method can hardly be considered for other religious groups.

In his chapter, *Alessandro Ferrari* focuses on the 'Islamic question' that in Italy, according to Ferrari, seems to be a 'hibernating reality' contradicting the fast-moving social dynamics and reflecting a broad 'continental involution' in the protection of religious freedom. Ferrari notes that, for the Muslim question in Italy, there is an attraction to the 'Catholic paradigm' based on a 'unitary Islamic representation' that contradicts the variations existing within Islamic denominations that are also strongly intertwined with and influenced by foreign entities. Ferrari recalls the unlimited political discretion and ambiguous bureaucracy behind the recognition in Italy of religious denominations' legal personality. In this regard, Ferrari analyses the requirements relating to the asset of the association and to the criterion of 'numerosity' coupled, at times, with the inertia of the public authorities. By noting that the Muslim communities in Italy have so far preferred a generic private appearance rather than a specific recognition, Ferrari questions whether the problem does not lie, in the end, with the right to religious freedom as such. Quoting Silvio Ferrari – the author suggests the need to "de-Islamise" the Islamic question to grasp the similarities between this and all other religious experiences whose needs had already been taken into consideration – and often positively satisfied – by European legal systems.

Kiryl Kascian and *Hanna Vasilevich* dedicate their chapter, written before the Russian military campaign against Ukraine, to the analysis of interactions of the Russian Orthodox Church (ROC) with the Russian State as well as its role in society and as an agent that directly contributes to the implementation of Russia's migration policies. As the authors point out, the role of the ROC in Russian society significantly increased after the collapse of the USSR with the ROC ignoring the multi-confessional character of the Russian society to actively promote Russian civilizational nationalism by combining religious and ethnocultural aspects. Although the State is secular in nature, it closely cooperates with the ROC in areas such as the integration of labour migrants and returned compatriots. In this regard, the authors analyse textbook material used by the ROC in their work with migrants and argue the ROC not only ignores the ethnic and confessional diversity of Russia's society but fosters conformity with the existing cultural order. Consequently, this approach impedes on the rights of migrants to preserve their identity and traditions.

Analyzing the various contributions of this volume, *Silvio Ferrari* discusses "some thematic knots that in different forms underlie many of them". At the outset of his conclusions, Ferrari notes that only a balanced triangular combination between freedom, equality and diversity can lead us toward an integrated society, namely a society that, as described by the editors of the volume, recognizes the dignity of different lifestyle choices and traditions while ensuring equitable access to rights and resources. On legal pluralism and the freedom to choose between equality and diversity, notwithstanding the assumption that the limit to the State's recognition of legal pluralism lies with inalienable rights, he warns us that this category of rights must be handled with caution, as in the case of women's self-determination. Ferrari persuasively argues that, in this case, the solution lies in women's empowerment through long-term processes of cultural, social and economic promotion rather than in strengthening women's protection through legislative interventions.

Ferrari suggests that the provision of secular alternatives to religious choices allowed by the legal system is crucial for creating a sustainable legal pluralism that respects the right to freedom of thought, conscience, and religion. He argues that the agreement system between the State and religious organizations should be adapted to new needs and to limit discretionary power in deciding whether and when to enter into agreements. Ferrari concludes by noting that a new discrepancy has been created between those religious minorities that have entered an agreement with the State and other minorities without agreements, and this 'new fault line' should be addressed to avoid tensions and further inequalities.

Bibliography

Bader, V., "The Governance of Islam in Europe. The Perils of Modelling", (2007) 33(6) *Journal of Ethnic and Migration Studies* 871–886.

Bader, V., "Post-Secularism or Liberal-Democratic Constitutionalism?", (2012) 5(1) *Erasmus Law Review* 5–26.

Barker, F., *Nationalism, Identity and the Governance of Diversity. Old Politics, New Arrivals* (London, Palgrave Macmillan, 2015).

Bauböck, R., *Transnational Citizenship* (London, Edward Elgar Publ., 1994).

Cesari, J., "Introduction" in J. Cesari and J. Casanova (eds.), *Islam, Gender and Democracy in Comparative Perspective* (Oxford, Oxford University Press, 2017).

Crepaz, K., *"Old" and "New" Minorities – Regional synergies, differences and perspectives,* Project Report: MinMig – Accommodating Linguistic, Religious and Cultural Diversity Through a Comparative Analysis of Minorities' and Migrants' Claims (Bolzano, Eurac Research, 2011), accessed September 20, 2023, https://zenodo.org/record/5656645#.YsF5GoRBw2w.

Doe, N., *Law and religion in Europe. A comparative introduction*, Ed. 1 (Oxford, Oxford Univ. Press, 2011).

Eck, D.L., "What is Pluralism?" (2006) The Pluralism Project, Harvard University, accessed September 20, 2023, http://pluralism.org/what-is-pluralism/.

Ferrari, S., "The Protection and Promotion of Religious Minorities in the EU Countries. a Perspective from Law and Religion" in *European Consortium for Church and State Research, the Legal Status of Old and New Religious Minorities in the European Union* (Granada, Comares, 2021).

Hasmath, R., *Managing Ethnic Diversity. Meanings and Practices from an International Perspective* (Toronto, University of Toronto, 2011).

Hochschild, J. *et al.* (eds.), *Outsiders no More? Models of Immigrant Political Incorporation* (Oxford, Oxford University Press, 2013).

Jacob-Owens, T., "Immigration and Multicultural Citizenship in Europe: Insights from the Framework Convention for the Protection of National Minorities", (2021) 29(1) *International Journal on Minority and Group Rights* 167–197.

Joppke, C., *The Role of the State in Cultural Integration: Trends, Challenges, and Ways Ahead* (Washington, DC, Migration Policy Institute, 2012).

Kalb, H., Potz, R., and Schinkele, B., *Religionsrecht* (Wien, WUV-Univ.-Verl, 2003).

Kymlicka, W., *Multicultural Odysseys: Navigating the New International Politics of Diversity* (Oxford, Oxford University Press, 2009).

Krishnaswami, A., *Study of Discrimination in the Matter of Religious Rights and Practices*, E/CN.4/Sub.2/200/Rev. 1 (United Nations, New York, 1960).

Malloy, T. H., "Conceptualizing Democratic Diversity Management for Multicultural Societies: Theories of Society and Law", (2008) 6 *European Yearbook of Minority Issues* 281–306.

Marko, J., *Autonomie und Integration* (Vienna, Cologne, Graz, Böhlau, 1995).

Marko, J., "The Law and Politics of Diversity Management: A Neo-Institutional Approach", (2006) 6 *European Yearbook of Minority Issues* 251–280.

Marko, J., "Ethnopolitics: The Challenge for Human and Minority Rights Protection" in C. Corradetti (ed.), *Philosophical Dimensions of Human Rights: Some Contemporary Views* (Dordrecht, Heidelberg, Springer, 2012).

Medda-Windischer, R., *Old and New Minorities: Reconciling Diversity and Cohesion. a Human Rights Model for Minority Integration* (Nomos, Baden-Baden, 2008).

Medda-Windischer, R., "Integration of New and Old Minorities: Beyond a Janus-faced Perspective", (2017) 14 *European Yearbook of Minority Issues*.

Medda-Windischer, R., "Militant or Pluralist Secularism? the European Court of Human Rights Facing Religious Diversity", (2017) 45(3–4) *Religion, State and Society*.

Medda-Windischer, R., "The Nexus of Old and New Minorities" in T. H. Malloy and C. Boulter, (eds.), *Minority Issues in Europe: New Ideas and Approaches*, Vol. 2 (Berlin, Frank & Timme, 2019).

Medda-Windischer, R. and Crepaz, K., "Fundamental Rights and Non-EU Minorities: from an Ambiguous Concept to an Integrated Society?", in T. H. Malloy and B. Vizi (eds.), *Research Handbook on Minority Politics in the European Union* (London, Edward Elgar Publ., 2022).

Modood, T., "Muslims, Religious Equality and Secularism" in G.B. Levey (ed.), *Secularism, Religion, and Multicultural Citizenship*, Ed. 1 (Cambridge, Cambridge Univ. Press, 2009).

Modood, T., "Moderate Secularism and Multiculturalism", (2009) 29(1) *Politics* 71–76.

Modood, T., "Rethinking Political Secularism: the Multiculturalist Challenge", (2021) 55(1) *Patterns of Prejudice* 115–124.

Modood, T. and Kastoryano, R., "Secularism and the Accommodation of Muslims in Europe" in T. Modood *et al.* (eds.), *Multiculturalism, Muslims and Citizenship: A European Approach* (New York, Routledge, 2006).

Parekh, B., "Integrating Minorities in a Multicultural Society" in U.K. Preuss and F. Requejo (eds.), *European Citizenship, Multiculturalism, and the State* (Baden-Baden, Nomos, 1998).

Pero, D. and Solomos, J., "Migrant Politics and Mobilization: Exclusion, Engagements, Incorporation", (2010) 33(1) *Ethnic and Racial Studies*.

Rawls, J., *A Theory of Justice* (Cambridge, Harvard University Press, 1971).

Rawls, J., *Political Liberalism* (New York, Columbia University Press, 1993).

Robbers, G., "State and Church in the European Union" in G. Robbers (ed.), *State and Church in the European Union*, 2. ed. (Baden-Baden: Nomos, 2005).

Rodriguez-Garcìa, D., "Beyond Assimilation and Multiculturalism: a Critical Review of the Debate on Managing Diversity", (2010) 11 *International Migration and Integration*.

Scott, J.W., *Sex and Secularism* (Princeton, NJ, Princeton University Press, 2018).

Taylor, C. and Gutmann, A., (eds.), *Multiculturalism and "the politics of recognition". An Essay* (Princeton, NJ, Princeton University Press, 1992).

Thornberry, P., *International Law and the Rights of Minorities* (Oxford, Clarendon Press, 1991).

Turner, B.S., *Religion and Modern Society. Citizenship, Secularisation and the State* (Cambridge, Cambridge University Press, 2011).

United Nations Special Rapporteur on Minority Issues, *Effective Promotion of the Declaration on the Rights of Persons Belonging to National or Ethnic, Religious and Linguistic Minorities*, Report to the UN General Assembly, (15 July 2019) A/74/160, available at https://undocs.org/A/74/160.

Wonisch, K., "Religion, Gender and Law: A Tense Relationship" in J. Marko *et al.* (eds.), *Religious Diversity, State and Law* (Leiden, Brill, 2023).

Xanthaki, A., "Multiculturalism and International Law: Discussing Universal Standards", (2010) 32 *Human Rights Quarterly* 21–48.

Xanthaki, A., "Against Integration, for Human Rights", (2016) 20(6) *The International Journal of Human Rights* 815–838.

CHAPTER 1

Regulation of Muslim Religious Minority Groups and the European State: The Unique Case of Legal Pluralism in Greece

Kyriaki Topidi

1 Introduction

The management of cultural and religiously diverse societies, particularly in the area of family affairs, has acquired global resonance. It may be misleading, however, to assume that even in cases where exposure to religious and cultural difference is historically rooted, solutions are settled and readily available.[1] Indeed, legal systems regulating the relationship between state law and religious norms (as well as the broader relationship between the state and religion) are largely products of historical processes and the quest for 'social equilibrium points',[2] which can (and should) involve continuous debate and adjustments. In fact, the more societies are becoming culturally and religiously pluralized, the less state identification with one religious group becomes politically sustainable.[3]

Since the 1990s, governance, covering law production by an expanding range of private and public organisations (including NGOs and corporations), has stood in a 'symbiotic' relationship with legal pluralism.[4] In some cases, non-state law has been moving closer to state law and in some, it has distanced itself from it. As such, management strategies of normative plurality are known to pose important challenges for legal systems for all categories of legal systems. Judicial functions, in particular, have been increasingly privatized,[5]

1 C. Rautenbach, "The Modern-day Impact of Cultural and Religious Diversity: Managing Family Justice in Diverse Societies", (2014) 17 (1) *PER/PELJ* 521–553, at 522.

2 Expression borrowed from W.C. Durham, "State Reactions to Minority Religions: A Legal Overview" in D. Kirkham (ed.), *State Responses to Minority Religions*, (Farnham, UK, Ashgate, 2013), at 10.

3 W.C. Durham, "State Reactions to Minority Religions" *supra*, at 9.

4 K. von Benda-Beckmann and B. Turner, "Legal Pluralism, Social Theory and the State", (2018) 50(3) *Journal of Legal Pluralism and Unofficial Law* 255–274, at 260.

5 F. C. Gonzalez, "The Legal Self-Regulation of Religious Groups: Tackling the Challenges of Legal Pluralism in Theory and Practice", (2014) 21 *RECODE Working Paper Series*, at 1.

 | DOI:10.1163/9789004446816_003

opening a growing space of regulatory functions for states to address intercultural and interreligious relations. Claims towards self-regulation from minority religious groups are, however, not necessarily new, as the Greek context on legal pluralism will show, even within a European context. Both current and past such claims share the questioning of the state monopoly in the production, interpretation and application of law. They also stress the search for the limits of the compromises that can be made on the formal guarantees of state law and fundamental rights, when confronted with diverging cultural and religious norms. Within these scenarios, 'regulation does not reside in the state, but more broadly, in everyday life and its social realms'.[6] In many ways, thus, the state cannot be neatly separated from social life (and lived religion) and the challenge often becomes to identify the ways in which entanglement between state affairs and social institutions affects the status and positionality of religious minorities.[7] Because of this kind of entanglement, it is important to consider religious minorities in the context of the broader web of their relations with the state and other civil actors, not forgetting that religious minorities are themselves actors.[8]

From a legal pluralist perspective, the co-production of norms by various actors raises two issues: a theoretical one that focuses on whether, and if so to what extent, the 'production' of law should be the exclusive privilege of the state, and second, a more empirical issue on how to manage in practical terms non-homogenous and potentially conflicting sources of legal authority and their outcomes.[9] The latter aspect and the regulative practices devised by states, on the basis of religious belief, are more specifically the focus in the present contribution, with emphasis on state-endorsed religious arbitration with recognized legal effects.[10] When discussing the role of the state in such a scenario, the dynamics between the state and religious minorities also

6 L.G. Beaman, "Expanding the Scope of Regulation: Some Reflections on Religious Minorities in Canada", in D. Kirkham (ed.), *State Responses to Minority Religions* (Farnham, UK, Ashgate, 2013), at 229.

7 *Ibid.,*, at 218.

8 *Ibid.,*at 225.

9 F. C. Gonzalez, The Legal Self-Regulation of Religious Groups" *supra,* at at 2.

10 For the purposes of the present analysis, 'religious arbitration' can be defined as: "A *voluntary* dispute resolution process, conducted according to religious principles (…). It can refer to processes that are binding, or non-binding; to actions that are highly formal, or highly informal; and to processes that are intended to serve as a prelude to court action, a partial substitute for court action, or a complete substitute." (emphasis added) See N. Walter, "Religious Arbitration in the United States and Canada", (2012) 52(2) *Santa Clara Law Review*502–569, at 503–504.

inevitably invite a reconfiguration of the concepts of state sovereignty, minority protection and individual rights.[11]

In a widely cited legal case, distant from European jurisdiction, Justice Sachs of the South African Constitutional Court in *Christian Education South Africa v Minister of Education*[12] eloquently and accurately described the regulation and governance dilemma for states, as far as religious identity and freedom exercised is concerned, as follows:

> The underlying problem in any open and democratic society based on human, dignity, equality and freedom in which conscientious and religious freedom has to be regarded with appropriate seriousness, is how far such democracy can and must go in allowing members of religious communities to define for themselves which laws they will obey and which not. Such a society can cohere only if all its participants accept that certain basic norms and standards are binding. Accordingly, believers, cannot claim an automatic right to be exempted by their beliefs from the laws of the land. At the same time, the State should, wherever reasonably possible, seek to avoid putting believers to extremely painful and intensely burdensome choices of either being true to their faith or else respectful of the law.

The primary aim of this contribution is to reflect on the regulatory arrangements and practices of the Greek state in the case of its historically present Muslim minority with emphasis on the area of family law. To do so, the first step of the analysis will be to present a brief overview of legal pluralism as a frame for the management of religious difference, stressing the kinds of questions that it poses for states and state law. The second stage of the discussion will introduce the distinct (within Europe) case of the Greek pluralist legal system, explaining both the past and present backgrounds of the prevailing arrangements. Within this frame, the case that reached the European Court of Human Rights of *Molla Sali v Greece* will be used in a double role: first, to outline in a socio-legal sense the type of legally plural arrangements prevailing in the case at hand; and second, to explore the European Court of Human Rights' position vis-à-vis legal pluralism and sharia law in Europe. The final part of the discussion will evaluate the legal approach of the Greek state in dealing with

11 F. C. Gonzalez, "The Legal Self-Regulation of Religious Groups" *supra*, at 9.

12 2000 4 SA 757 (CC) at para. 35.

religious plurality and transpose it to the broader critical frame of a relevant paradigm for diversity management.

2 Legal Pluralism as a Frame for the Management of Religious Difference

Legal pluralism describes the co-existence of more than one body of law within the same social or geographical space.[13] While within a given legal system only one body of law may be recognized as state law, others may still run in parallel to that system but not be considered part of the official law.[14] From the point of view of religious groups, however, the perception (and expectation) of law within religious groups often differs greatly from a state-centric one: law in these contexts operates commonly as a 'folk concept'[15] suggesting law's role as a regulator of community conduct, tightly connected to the perpetuation of religious customs.[16] This 'vision' of law largely escapes the confines of the private sphere and has been moving to the public one, even in the European context. This is why an actor-oriented analysis of how the private individual exercises (or not) religious rights as an expression of power/agency is necessary though a particularly complex endeavour, when trying to understand what makes and un-makes the power of state legal regulation.

There is abundant theoretical and empirical argumentation in contemporary socio-legal scholarship that claims that modern state governance can no longer ignore non-state normative commitments and community affiliations, especially when these highlight the (in)-efficiency of state law.[17] In fact, the

---

13 F. von Benda-Beckmann, "Who's Afraid of Legal Pluralism?" (2002) 47 *Journal of Legal Pluralism* 37–83, at 37.

14 F. and K. von Benda-Beckmann, "The Dynamics of Change and Continuity in Plural Legal Orders", in (2006) 53/54 *Journal of Legal Pluralism and Unofficial Law*, Special Double Issue 1–44, at 18.

15 M. Malik, *Minority Legal Orders in the UK: Minorities, Pluralism and the Law*, (London: British Academy Policy Centre, 2012) at 11.

16 *Ibid.*, at 11.

17 Chiba's tripartite classification distinguishes in this respect between 'official law', defined as "the legal system authorized by the legitimate authority of a country", 'unofficial law', defined as the legal system which is 'not officially authorized by the official authorities but (...) by the general consensus of a certain circle of people', and of 'legal postulates' understood as 'the system of values and ideals specifically relevant to both official and unofficial law'. See M. Chiba, "Three Dichotomies of Law in Pluralism" in P.Sack, and J. Aleck, (eds.), *Law and Anthropology*, (New York, New York University Press, 1992), at 173, 178.

more critical strands of this type of scholarship, labelled as *critical legal pluralism,* advance that even apparently marginalized actors (e.g. members of a religious minority community) may contribute in shaping the normative frameworks in which they live.[18] Different categories and types of legal subjects, thus, produce law, as much as official law-making instances.

From a governance perspective and using a more anthropological understanding of law as both an enabling and a constraining tool,[19] especially in scenarios of normative conflict, religious diversity management models reveal indeed the plural nature of law in relation to individuals and religious communities within multicultural societies. They also unveil the impact of the globalization of law and the evolution towards new forms of diversity governance where law is negotiated both internally and externally.[20]

Most commonly, state regulation of family affairs ranges from formal *authorization* and recognition within state law, to *delegation* to cultural and religious communities and their institutions with subsequent partial or fuller recognition by the state and then to *purposive abstention*, where moral and social obligation of families do not acquire the force of state law although the state can intervene when community interests and fundamental rights are threatened.[21] In the last model, the state abstains from intervention and by doing so increases group autonomy on a voluntary basis. The notions of *consent* and *voluntariness* are, however, crucial components to weigh, as community practices are not always freely adhered to. The rigid demarcation between religious and secular authority is known to often operate at the disadvantage of vulnerable groups within the cultural/religious minorities, as will also be shown later in this paper.[22] Self-determination and gender-discrimination are focal points within these processes. They remain both controversial for states (and their agencies such as courts) but also for the communities themselves, given the internal diversity of these groups. In any case, it should be stressed that cultural differences require legal protection beyond the individual dimension of human/minority rights violations, especially to the extent that members of

18 A. Campbell, "Wives Tales: Reflecting on Research in Bountiful", (2008) 23 *Canadian Journal of Law and Society* 121–141, at 123.

19 F. and K. von Benda–Beckmann, "The Dynamics of Change and Continuity in Plural Legal Orders" *supra,* at 3.

20 *Ibid.*, at 10.

21 J. Eekelaar, "Law and Community Practices" in M. Maclean and J. Eekelaar (eds.), *Managing Family Justice in Diverse Societies* (Oxford, UK, Hart Publishing, 2013).

22 C. Rautenbach, "The Modern-day Impact of Cultural and Religious Diversity" *supra,* at 535.

religious and cultural minority groups are in fact embedded in their communities and not single agents in their claims of recognition/justice.[23]

But how much plurality can a legal system manage? The answer to the question is by no means a straightforward one. The expectation from the state is at best to facilitate plural normative interactions but these movements ought to happen in 'dialectical and iterative interplay'.[24] The solution, therefore, of distinguishing between the public and private sphere in order to safeguard the neutrality of the state (and the public sphere) appears today artificial, divisive and subjective.[25] State law and non-State normative orderings are no longer two neatly separated entities.[26] They coexist and shape each other, but just like the boundaries between state and society, they are blurred.

It should not be assumed, however, that religious legal orders are uniform: to the contrary, they are plural, pluri-vocal loaded in many cases with intense asymmetries of power leading to the imposition of solutions deemed to become the 'governing norm'.[27] The risk here is that legal pluralism may become victim of instrumentalization in similar ways that state law itself may be 'used': often for political or moral purposes, it may be manipulated to apply pressure for the recognition of legal orders by the state and may invoke in that context intense debate when it implies the recognition of morally intolerable values (e.g. gender inequality).[28] As importantly, within legal pluralism, the idea that consent is at the basis of obedience to law has been questioned,[29] with legal pluralism bringing to light conflicts between and within non-state normative orders as the source of both obedience and disobedience towards (State) law.

But legal pluralism is also inherently connected with multiculturalism insofar as contemporary societies struggle with globalization, labour mobility, immigration flows and their pluralizing effects. The discussion around the two

23 P. Shah, "Shadow Boxing with Community Practices" in M. Maclean and J. Eekelaar (eds.), *Managing Family Justice in Diverse Societies* (Oxford, UK: Hart Publishing, 2013).

24 P. Schiff Berman, *Global Legal Pluralism: A jurisprudence of law beyond borders*, (Cambridge, Cambridge University Press, 2014), at 25.

25 S. A. Ercan, "Democratizing Identity Politics: A Deliberative Approach to the Politics of Recognition" in D. A. Gozdecka and M. Kmak (eds.), *Europe at the Edge of Pluralism* (Cambridge, Intersentia, 2015) 13–26, at 16.

26 M. Chiba, "Three Dichotomies of Law in Pluralism" *supra* and Y. Sezgin, "Theorizing Formal Pluralism: Quantification of Legal Pluralism for Spatio-Temporal Analysis", (2004) 50 *Journal of Legal Pluralism*, 101–118, at 102.

27 Expression borrowed from M. Malik, *Minority Legal Orders in the UK supra*, at 25.

28 F. von Benda-Beckmann, "Who's Afraid of Legal Pluralism?" *supra*, at 45.

29 On the point, see G. Barzilai, "Beyond Relativism: Where is the Political Power in Legal Pluralism?", (2008) 9.2 *Theoretical Inquiries in Law* 395–416, at 402.

concepts is, therefore, connected to a deeper cause (or fear): the perceived or actual erosion of shared values and the threatened or actual fragmentation of the public sphere, both leading to the decline of shared forms of citizenship.[30] Particularly relevant here is the question of the division between public and private realms of religious belonging and exercise, already mentioned. Liberal societies and their governments rely on this binary differentiation and claim from the State and its law to act as a "neutral" presence within society for the common good. But what if State law is seen as an extension of one community (normally, but not always, the demographic majority) or is indeed inseparable from one religious normative ordering (e.g. in theocracies) and/or is not structured according to the public/private separation?[31]

From yet another angle, legal pluralism in contemporary societies challenges also modern conceptualisations of State law. Here the key argument is that territorially defined states are no longer the sole source of legal norms, not that they ever enjoyed exclusivity. A new, fluid norm development track is developing in the global legal arena that acknowledges multiple community affiliations, particularly relevant in the light of current migratory movements of population in the European continent and beyond.[32] The challenge remains to explore how the notion of identity and religious difference can be 'spatialized' in ways that address the complexity of these processes.[33]

Yet, the role of the State in this context is still essential and a lot depends on how it positions itself in the debate on the need to create demarcating lines between "us" and "them". The process of line drawing involves, apart from power, the questioning of the extent to which the State (just like law) retains its capacity to reflect its conception of membership to the actual community in all its diversity on the ground[34] and at what cost this happens, if at all.

---

30 B. S. Turner and J. T. Richardson, "The Future of Legal Pluralism" in A. *Possamai et al.*(eds.), *The Sociology of Shari'a: Case Studies from around the world*, (Cham, Switzerland, Springer, 2015), at 311–312.

31 B. Z. Tamanaha, "A Framework for Pluralistic Socio-Legal Arenas" in M-C. Foblets *et al.* (eds.), *Cultural Diversity and the Law: State Responses from Around the World* (Bruxelles, Bruylant, 2010,), at 399.

32 See indicatively, P. Schiff Berman, *Global Legal Pluralism: A jurisprudence of law beyond borders* (Cambridge, Cambridge University Press, 2012).

33 See A. Sarat and T. R. Kearns (eds.), *The Unsettled States of Human Rights: An Introduction, in Human Rights: Concepts, Contests, Contingencies*, (Ann Arbor, University of Michigan Press, 2001) at 1 and 13 that argue in favour of a new understanding of culture that takes account of the internal plurality of cultures and their fragmentation.

34 P. J. Spiro, "The Boundaries of Cosmopolitan Pluralism", (2005) 51 *Wayne L. Rev.* 1261–1269, at 1261, 1264.

3 The Idiosyncratic Case of Greece: between Ideological Perplexity and Institutional Uncertainty

3.1 *Background*

Revival of research interest in what constitutes a unique scenario of state-recognized implementation of sharia law in Europe reached its peak in connection with the intensified Muslim presence in the European continent as a result of immigration. The Greek case is, however, of a different kind to the establishment of Muslim communities through waves of immigration. In contrast to Western Europe, where Islam is framed in largely colonial terms, modern Greece is characterized by an almost reversed association of Islam with occupation and 'enslavement'.[35] Labelled appropriately as 'neo-milletism',[36] the special status of Muslims in Greece is connected to the legacies of the Ottoman Empire and several centuries of co-existence of the two groups.[37] A question, nevertheless, still stands today: does state recognition of sharia in Western Thrace constitute an effective paradigm towards religious pluralism and the protection of multiple identities?

For the most part also a linguistic minority that speaks Turkish, the historical Muslim minority of Western Thrace is not uniform: among an estimated 100,000–120,000 of Muslims, 50 per cent have Turkish origin, 35 per cent are Pomaks, expressing Pomak identity and speaking a Bulgarian dialect, and another 15 per cent express Roma identity speaking either Romany or Turkish.[38] The groups in question operate their own institutions (e.g. mosques, schools, associations). Their enjoyment of rights as minorities are, however, territorially limited to Thrace, including the application of sharia as personal law, for family matters.[39] In simpler terms, if they move to other parts of the country, these special rights are no longer available to them.

At the outset, it should be stressed that the historical presence of a Muslim minority within Greece is construed around the fusion of ethnic with religious

35 E. Kostopoulou, "From Mosque to Mosque: Past and present images of Islamic Space in Greece", (2016) 44(5) *Nationalities Papers* 826–846, at 827. She labels it as a "symbol of dominance over victimized Christians" (*Ibid.*, at 829).

36 Term borrowed from A. Ziaka, "Greece – Debate and Challenges" in M.. Berger (ed.), *Applying Sharia in the West: Fact, Fears and the Future of Islamic Rules on Family Relations in the West* (Amsterdam, Amsterdam University Press, 2013) 125–138, at 125.

37 For a brief historical overview, see *Ibid.*, at 126–127.

38 A.N. Anagnostopoulos, *Orthodoxy and Islam: Theology and Muslim-Christian Relations in Modern Greece and Turkey*, (London, Routledge, 2017), at 104.

39 There are currently three state recognized sharia courts, presided by muftis, in Western Thrace, located in Xanthi, Komotini and Didymoteicho, respectively.

identity, applied to both historical minorities and more recent immigrants.[40] This fusion is largely the product of identity and nation-building processes built in juxtaposition to a 'religious Other', Muslims. This particular trajectory also explains the dominance and embeddedness of the Greek Orthodox Church as the 'national church' in the Greek legal order.[41]

The dualistic dimension of identities as religious and ethnic does not favour nuances in the self-identification of other ethnic groups of Muslim faith, namely the Roma and Pomaks, also present in the same territory, who are subjected to a process of 'turkification'.[42] The combination of historical repression from Athens and assistance from Ankara has created considerable complications in that respect: the Greek policy towards the Muslim Roma communities of Western Thrace, for example, has aimed at carving out a separate Muslim identity for the group in order to show that a considerable proportion of the Muslim minorities is not ethnically Turkish.[43] In more substantive terms, the 'competition' between states towards national identity 'patronage' ignores the religious dimension of Muslim Roma and Pomak self-determination, which has been ambiguous and in any case distant from a strictly pious practice of Islam.[44]

In contemporary terms, there is a basic distinction between the Muslims of Western Thrace, that hold Greek citizenship (also labelled as 'Old' Islam) and recently arrived immigrants and asylum seekers (called 'New' Islam) that do not hold the state's citizenship.[45] 'New Islam' is constituted by majority by South Asian groups, in particular originating from Pakistan and Bangladesh.[46]

40 See the case-law before the European Court of Human Rights on behalf of associations wishing to use the term 'Turkish' in their names (ECtHR, *Bekir Ousta and Others v Greece*, Appl. No.35151/05; ECtHR, *Turkish Association of Xanthi and Others v Greece*, Appl. No. 26698/05; ECtHR, Emin and Others v. Greece, Appl. No. 34144/05). See also the *Report of Thomas Hammarberg*, Commissioner for Human Rights of the Council of Europe on Greece, 8–10.12.2008.

41 Article 3 of the Greek Constitution declares as 'prevailing religion' the Eastern Orthodox Church of Christ, which is additionally considered a legal entity of public law.

42 A. Ziaka, "Greece – Debate and Challenges" *supra*, at 128.

43 A. Zenakos and M. Alevizopoulou, "Identity Geopolitics: Nation, Faith, and the Roma of Western Thrace", *BIRN*, 31 May 2021, available at: https://balkaninsight.com/2021/05/31/identity-geopolitics-nation-faith-and-the-roma-of-western-thrace/.

44 *Ibid.*

45 K. Tsitselikis, "Muslims in Greece: A Legal Paradox and a Political Failure", in N. Oberauer, Y. Prief, U. Qubaja (eds.) *Legal pluralism in Muslim contexts* (Leiden/Boston, Brill, 2019), at 65. In the absence of reliable statistics, recent immigrants constitute close to 10 per cent of the total population and range close to 1 million, with predominant countries of origin being Afghanistan, Pakistan, Bangladesh, Iraq and Syria.

46 While Albanians are numerically the largest ethnic minority group in Greece (66 per cent of the total number of immigrants) they are not considered within the categorisation

Despite, however, the historical interaction with the so-called 'Old Islam' – referring to the Muslim minority in Western Thrace – there has been resistance from the Greek state to provide religious freedoms to the 'New Islam' (i.e. immigrants). The latter groups comprise approximately 9 per cent of the total resident population in Greece.[47] A numerical increase of this group was noted between 2015–2017, at the apex of the immigration waves from Syria to Europe, but which also coincided with the country's ongoing economic crisis and, as importantly, with the rise of far-right parties and policies.[48] Religion for Muslim immigrants in Greece is practiced for the most part within informal mosques and there has been a growing fragmentation of mosque attendance along ethnic lines, reflecting indirectly the different Islamic traditions practiced.[49]

The *Molla Sali* case originated from a claim of a Muslim woman of Greek origin, part of the only recognized religious minority, from Western Thrace. The frame of the *Sali* legal case is predictably loaded with elements of nationalism, as relations between Greece and Turkey are systematically approached as identity clashes between two competing national ideologies. Historically, the minority in Thrace is governed by the 1923 Treaty of Lausanne that created reciprocal obligations between the two neighbouring states regarding religious and linguistic status. The Treaty has exclusive territorial application in Thrace and beyond it is no application (i.e. a Muslim marriage cannot be registered outside Thrace). State-endorsed Muslim autonomy on the Greek side includes government-appointed muftis (with an additional two elected by parts of the community although not recognized by the Greek State), with until recent legislative amendments in 2018, compulsory jurisdiction in certain family matters. It also extends to minority schools offering bilingual education, dedicated Muslim property regimes administered by special councils appointed by the

of 'New Islam' in Greece as they have either converted to Christian Orthodoxy or do not practice Islam at all (See E. Gemi, "GREECE – Country Report of the GREASE Project", available at: http://grease.eui.eu/wp-content/uploads/sites/8/2019/11/Greece-Report.pdf, November 2019, at 7).

47 See the latest 2023 statistics for a breakdown by nationality at Greek Ministry of Migration and Asylum, available at: https://migration.gov.gr/wp-content/uploads/2023/08/Report_A_June-2023_International-Protection_NEW.pdf. Muslims are the largest religious minority followed by the Roman Catholic and the Jewish communities.

48 The example of the (now dismantled) Golden Dawn party is characteristic of the trend.

49 E. Gemi, "GREECE" *supra*, at 7. A state-sponsored mosque was opened in 2020 in Athens, following much controversy.

government, political and associative representation and activities, as well as cultural and religious rights.[50]

3.2 *The Model of State-Endorsed Legal Pluralism: Legal Pluralism as Segregation?*

At the basis of the model of religious legal pluralism in Greece, one finds the institution of *muftis*. The function of the *mufti* as a religious leader of the Muslims in Western Thrace is supplemented by his role as interpreter-judge of sharia. He presides over special religious courts and his field of jurisdiction concerns family matters and inheritance, although the greatest part of the daily operations of religious minority courts revolves around divorce. He is considered a civil servant of the Greek state and appointed by Presidential decree (Article 11 of the Convention of Athens). By consequence, he is also paid by the Greek State.[51] His decisions cannot contravene the Constitution and as of the latest legal amendment in 2018,[52] his judicial competence is optional as Greek Muslims can choose to address either civil courts or Islamic jurisdictions, in which case the express consent of parties involved is necessary. As a general rule, under the new legal framework, civil courts will have competence by default unless litigant parties decide jointly otherwise. Wills of succession drafted by Muslims will enjoy the same protection of civil law.

The practice of *muftis*' decision-making has commonly entailed gender discrimination violations.[53] In that sense, it affirms the broader and more global concern over religious arbitration mechanisms becoming a 'judicial ghetto' for vulnerable members of Muslim communities, even beyond the immigration context.[54] This is for several reasons: the applicable Sharia-inspired principles

50 For an overview, see K. Tsitselikis, "Muslims in Greece: a Legal Paradox and a Political Failure" in N. Oberauer *et al.* (eds.), *Legal Pluralism in Muslim Contexts* (Leiden: BRILL, 2019), at 67–69.

51 The question of the election of muftis has been revived since the 1980s; part of the Muslim community supports his election by the community itself rather than being appointed by the Greek State. Indirectly, such an election process can be construed as conducive to the reform/modernization or even abolition of sharia, especially given the declared incompatibility of sharia with the European Convention for Human Rights (see ECtHR, *Refah Partisi v Turkey*, Appl. Nos 41340/1998, 41342/1998, 41343/1998, 41344/1998, judgment of 13 February 2003). At the same time, his election is part and parcel of a wider political bargaining power attached to the post, especially since Turkey supports the elected muftis (see A. Ziaka, "Greece – Debate and Challenges" *supra*, at 131). The community remains divided on the issue.

52 Law No. 4511/2018 on *Muslim Religious Clerics*, Official Gazette of the Hellenic Republic, 15 January 2018, Issue A.

53 K. Tsitselikis, "Muslims in Greece" *supra*, at 70.

54 F. C. Gonzalez, "The Legal Self-Regulation of Religious Groups" *supra*, at 4.

within the muftis' decisions are not standardized or codified. This leaves considerable room for discretion to the religious judge. Procedurally, these instances are not always in line with fair trial guarantees (Article 6 ECHR), neither do they abide to due process, as legal representation before them is not necessary. Finally, the review of the merits of the *muftis*' decisions by state courts is not efficient. Commonly in the past, Greek civil courts have resisted review of *mufti* decisions and remanded cases back to the religious fora. Pre-*Sali,* using the frame of the application of sharia principles in family affairs as a set of provisions designed to function as a minority protection mechanism, the choice of jurisdiction between a state and a religious forum was taken away from Muslim claimants by enforcing a de facto exclusivity of *mufti* jurisdiction.[55] The conservative stance of civil courts vis-à-vis *mufti* jurisdiction can be justified on the basis of political/security concerns connected to the tense relationship between Greece-Turkey. By treating sharia law as 'special law' and exempting it from constitutional review, they have contributed to creating a 'segregated' judicial scope of application of sharia.

The question raised in the context of the *Sali* case is therefore crucial: when dealing with legal pluralism and state-recognized adjudicatory mechanisms, where should the line be drawn between respect of cultural and religious identity and non-discrimination? The most common response to this question supports the formally recognized co-existence of multiple legal systems within a state, provided that the right to exit/opt-out is available. By extension, the notion of consent of the member of the cultural/religious minority member is necessary. The discretion of the State to impose a forum on a religious minority claimant is, therefore, not an option (by mandating the choice of the appropriate forum) as the *Sali* case showed.

Analysis of legal pluralist diversity management scenarios, however, rarely stops here: social and political factors apply in addition to the purely legal considerations. For the case of the Muslim minority in Thrace, political factors, as already stated are particularly salient as they tend to replicate tensions between the Greek and Turkish states rooted in historical claims and counter-claims. Social factors are equally complex. This is particularly so when there is a track record of intersectional discrimination affecting Muslim (female) claimants. The UN Human Rights Committee has noted in the recent past the need to 'increase the awareness of Muslim women of their rights and the availability of remedies, and to ensure that they benefit from the provisions of

---

55 As Tsitselikis notes, however, neither the Treaty of Athens (1923), nor the Treaty of Sevres (1920/23) or the Treaty of Lausanne (1923) stipulate compulsory jurisdiction of the mufti. K. Tsitselikis, "Muslims in Greece" *supra.*

Greek Civil law'.[56] While recent empirical data on the use that Muslim community members, in particular women, make of religious courts in Western Thrace are not available, it can be claimed that for reasons of social stigmatization or pressure, female members of these communities may avoid resorting to state civil courts.[57]

3.3. *The Findings of the European Court of Human Rights (ECtHR) in* Molla Sali

Factually, *Molla Sali* concerned a Muslim woman of Greek citizenship that challenged the decision of the Greek courts[58] to be compelled to apply Muslim inheritance principles to her deceased's husband estate, despite the latter having established a valid will under Greek civil law. Although the case was of limited practical impact,[59] it deserves methodological de-construction to show the position of the Court on the broader question: the Court had already recognized previously that imposing a certain judicial system on individuals on the basis of their religious affiliation is not compatible with the European legal order.[60] In essence, the question before it in *Sali* was centered on how to accommodate within liberal legal contexts laws of a non-liberal character. More than that, the de facto compulsory use of religious fora to settle family law claims was claimed by the Greek state as a minority protection measure rooted in international law bilateral commitments. In other words, preserving one's minority identity should come at the cost of a violation of equality and direct discrimination, following the arguments of the Greek state.

The interpretation of Article 9 ECHR on religious freedom, according to the Court, does not impose a legal duty on individuals to comply with religious law. The general duties of the State in the framework of the protection of religious

56 Human Rights Committee (ICCPR), *Report on Greece – Concluding Observations*, 24 April 2005, CCPR/CO.83/GRC, at para.8.

57 A. Ziaka reaches a similar conclusion although more recent data is missing. A. Ziaka, "Greece – Debate and Challenges" *supra,* at 131.

58 At the basis of the complaint was the Greek Court of Cassation decision 1862/2013 denying the right of the Muslim Greek applicant to enforce a legally valid will under Greek Civil law and enforce, against her will, the application of sharia rules on the matter.

59 Greek law was amended while the case was being heard in Strasbourg aligning the Greek law's scope of application with the Court subsequent findings.

60 ECtHR, *Refah Partisi v Turkey*, Appl. Nos 41340/1998, 41342/1998, 41343/1998, 41344/1998, judgment of 13 February 2003, paras. 126–128.

freedom is essentially to act neutrally and impartially when exercising regulatory power.[61] Its main finding in *Sali* can be summarized as follows:

> [A]ccording to its case-law, freedom of religion does not require the Contracting States to create a particular legal framework in order to grant religious communities a special status entailing specific privileges. Nevertheless, a State which has created such a status must ensure that the criteria established for a group's entitlement to it are applied in a non-discriminatory manner.[62]

The Court did not, however, respond directly to the core issue. It chose to treat the matter as a property case related to discrimination *by association* (Article 1 of Protocol 1 together with Article 14). The legal question was formulated as follows: "whether there was a difference in treatment potentially amounting to discrimination as compared with the application of the law of succession, as laid down in the Civil Code, to those seeking to benefit from a will as drawn up by a testator who was not of Muslim faith." (para. 86.) The Court then concluded that: "Refusing members of a religious minority the right to voluntarily opt for and benefit from ordinary law amounts not only to discriminatory treatment but also to a breach of a right of cardinal importance in the field of protection of minorities, that is to say the right to free self-identification. It must be respected both by the other members of the minority and by the State itself" (para.157). In this context, the right to self-determination of ethnic, religious and linguistic communities can be understood in line with the UN Declaration on the Rights of Persons Belonging to National or Ethnic, Religious and Linguistic Minorities (Article 2(1)) as "the right to enjoy their own culture, to profess and practice their own religion and to use their own language, in private and in public, freely and without interference or any form of discrimination."[63]

The Court left aside any consideration of systematic or intersectional discrimination of a member of the Muslim minority. It also did not consider any dimension of the right to freedom of religious belief. By extension, therefore,

61 See indicatively the ECtHR cases of *Metropolitan Church of Bessarabia and Others v Moldova*, Appl. No. 45701/99, judgment of 13 December2011 (paras. 115–116); *Manoussakis and Others v Greece*, Appl. No. 18748/91, judgment of 26 September1996; *Bayatyan v Armenia*, Appl. No. 23459/03, judgment of 7 July2011.

62 ECtHR, *Molla Sali v Greece*, Appl. No. 20452/14, judgment of 19 December2018.

63 G.A. Res. 47/136 of Dec. 18, 1992, 47 U.N. GAOR Supp. (No.49), at 210, UN Doc A/Res/47/135 (1992).

it left untouched the issue of the role of the state in a contemporary religiously diverse European society.[64] Prior available legal precedent related to a right to property claim but seen through the prism of discrimination by association also resisted the consideration of past discrimination.[65] There, the court simply narrowed the state's margin of appreciation when applying restrictions to the right to property. Seen exclusively as a case of personal autonomy and self-identification, the findings of the Court in the *Sali* case avoided the discussion in more detail of the clash between religious freedom and fundamental rights. The judgement also offered little clarity for states on how to avoid and/or appease 'culture wars'.

Overall, the European mono-legal approach, centered around the principle of equality as a fundamental principle of a legal system, is tested in the case of Greece, and *Molla Sali* more specifically. The approach is applied, however, in a plural legal system producing mixed results, which the Court in Strasbourg acknowledges by stating that a state 'may feel required as a matter of freedom of religion to create a particular legal framework in order to grant religious communities a special status entailing special privileges'.[66] What is missing are guidelines for states that precisely are pluri-legal and committed to fundamental rights (through the respect of the Convention).

4 Diversity Management and Self-regulation of Muslim Minorities in Greece: the 'Right' Paradigm for Europe?

The 2001 UNESCO Universal Declaration on Cultural Diversity approaches culture 'as the set of distinctive spiritual, material, intellectual and emotional features of society or a social group (...) that encompasses, in addition to art and literature, lifestyles, ways of living together, value systems, traditions and beliefs'.[67] According to the same text, states should 'ensure harmonious interaction among people and groups with plural, varied and dynamic cultural identities as well as their willingness to live together'.[68] This kind of framework poses at least two fundamental sets of concerns: first, from the perspective of the state, the concern on how much regulation is required in each case,

64 R. Uitz, "The Vices of Leaving This Undecided", *Int'l J. Const. L. Blog*, 3 January 2019, available at. http://www.iconnectblog.com/the-vices-of-leaving-this-undecided/

65 See ECtHR, *Guberina v. Croatia*, Appl. No. 23683/13, 22 March 2016.

66 At para. 155 of the judgement.

67 Preamble of the UNESCO *Universal Declaration on Cultural Diversity* (2001).

68 *Ibid.*, Article 2.

especially in relation to family conduct, and second, and depending on the approach adopted for the first point, what are the implications of the state's approach for the cultural/religious minorities and their members.

At the same time, in our diverse societies, a 'new normal' tends to develop. The coexistence of multiple normative systems is not in itself new but the pressure for states to reconfigure their role, position and duties in scenarios of overlapping and conflicting legal orders is more recent. This is also a concern that largely escapes legal considerations and is heavily tainted by political ones. Sousa Santos has aptly summarized the situation in the early 2000s in these terms: "We live in a time of porous legality or legal porosity, multiple networks of legal orders forcing us to constant transitions and trespassing."[69] Modern states have resisted this type of 'trespassing' among norms because it places obstacles in nation-building and homogenizing processes but also because it may lead to violations of the principle of equality, although not in the Greek case.

The dynamics of self-regulation within the Muslim communities in Thrace show conservative trends which increase also the pressure for 'internal' reform of the traditionalist elements prevalent within the group itself. This type of reform, however, presupposes that the state proactively offers and guarantees 'external protection' mechanisms, unlike the ones shown in the *Molla Sali* case. It begs joint governance schemes between the state and minorities that aim to reverse the concentration of normative authority in the hands of those that resist change. Transmitting tradition is not necessarily incompatible with evolution. Leaving transformation to the agency of individual minority members, including through recourse to national and supra-national courts, is not sufficient and de-legitimizes a deliberative interpretation of the democratic processes.[70]

Acknowledging the rootedness of Islamic law practices among the Muslim communities in Western Thrace for historical and political reasons is not a self-sufficient policy or legal goal: when norms are used in circumstances that are different to the ones that they were designed for, it is the duty of the state and the affected communities to contextually justify their maintenance or else to proceed to their revision through deliberation, lest they agree on the slower

69 B. Sousa Santos, *Toward a New Legal Common Sense*, 2nd Edition, (Cambridge, Cambridge University Press, 2002), at 437.

70 F. C. Gonzalez, "The Legal Self-Regulation of Religious Groups" *supra*, at 11.

process of these norms losing their authoritative aura through social oblivion or discontinuation of their use. The latter option comes at the cost of a considerable number of violations suffered by the weaker segments of the groups concerned.

The Greek state, as has been shown, has been reluctant to become involved with the application of sharia, even when other fundamental rights of the members of these groups were at issue. In the absence of data that shed light on the reasons as to why Muslim women, by predominance, continue to resort to the muftis, the regulation of sharia courts in Western Thrace remains a puzzle: self-regulation raises a good number of concerns as the *Sali* case showed. The alternative of state-devised regulation is the currently applicable scenario in the Greek context which remains to be evaluated. As for the third option of full elimination of sharia courts, it would generate political claims from the Muslim minority and force the operation of the same fora unofficially and outside of State oversight. In addition, in the absence of an understanding of the use of agency on the part of the claimants before these fora and the degree of willingness to resist community pressure (to the extent that it is at the source of forcing them to resort to religious fora), it might be difficult to understand the needs of and evolution within religious minority groups.

5 Concluding Remarks

As states cease to be the main source of law, in light also of globalization and the expansion of transnational organisations and networks of actors, their position has changed too: from main lawmakers they are gradually shifting to mediators between 'above-the-state' and 'below-the-state' legal pluralisms.[71] So, while this (re)-pluralization of state law contributes to the flourishing of legal pluralist arrangements, the Greek case shows a calibration between state law and sharia which appears largely proceduralist and fits in the kind of normative 'mediation' described above. It addresses some of the issues arising out of the plural family law arrangements in Western Thrace. It reinforces by default the primacy of state law under the influence of human rights law. Soon after the 2018 legal reform entered into force, the number of decisions issued by muftis in Western Thrace dropped dramatically in 2019.[72] The law reform

71 M. Helfand, *Negotiating State and Non-State Law: The Challenge of Global Law and Local Legal Pluralism* (Cambridge, Cambridge University Press, 2015), at 5.

72 Y. Ktistakis, "Η Στάση των Πρωτοδικείων Θράκης έναντι των Αποφάσεων των Ιεροδικείων της Θράκης", [The Position of First Instance Courts faced with Religious Court Decisions in

also allowed the termination of religious marriages before civil courts, when applicants were precisely claiming the principle of default competence of civil courts. What remains unsolved is the religious termination of a religious marriage, especially where husbands resist it. In other terms, the need for certain women to be considered divorced in the eyes of their religious community and social entourage, which was at the source of their vulnerability in the first place, stands unadressed. As such, the liberal approach of placing individuals against their groups continues to be preferred. Such an approach is less informed from a socio-legal perspective.[73] This is because it affords less consideration to minority accommodation and by implication also reduces the likelihood of internal reforms for minority communities that systematically leave exposed to harm certain of their segments (e.g. women/children).

As states cannot shape or interpret religious traditions in direct ways, their duty is limited to respecting the autonomy of religious minorities. This autonomy is not, however, unlimited, as *Molla Sali* showed because alternative interpretations of religious norms and of self-identification with a given community should not be suppressed but on the contrary encouraged in the direction of more gender-sensitive interpretation of sharia.[74] Moreover, the conflicting interpretation of religious norms that enjoy state-law recognition should be viewed more holistically as a process depending on numerous factors: the 'problem' from a normative perspective tends (not always accurately) to be perceived as being located within Islam as such but political interests, local cultures, socio-economic background, gender dimensions as well as religious dogma shape the content and use of such norms.

From the perspective of the State, the Greek model in its post-2018 frame still struggles to resolve the issues of consent (i.e. to what extent those using religious judicial for a genuine wish to do so), of agency (i.e. on what basis members of a religious minority decide to forum shop between jurisdictions)[75] and of broader compatibility of human rights with Islamic family law, although in the *Sali* case this was relegated to a background consideration.

Within this framework, the contrast between 'Old Islam' in Greece, enjoying the possibility to use personal law aligned to its faith, and 'New Islam',

---

Thrace], available at: https://www.constitutionalism.gr/wp-content/uploads/2020/06/2020.06_Ktistakis-ierodikeia.pdf, 2020, at 2.

73 P. Shah, "Shadow Boxing with Community Practices" *supra.*

74 E. Verhas, *The Turkish Minority in Western Thrace: The Long Struggle for Rights and Recognition,* Minority Rights Group, (2019) at 15–16, available at: https://minorityrights.org/wp-content/uploads/2019/10/MRG_Rep_WThrace_EN_Sept19.pdf.

75 In Molla Sali, the financial incentive was for example obvious.

in constant struggle to enforce basic religious freedoms, despite progress, is striking: from a diversity management perspective, the size of 'New Islam' is considerably larger than that of the historic Muslim minority communities. The Greek state will, therefore, be confronted with a vast array of issues such as the need for creation of favourable conditions for interreligious dialogue, the modalities of external funding streams for Muslim religious activities or the broader issue of oversight of religious expressions in the public sphere. Without a formalized public engagement framework for all sides concerned, these and other related issues can revert to risks of persistent normative conflict and societal disruptions and disorder.

Bibliography

Anagnostopoulos, A.N., *Orthodoxy and Islam: Theology and Muslim-Christian Relations in Modern Greece and Turkey*(London, Routledge, 2017).

Barzilai, G., "Beyond Relativism: Where is the Political Power in Legal Pluralism?", (2008) 9(2) *Theoretical Inquiries in Law* 395–416.

Beaman, L.G., "Expanding the Scope of Regulation: Some Reflections on Religious Minorities in Canada" in D. Kirkham (ed.), *State Responses to Minority Religions*(Farnham, UK, Ashgate, 2013).

Boaventura, S. S., *Toward a New Legal Common Sense*, 2nd Edition, (Cambridge, UK, Cambridge University Press, 2002).

Campbell, A., "Wives Tales: Reflecting on Research in Bountiful", (2008) 23 *Canadian Journal of Law and Society* 121–141.

Chiba, M., "Three Dichotomies of Law in Pluralism" in Sack, P., and Aleck, J. (eds.), *Law and Anthropology* (New York, New York University Press, 1992).

Colom Gonzalez, F., "The Legal Self-Regulation of Religious Groups: Tackling the Challenges of Legal Pluralism in Theory and Practice"', (2014) 21 *RECODE Working Paper Series*.

Durham, W.C., "State Reactions to Minority Religions: a Legal Overview" in D. Kirkham (ed.), *State Responses to Minority Religions* (Farnham, UK, Ashgate, 2013).

Eekelaar, J., "Law and Community Practices" in M. Maclean and J. Eekelaar (eds.), *Managing Family Justice in Diverse Societies* (Oxford, UK, Hart Publishing, 2013).

Ercan, S.A., "Democratizing Identity Politics: a Deliberative Approach to the Politics of Recognition" in D. A. Gozdecka and M. Kmak (eds.), *Europe at the Edge of Pluralism* (Cambridge, Intersentia, 2015).

Gemi, E., GREECE – Country Report of the GREASE Project (November 2019), available at: http://grease.eui.eu/wp-content/uploads/sites/8/2019/11/Greece-Report.pdf.

Helfand, M., *Negotiating State and Non-State Law: the Challenge of Global Law and Local Legal Pluralism* (Cambridge, UK, Cambridge University Press, 2015).

Human Rights Committee (ICCPR), Report on Greece – Concluding Observations, 24/04/2005, CCPR/CO.83/GRC

Kostopoulou, E., "From Mosque to Mosque: Past and present images of Islamic Space in Greece", (2016) 44(5) *Nationalities Paper* 826–846.

Ktistakis, Y., "Η Στάση των Πρωτοδικείων Θράκης έναντι των Αποφάσεων των Ιεροδικείων της Θράκης", [The Position of First Instance Courts faced with Religious Court Decisions in Thrace] (2020) available at: https://www.constitutionalism.gr/wpcontent/uploads/2020/06/2020.06_Ktistakis-ierodikeia.pdf.

Malik, M., *Minority Legal Orders in the UK: Minorities, Pluralism and the Law* (London, British Academy Policy Centre, 2012).

Rautenbach, C., "The Modern-day Impact of Cultural and Religious Diversity: 'Managing Family Justice in Diverse Societies'", (2014) 17 (1) *PER/PELJ* 521–553.

Sarat, A. and Kearns T.R. (eds.), *The Unsettled States of Human Rights: An Introduction, in Human Rights: Concepts, Contests, Contingencies* (Ann Arbor, University of Michigan Press, 2001).

Schiff Berman, P., *Global Legal Pluralism: A Jurisprudence of Law beyond Borders* (Cambridge, UK, Cambridge University Press, 2012).

Sezgin, Y., "Theorizing Formal Pluralism: Quantification of Legal Pluralism for Spatio-temporal Analysis", (2004) 50 *Journal of Legal Pluralism* 101–118.

Shah, P., "Shadow Boxing with Community Practices" in M. Maclean and J. Eekelaar (eds.), *Managing Family Justice in Diverse Societies* (Oxford, UK, Hart Publishing, 2013).

Spiro, Peter J., "The Boundaries of Cosmopolitan Pluralism", (2005) 51 *Wayne L. Rev.* 1261–1269.

Tamanaha, B.Z., "A Framework for Pluralistic Socio-legal Arenas" in M-C. Foblets *et al.* ln (eds.), *Cultural Diversity and the Law: State Responses from Around the World* (Bruxelles, Bruylant, 2010).

Tsitselikis, K., "Muslims in Greece: a Legal Paradox and a Political Failure" in N. Oberauer *et al.* (eds.), *Legal Pluralism in Muslim Contexts* (Leiden/Boston, Brill, 2019).

Turner, B.S. and Richardson, J. T., "The Future of Legal Pluralism" in A. Possamai *et al.* (eds.), *The Sociology of Shari'a: Case Studies from around the world* (Cham, Switzerland, Springer, 2015).

Uitz, R., "The Vices of Leaving this Undecided", (2019) *Int'l J. Const. L. Blog*, available at: http://www.iconnectblog.com/the-vices-of-leaving-this-undecided/.

Verhas, E., "The Turkish Minority in Western Thrace: the Long Struggle for Rights and Recognition", (2019) *Minority Rights Group* 15–16, available at: https://minorityrights.org/wp-content/uploads/2019/10/MRG_Rep_WThrace_EN_Sept19.pdf.

von Benda-Beckmann, F. and K., "The Dynamics of Change and Continuity in Plural Legal Orders", (2006) 53/54 *Journal of Legal Pluralism and Unofficial Law*, Special Double Issue 1–44.

von Benda-Beckmann, F., "Who's Afraid of Legal Pluralism?", (2002) 47 *Journal of Legal Pluralism* 37–83.

von Benda-Beckmann, K. and Turner, B., "Legal Pluralism, Social Theory and the State", (2018) 50 (3) *Journal of Legal Pluralism and Unofficial Law*, 255–274.

Walter, N., "Religious Arbitration in the United States and Canada", (2012) 52(2) *Santa Clara Law Review* 502–569.

Zenakos, A. and Alevizopoulou, M., "Identity Geopolitics: Nation, Faith, and the Roma of Western Thrace", (2021) *BIRN*, available at: https://balkaninsight.com/2021/05/31/identity-geopolitics-nation-faith-and-the-roma-of-western-thrace/.

Ziaka, A., "Greece – Debate and Challenges" in M. Berger (ed.), *Applying Sharia in the West: Fact, Fears and the Future of Islamic Rules on Family Relations in the West* (Amsterdam, Amsterdam University Press, 2013).

CHAPTER 2

Women and Sharia Law in the UK

Elham Manea

1 Introduction[1]

The concept of legal pluralism has been a subject of research by legal anthropologies and legal and Islamic studies' scholars. It has also been a contested subject matter between two theoretical points of view, one that argues for state's monopoly on legal productions and a monistic conception of law; and another that conceptualises law as more plural, not located entirely in the state.Defined by Jacques Vanderlinden in 1972 as "the existence within particular society of different legal mechanisms applying to identical institutions",[2] legal pluralism has currently started to attract attention in Europe. The presence of different groups of immigrants has raised the question of whether they should be treated differently according to their religious or original national laws. At the heart of the discourses taking place currently on legal pluralism lies the question of how to balance equality and difference.[3]

Two theoretical points of view in this regard stand out. The first theoretical orientation advocates legal centralism in the state, considers it to be the basic foundation on which liberal-democratic nations rely on, argues for the state's monopoly on legal productions and a monistic conception of law and warns all the same of depriving the state of its capacity as a social actor. It also highlights the negative consequences of legal pluralism on weak groups within the minorities, such as women and children and insists on equal protection of rights within one society through the application of a 'single and comprehensive vision of justice'. The second theoretical standpoint argues for legal pluralism, maintains that legal centralism is more relevant within a Western model of Jurisprudence, that it ignores the experience of non-Western nations. Accordingly, legal pluralism indicates that state law is only one of many levels,

1 The core of this chapter is based on an update of sections from the author's book *Women and Sharia Law: The Impact of Legal Pluarlism in the UK* (London, I.B. Tauris, 2016).

2 G. Woodman, "The Idea of Legal Pluralism", in B. Dupret *et al* (eds.), *Legal Pluralism in the Arab World* (The Hague, Kluwer Law International, 1999), at 4.

3 P. Shah, *Legal Pluralism in Conflict: Coping with Cultural Diversity in Law* (London, Glasshouse Press, 2005), at ix.

 | DOI:10.1163/9789004446816_004

and it means a plurality of social fields and producer of norms, which are in partial interaction with each other. It also insists that legal pluralism is the adequate system that guarantees the protection of minorities' rights and their entitlement to be different.[4]

This discussion, which concerns itself with describing legal and social realities in Western and non-Western states, has rarely touched on the political function of legal pluralism. My research in Middle Eastern societies indicates a political function that intersects with divided societies in the post-colonial era. The system of legal pluralism in family laws, while discriminating against women, is the tool that has helped perpetuate the very social division of Arab societies: it has kept society divided, hindering intermarriage between Sunnis and Shiites, Christians and Muslims and Jews, superior tribes and inferior tribes, etc. In the process, it kept the traditional base of power of Arab authoritarian regimes intact and has sabotaged nation building and the development of a national identity. This political function was also highlighted by the research conducted by Yüksel Sezgin.[5]

Another dimension that deserves our attention is how legal pluralism contributes to the rise of what one could call parallel/or closed societies/communities, and most importantly how the interaction between the two (application of legal pluralism and closed communities) reflects on the rights of members of these closed communities within the state, especially from a human rights perspective.

Just like legal pluralism, the concept of parallel societies has been a subject of contention. From a theoretical point of view, however, it is important to differentiate between two levels of perspective:

4 D. MacEoin, *Sharia Law or 'One Law for All'?* (London, CIVITAS, Institute for the Study of Civil Society, 2009); J. Rawls, *A Theory of Justice* Revised Edition (Cambridge, Belknap Press of Harvard University Press, 2005); R. Dworkin, *Law's Empire* (Cambridge, Belknap Press of Harvard University Press, 1986); I. Yilmaz, *Muslim Laws, Politics and Society in Modern Nations States: Dynamic Legal Pluralism in England, Turkey and Pakistan* (Farham, England, Ashgate Publishing Limited, 2005); W. Menski, *Comparative Law in a Global Context: the Legal Systems of Asia and Africa,* Second Edition (Cambridge, Cambridge University Press, 2006); B. Dupret *et. al.* (eds.), *Legal Pluralism in the Arab World, supra*; M. Kemper and M. Reinkowski, (eds.), *Rechtspluralismus in der islamischen Welt: Gewohnheitsrecht zwischen Staat und Gesellschaft* (Berlin, Walter de Gruyter, 2005).

5 See E. Manea, *The Arab State and Women's Rights: The Trap of Authoritarian Governance* (London, Routledge, 2011); E. Manea, *Women and Shari'a Law, supra*; see also Y. Sezgin,*Human Rights under State-Enforced Religious Family Laws in Israel, Egypt and India,*Cambridge, UK, Cambridge University Press, 2013).

a) The de jure level where different types of legal systems are applied by the state to different ethnic communities within its boundaries. Accordingly, the state itself seems to designate these communities as distinct and different, as with the case for instance of religious minorities in Islamic states, native Indians in the United States and Canada and members of ethnic minorities/migrants in Britain and Germany;
b) The de facto level where different (written and/or unwritten) rules of behavior and values seem to distinguish a community from its general society.

Within Middle Eastern area studies, the concept of parallel societies was first introduced in research investigating the Ottoman Empire's system of legal pluralism. Under the Ottoman's *millet system* in Greater Syria for example, 'recognised' religious groups were organised into relatively self-contained autonomous communities, each operating under its own religious laws and customs, each was directed by a religious leader, and each assumed social and administrative functions concerning diverse matters, among them issues of marriage and divorce. Syrian Christian communities were covered by this system and they retained a high degree of autonomy. Consequently, Syrian Christians, in their diverse denominations, lived in separate parallel societies whose leaders were given absolute authority in administering the affairs of their community, including family matters.[6] Albert Hourani used the term "closed communities" to describe these parallel societies in Syria, where each community was "a world, sufficient to its members and exacting their ultimate loyalty. The worlds touched, but did not mingle with each other; each looked at the rest with suspicion and even hatred".[7]

Within a European context, on the other hand, the concept of parallel societies has taken a new dimension with the demographic change that has taken place in European countries. Waves of immigrants moved to Western European societies in the fifties and sixties of the last century for different reasons: some came because of economic reasons (workers from Southern Europe and Turkey helping in rebuilding Germany and Austria during its years of economic boom) and others as members of previous colonies of their hosted states (North Africans in France and Indians and Pakistanis in the United Kingdom). Another wave of migration followed in the eighties, nineties, and the first two

6 E. Manea, *The Arab State and Women's Rights, supra*, at 41–42; Encyclopedia Britannica Online, s.v. "Ottoman Empire," accessed September 2, 2023, https://www.britannica.com/place/Ottoman-Empire.

7 E. Manea, *Women and Shari'a Law*, at 55; M. A. Faksh, Mahmud, "The Alawi Community of Syria: A New Dominant Political Force", (1984) 20 (2) *Middle Eastern Studies*, at 138.

decades of the 21st century as a result of the wars and political upheavals, in places like Yugoslavia, Sri Lanka, and Somalia, Iraq, Syria.

The new groups of immigrants started to organise themselves along ethnic and religious lines and created in some European societies separate cultural and social entities, sometimes functioning with different cultural norms than those prevalent in the society. The debate on parallel societies and/or the construction of 'parallel societies' as an 'image of the other' have been debated in Germany since the German sociologist Wilhelm Heitmeyer first used the term in the early 1990s and was later criticized by several scholars, such as Wolfgang Kashuba.[8]

Calls for the introduction of forms of Islamic Law, Sharia, into European and North American legal systems have often been made by three groups of people. First, from Islamic organisations which often represent a traditional if not conservative reading of Islam. Second, from high European or North American officials or figures, who seem to be genuinely concerned about the integration of Muslim communities in their respective countries, and consider the move inevitable for any "successful" integration of Muslims. Third, from within the circle of legal anthropology academics, who are leading a theoretical and intellectual discourse on the state. As seen earlier, at the heart of the issue is a debate on legal pluralism, defined by Vanderlinden as "the existence within particular society of different legal mechanisms applying to identical institutions".[9] Legal pluralism has currently started to attract attention in Europe. The presence of different groups of immigrants has raised the question of whether they should be treated differently according to their religious or original national laws. At the heart of the discourses taking place currently on legal pluralism lays the question of how to balance equality and difference.[10]

Members of the above-mentioned categories are often of the opinion that weak legal pluralism is just one out of many instruments for resolving conflicts, and that it is an extension of a right already given to the Jewish minority: a right to arbitration tribunals in a system called Beth Din (for example in

8 For more information on this discourse please see W. Kashuba, "Wie Fremde gemacht werden", *der Tagesspiegel*, January 14, 2007, accessed September 02, 2023, https://www.tagesspiegel.de/meinung/wie-fremde-gemacht-werden-1435909.html; W. Kaschuba,, "Ethnische Parallelgesllschaften: Zur kulturellen Konstruktion des Fremden in der europäischen Migration", (2007) 1 *Zeitschrift für Volkskunde* 65–85; B. Heininger, *Ehrenmord und Emanzipation: Die Geschlechterfrage in Ritualen von Parallelgesellschaften* (Berlin, LIT Verlag, 2009); W. Schiffauer, *Parallelgesellschaften* (Bielefeld, transcript Verlag, 2008).

9 B. Dupret *et. al* (eds.), *Legal Pluralism in the Arab World, supra.*

10 P. Shah, *Legal Pluralism in Conflict: Coping with Cultural Diversity in Law* (London, Glasshouse Press, 2005), at ix.

Britain, Germany and Switzerland). Members of the above-mentioned categories also emphasise that this instrument of conflict resolution is voluntary, that they only support it with safeguards that ensure respect for human rights, especially for women's rights. Accordingly, if a member of a religious minority does not want to be ruled by these laws, all she or he has to do is to opt out of these legal instruments and leave the religious community.[11] And they often argue that the Western legal tradition, which is based on legal centralism and state monopoly over legal productions and a monistic conception of law (the basic foundation on which liberal-democratic nations are instituted) is Euro-American centric and ignores the experience of non-Western nations.[12]

Those calling for soft legal pluralism in the UK are often shaped by strong or weak cultural relativism. The strong cultural relativists hold that 'culture is the *principal* source of the validity of a moral right or rule [...] the presumption is that rights (and other social practices, values, and moral rules) are culturally determined'.[13] The weak cultural relativists, on the other hand, assert that 'culture may be an *important* source of the validity of a moral right or rule. Universality is initially presumed, but the relativity of human nature, communities, and rights serves as a check on potential excesses of universalism'.[14]

Absent from this plea for the introduction of Islamic law is the actual experience with legal pluralism in non-Western countries specifically with its often grave political and human rights consequences. Also absent is clarity about the type of Islamic law being used in this so-called method of conflict resolution. No one considers the social context within which this law is being implemented. The diversity and multitude of positions towards Islamic law, the critical discourse in Islamic countries among civil society actors and

11 See for example the government-commissioned report by the then Canadian Attorney General and Minister Responsible for Women's Issues Marion Boyd suggesting that faith-based arbitration continue as long as safeguards were introduced and are conducted voluntarily. M. Boyd, *Dispute Resolution in Family Law: Protecting Choice. Promoting Inclusion*, Report prepared for the Attorney General and Minister Responsible for Women's Issues, December 2004, at133.

12 It should be mentioned that since 1881, Greece has formally integrated Muslim Family Laws into its legal system. The work of sharia councils in Greece is a result of bilateral treaties between the Greek and Ottoman (later Turkish) governments in the late 19th and early 20th centuries. Greece continues to officially recognize the jurisdiction of three Muslim muftis. See Y. Sezgin, "Muslim Family Laws in Israel and Greece: Can Non-Muslim Courts Bring about Legal Change in Shari'a?", (2018) 25 (3) *Islamic Law and Society*, 25(3)243–246.

13 J. Donnelly, "Cultural relativism and universal human rights", (1984) 4 *Human Rights Quarterly*, at 401.

14 *Ibid.*

intellectuals, and their attempts to change Islamic laws: none of this seems to be relevant to their discourse. Indeed, the discourse is very academic and theoretical, ignoring the settings or circumstances within which women are living in closed societies. It is as if Muslim women, Muslims and Islam itself had been crafted and constructed separate from their historical, political, social and religious contexts.

Also absent from their discourse is an awareness of the role that two forms of Islamism[15] – societal and political – plays in promoting this development, or of their totalitarian agenda. I will come back to this point later in this chapter.

2 Legal Pluralism in the UK

The United Kingdom allows the application of Islamic law in family affairs in Sharia councils and Muslim arbitration tribunals. British Muslims[16] are not the only group that resort to their religious laws. Jewish and Hindu laws are also used as well. My research however focuses on the Muslim separate legal system that exists.

15 Islamism is a religious far right ideology. The ideology seeks domination and a world order that is based on a theocratic concept of state and society. It has diverse currents but can be divided into two main forms neo-fundamentalism (societal Islamism), and political Islamism. *Neo-fundamentalism* (*societal Islamism*) is a set of modern movements that sprang up in the eighteenth century, promoting a fundamentalist extremist form of Islam; in essence they were created as a reaction to the challenges of modernity. Wahhabi Salafi Islam and Deobandi Islam are two examples of this form. The second form is *political Islamism*, basically a political ideology grounded in interpretations of neo-fundamentalism. Hence the Muslim Brotherhood, which is the prototype of political Islamism, is Salafi in its religious creed. Jamaat-e-Islami and Millî Görüş are the twin sisters of the Muslim Brotherhood, in South Asia and Turkey respectively. See E. Manea, *The Perils of Nonviolent Islamism* (New York, Telos Press, 2021).

16 The Muslim population is divided into 14 nationalities. The majority, about two thirds, have South Asian roots: they are from Pakistan or Bangladesh, followed by India. The rest come from Afghanistan, Algeria, Bangladesh, Egypt, Iran, Iraq, Morocco, Nigeria, Pakistan, Saudi Arabia, Somalia and Turkey. Heterogeneity in their denomination, languages and ethnicities is a key characteristic. Despite this heterogeneity, a process that started in the 1950s led to the construction of the so-called 'Muslim community' and hence the introduction of legal pluralism in the UK. For more information see Change Institute, *Summary Report: Understanding Muslim Ethnic Communities* (London, Change Institute, Department for Communities and Local Government, 2009), at 19–23.

The number of Sharia Councils is unknown and ranges from 35 to 85 councils.[17] These are not subject to any state supervision, they deny access to legal advice and legal assistance, appeals to their decisions are not possible and their focus is on family disputes. The majority of their applicants are women, who seek a religious divorce from their husbands. Muslim Arbitration Tribunals apply Islamic Law under the British Arbitration Act of 1996 and therefore their judgments are legally binding. Both parties must agree first to arbitration. There are indications that these tribunals, just like the councils, have turned into parallel legal structures. They arbitrate on family disputes, domestic violence and even in cases of child abuse.[18]

Four factors played a central role in the creation of these parallel legal structures in the UK, and part of the process entailed the construction of a Muslim community.

2.1 *First, Legacy of the Colonial Era: Former Colonial Policies towards Colonies/Protectorates*

As colonial Britain ruled and administered its colonies and protectorates it established specific policy measures, which continued as Britain became a post-colonial nation. First, within its various colonies and protectorates, Britain often used intermediaries to establish indirect control. Second, it often refrained from interfering in the social customs of its colonies and protectorates, at the same time fostering systems of legal pluralism.[19]

In the Arabian Peninsula, these intermediaries could have been sheikhs, sultans or emirs. Within British India, more relevant to our discussion are the political leaders who attained power by presenting themselves as the exclusive representatives of what they wished to define as a 'religious community'. Through this process, heterogeneous populations were combined and homogenised on the basis of a sociological definition of what Kepel calls their 'Muslimness'.[20]

These leaders were promoting a political agenda: they wanted to carve their own state, Pakistan, out of India. Meanwhile, colonial Britain had an interest

17 For more information on the work of Sharia Councils, see B. Samia, *Muslim Women and Shari'ah Councils: Transcending the Boundaries of Community and Law* (London, Palgrave Macmillan, 2012).

18 See E. Manea, *Women and Shari'a Law, supra.*

19 E. Manea, *Regional Politics, supra,* at 24; E. Manea, *The Arab State, supra,* at 59.

20 G. Kepel, *Allah in the West: Islamic Movements in America and Europe* (Cambridge, UK, Polity Press, 1997), at 94–95.

in weakening Indians' nationalist aspirations using the strategy of divide and rule. This worked, as the historian David Page explains:

> By treating the Muslims as a separate group, [the colonial government] divided them from other Indians. By granting them separate electorates, it institutionalised that division. This was one of the most crucial factors in the development of communal politics. Muslim politicians did not have to appeal to non-Muslims; non-Muslims did not have to appeal to Muslims. This made it difficult for a genuine Indian nationalism to emerge. [21]

Thus we see that the colonial British frequently used the policies of governing through intermediaries and developing a communalism that combined diverse groups into one for political reasons.

Likewise, legal pluralism was not foreign to colonial British policies. In fact, the system had a political function: it facilitated the fragmentation of the colonial societies. For example, in British India the legal system resolved family disputes according to the Warren Hastings Act II of 1772, adopted as the Regulation of 17 April, 1780 and enacted in Section 27. The act stated that 'in all suits regarding inheritance, succession, marriage, caste, and other religious usages or institutions, the laws of the Qur'an with respect to Mohammadans [Muslims] and those of the Shastras with respect to Gentoos [Hindus], shall be invariably adhered to'.[22]

Similarly, Aden in today's south of Yemen – under British rule since 1839 and granted the status of colony in 1937 – was to follow in the footsteps of the legal system in India, which was similar in its essentials to those that existed in other British colonies. The colonial legal and judicial system tried all cases of legal infringement and heard them in English. But in matters pertaining to marriage, divorce and inheritance, religious and customary stipulations remained

---

21 D. Page, *Prelude to Partition: The Indian Muslims and the Imperial System of Control (1920–1932)* (Delhi: Oxford University Press, 1982), at 260, quoted in G. Kepel, *Allah in the West, supra,* at 95.

22 E. Manea, *The Arab State, supra* at 63; Warren Hastings Act II of 1772, in K.P. Saksena, *Muslim Law as Administered in India and Pakistan*, 4th ed. (Lucknow, Eastern Book Company, 1963), at 41; R. Z. Said, *The Making of the Modern Gulf States: Kuwait, Bahrain, Qatar, The United Arab Emirates and Oman* (London, Unwin Hyman, 1989); K. Pieragostini, *Britain, Aden and South Arabia: Abandoning Empire* (New York, St. Martin's Press, 1991), at 21; M. Molyneux, *State Policies and the Position of Women Workers in the People's Democratic Republic of Yemen, 1967–1977* (Geneva, International Labour Office, 1982), at 246.

in force. Starting in 1840, the General Government of Bombay decided that laws, which were 'purely social or religious', should continue to be the concern of the Muslim *qadis* (judges). Religious minorities in Aden, such as Jews and Hindus, were allowed to have their separate religious courts to resolve their family disputes.[23]

2.2 *Second, the British Understanding of Nationality*

While communalism, the use of intermediaries, and legal pluralism were established policies in colonial Britain, the British understanding of nationality and citizenship further paved the way for what was to come in the post-colonial UK.

Britain does not understand nationality and citizenship as a homogeneous concept. Instead, political identity is expressed by various national identities existing side by side: English, Scottish, Welsh and Irish. Citizenship as such is the sum of various different nationalities. Gilles Kepel was quick to see how this concept of citizenship created the conditions within which the political system received the immigrant populations coming into Britain after their former colonial territories became independent. These immigrants were not required to assimilate into the dominant society. Instead they were granted a parallel status, similar to that of the Welsh and Scottish nations, which already existed at the time.[24]

These two specific features of the British context created the setting within which new immigrants coming from former colonies moved to the UK in the 1950s.

2.3 *Third, Measures Taken by Islamist Movements, Societal or Political*

The parallel status that the British government gave to South Asian migrants was cemented by actions and measures taken by members of the two types of Islamist movements: societal and political Islamism.[25]

Before elaborating on this point further, a definition of the two types of Islamism is warranted. Societal Islamism refers to puritanical religious

23 Z. H. Kour, *The History of Aden 1839–1872* (London, Frank Kass, 1981), at 88.

24 G. Kepel, *Allah in the West, supra,* at 98.

25 We should be careful not to confuse Islam, a world religion and a civilization with various traditions and diverse history, with Islamism– a far right religious ideology based on the absolute indivisibility of the trinity din (religion), dunya (life), and dawla (government). This indivisibility is supposed to be permanent and eternal. The ultimate goal is to bring this trio into a totalitarian order, not only at the local level but also on a global scale. See M.Mozaffari, "What Is Islamism? History and Definition of a Concept," (2007) 8 (1) *Totalitarian Movements and Political Religions* 21–24.

movements, such as Salafi and Deobandi movements, which concern themselves with changing social behaviours on the basis of their rigid worldviews, call for an Islamic mode of life, separate their followers from the wider society, and refrain from political engagement. This type focuses on behaviour, insisting on strict adherence to a range of ritual and personal behavioural practices, especially worship, dress and everyday conduct. In short, these movements insist on implementing the Shari'a, as they interpret it, in a strict and literal manner. However, unlike political Islamist movements, they lack a systematic political ideology and are not concerned with state building, at least not at this stage. Political Islamism, on the other hand, is an ideology, a modern ideology that seeks to use the state's political power as a means of changing and transforming existing societies. It is based on a fundamentalist interpretation of Islam. Power is only a means to an end; its goal is revolutionary change compelled by a vision of a puritanical society and state, a society that is governed by God's law, not laws made by men and women. It envisions a state where identity and citizenship are based on and defined by religious affiliation and observance. Consequently, universal human rights, citizenship rights, and minority, LGBT and women's rights are often violated. There are two main political movements that embody the ideology of political Islam: the Muslim Brotherhood, created in Egypt in 1928 by Hassan al-Banna, a primary school teacher; and the Jamaat-e-slami, created in British India in1941 by Abul A'la Maududi, an Indian-born journalist who later moved to Pakistan. From these two sprang other groups, both violent and non-violent.[26]

In the UK, the main strands of societal Islamism had worked persistently since the 1950s to create a Muslim identity among south Asian communities – an identity that ultimately separated 'Muslims' from the general British society. Concurrently, different foundations and organisations following the ideology of political Islamism were created in the early 1960s, primarily to promote and mainstream the concepts of political Islamism. Though they pleaded for Muslims to participate actively in British society, they did so by making demands for Islamist exceptionalism.

26 E. Manea, *Women and shari'a law, supra,* at 143–163; E.Manea, "In the Name of Culture and Religion: The Political Function of Blasphemy in Islamic States", (2016) 27 (1) *Islam and Christian–Muslim Relations*, at 122.; O.Roy, *Islamic Radicalism in Afghanistan and Pakistan.* UNHCR Emergency and Security Service WRITENET Paper No. 06/2001 (Paris, CNRS, January 2002), at 4; accessed July 01, 2015, available at: http://www.refworld.org/pdfid/3c6a3f7d2.pdf. B.D. Metcalf, *Traditionalist Islamic Activism: Deobandi, Tablighis, and Talibs* (Leiden, ISIM, 2002), at 2.

The ghettoising of Muslims that began started in the 1950s and 1960s was facilitated by the xenophobic reactions of landlords who refused to rent to 'Pakis'. Mosques representing the different strands of societal Islamism, specifically the Deobandi and Barelwi, were erected.[27] At the same time, scholars began to see a communalism expressed in what they called 'market segmentation'. Religious taboos were enacted, necessitating the need for halal food and Islamic financing. Supermarkets selling halal food and employing Muslim youth, whose assistants and cashiers wear a uniform with a veil, were also created around these mosques. Kepel researched this development since its inception, and observed it accurately:

> The organisation of communal networks around the first mosques thus allowed the immigrant Muslim communities to set in train a process of identity differentiation affecting all aspects of daily life.[28]

Differentiation took on a further dimension when associations connected to the Jamaat-e-Islami started to campaign actively for an Islamic, or rather Islamist, education, asking for revisions of the curriculum, and special conditions for Muslim students in public schools: halal food; permission for girls to wear trousers, tunics and veils; and separate prayer rooms for Muslims. They were most successful where they organised themselves to lobby local authorities.[29]

This lobbying succeeded in establishing a close working relationship with British authorities. For example, the Muslim Education Trust, created in 1966 by members of the Maududi movement, Jamaat-e-Islami,[30] was instrumental

---

27 Deobandi is an Islamic revivalist neo fundamentalist movement that formed during the late 19th century around the Darul Uloom Islamic seminary in the town of Deoband India. Its teaching is widespread in India, Pakistan, Bangladesh and in south Asian Muslim communities worldwide. The Barelwi movement is also a revivalist Sufi movement which appeared towards the end of the nineteenth century in the north Indian town of Bareilly as a reaction to the ideological attacks of the Deobandis. Despite its Sufi origins, experts argue that the movement has been radicalized in reaction to the Deobandi attacks against it. For more information see E. Manea, *Women and Shari'a Law, supra,* at chapter 5.

28 *Ibid.*, at 108.

29 *Ibid.*, at 110–111.

30 Jamaat-e-Islami, was created in British India in 1941 by Abul A'la Maududi, an Indian-born journalist who later moved to Pakistan. It is often described as the South Asian version of Muslim Brotherhood. It insists that Islam is not only a religion. It is a political system and a social order. It governs every aspect of society including politics. And Muslims have to surrender their wills to its stipulations. It aspires for the creation of an Islamic state that applies Islamic law, shari'a. See *Ibid.*, at chapter 5.

in pushing for an Islamic/Islamist educational agenda. According to its website, the trust was created to cater 'for the Islamic educational needs of the British Muslim children and advising their parents on how to bring up their children in an un-Islamic materialistic society'.[31]

The trust was successful in providing what it describes as 'practical help and advice to British education authorities, schools, educational bodies, Muslim parents and non-Muslim teachers, and a host of other people involved in education about the general and Islamic needs of Muslim pupils in British schools'.[32]

One achievement it boasts about is the preparation of the GCSE (General Certificate of Secondary Education) religious education (ISLAM) syllabus as a fully-fledged examination subject. The syllabus was approved by the then SEAC (Secondary Examinations and Assessment Council) and introduced by the erstwhile University of London Examinations and Assessment Council (ULEAC, now EDEXCEL). According to the trust, so far more than 25,000 pupils have taken the exam using this syllabus.[33]

Though the trust has a close working relationship with the British educational authorities, it is important to emphasise that the 'Islamic education' it has been promoting was designed to perpetuate a specific Islamic cultural identity and to prevent the assimilation of Muslim children into British society.[34] Significantly, it clearly propagates the political ideology of Islamism, especially the South Asian Jamaat-e-Islami ideology.

The question therefore arises: why did the British authorities take at face value the claim of these Islamist organisations and with them societal Islamists? This brings me to the fourth factor.

2.4 *Fourth, British Policies and the Use of Intermediaries to Get the 'Asian Vote'*

Slowly but steadily, across the later decades of the 1900s, a certain reality started to take shape. Consider the elements of the context: Citizenship was and is perceived as the sum of different nationalities, and the policies and conduct of post-colonial Britain were shaped by a colonial legacy of communalism and the need for intermediaries. In this context, the efforts of the societal and political Islamists to create a separate religious 'community' were bound to find a receptive audience in the British political establishment.

31 Cited in E.Manea, *Women and shari'a law, supra,* at 166.

32 *Ibid.*

33 *Ibid.*

34 G. Kepel, *Allah in the West, supra.*

The parallel status that was given to what would be called the 'Muslim community' took its full shape in the 1980s. Government policies, regardless of their ideological orientation, played a large role in the process that constructed and homogenised the diverse South Asian communities.

First, the conservatives, headed by Margaret Thatcher, created the policy of 'rolling back the state', and outsourcing public services to civil society actors. This process fostered partnerships between the state and civil society actors, especially faith organisations.[35]

Thatcher strongly believed in 'individual freedom and individual prosperity [...], in diversity of choice, [and] in the preservation of local rights in local communities'. But her concept of neo-liberalism and a limited role for the state was founded in her Christian beliefs and her conviction that the Church should take on strong functions in civil society.[36] Almost by default, this role was extended to other 'faith groups'.

Religion was also seen as a tool for facing social maladies within the British context.[37] In fact, in the 1980s some argued that the 'Muslim community's religiosity should be encouraged because it helped maintain relatively low crime rates' among 'young Asian men compared to their Afro-Caribbean counterparts'.[38]

Second, while the conservatives were urging a larger role for faith organisations, the Labour Party also played its part in constructing the Muslim community. Here the issue was getting votes. Labour needed to recruit from the Asian communities to compensate for the erosion of its traditional working-class electorate.[39] But when it recruited these voters, it used those same British colonial techniques of communalism and intermediaries. Early on, for example, it would recruit 'clan elders who could deliver votes en masse'. The assumption was that 'the elder would simply tell everyone in the clan to vote for their candidate'.[40] Slowly the 'Asian vote', also dubbed the 'ethnic vote', started being labelled the 'Muslim vote'.

35 J. Barbalet *et. al*, *Religion and the State: A Comparative Sociology* (London, Anthem Press, 2013), at 51.

36 M. Thatcher, "My kind of Tory Party", *Daily Telegraph*, January 30, 1975, accessed July 1, 2015, http://www.margaretthatcher.org/document/. For more about how Thatcher perceived the state, government, and the church see also her speech at St Lawrence Jewry, 4th March 1981, accessed July 01, 2015, http://www.margaretthatcher.org/document/104587.

37 Ghaffar Hussain, interview with author, St. Albans, August 06, 2013.

38 M. Mirza *et al*, "Living apart together" *supra*, at 25.

39 G. Kepel, *Allah in the West, supra*, at 112.

40 K. Malik, *From Fatwa to Jihad, supra*, at 68.

The need for intermediaries transcended the issue of votes. The racial tensions of the early 1980s highlighted what some local officials called the need for 'some new channel of communication' between local councils and the communities: 'something to compensate for the lack of political representation'.[41]

This new channel took the shape of religious intermediaries. For example, in 1981, to create this new channel, the Bradford local authority helped set up and fund the Bradford Council of Mosques, which would play later an important role in inciting resentment towards Salman Rushdie's *Satanic Verses*. Naturally, the council members belonged to the Deobandi, Barelwi and Jammat-e-Islami movements, the very advocates of societal and political Islamism that were pushing for a separate religious identity for the diverse South Asian communities.

Kenan Malik observes that the Council of Mosques was not primarily a religious organisation. Rather, it was set up to present itself as the true voice of the 'Muslim community' and to be the 'conduit between that community and the public bodies in the city'.[42]

A plethora of mosque-based social projects started to flourish: in the case of the Council of Mosques this included two centres for the elderly, a variety of workers offering advice, services for women in hospitals and clinics, and a series of centres for Muslim youth and the Muslim community. With these projects the council started to focus on demands for separate religious and cultural accommodations, such as separate Muslim schools, separate education for girls and serving of halal meat at schools. All these demands were met without much discussion.[43]

The newfound relationship between the local councils, the mosques and social service provision marginalised the more secular movements. Most importantly, it gave greater credibility to the conservative religious leadership within those communities. Likewise, this type of policy encouraged the emergence of a certain type of leader: one who has an interest in perpetuating the community boundary, since it makes him or her indispensable as an intermediary.[44]

Together, all of these factors and measures provided the backbone of the British policies of multiculturalism and its soft legal pluralism. Given that these measures focused on separation and even tribalism, it was not surprising that they led instead to the reality of plural monoculturalism. Multiculturalism

41 *Ibid.*, at 73.
42 *Ibid.*, at 72–75.
43 *Ibid.*, at 75–79.
44 G. Kepel, *Allah in the West, supra,* at 114–115.

was well intentioned but the efforts to develop it actually ingrained differences rather than celebrating what brings together different people from different backgrounds. It was focusing on what makes them separate and that separateness was promoted in policy measures. And when these efforts concerned South Asian communities, they were made in a political and Islamist context that homogenised people and reduced them to their religious identity.

Today, that separateness is seen and felt on a daily basis. I asked Tehmina Kazi, Director of British Muslims for Secular Democracy (BMSD), whether she agrees with the statement that multiculturalism led to a specific cultural separation between communities. Her answer reminded me of the closed communities of the Millet System of the Ottoman Empire:

> A separation of communities? Well if you go to places like Bradford and Oldham, even parts of East London, you will see a lot of communities that sort of rub together side by side. They are kind at best, they tolerate each other, and at worst there is sort of very little interaction and very little mixing. [There are …] lower rates of what I consider markers of integration such as interfaith marriages and [cross-cultural] relationships. For example, in whole swathes of Bradford you have Asian schools and Asian areas, and white schools and white areas and it is sad that these communities are disparate. They do not feel that there is anything bringing them together.[45]

Plural monoculturalism led to another outcome: a new generation of Muslims who identify themselves first as 'Muslim'. According to a 2009 study commissioned by the Department for Communities and Local Government on 'Muslim communities', the significance of ethnicity and faith in relation to identity has changed over the generations:

> For older generations in particular, affiliations relating to nation, clan, tribe, location of origin can all play as significant a part as faith identity and links with countries of origin remain strong. For younger respondents there are indications of a growing religiosity and a more pan-Muslim sense of identity that rejects other ethnic boundaries and practices seen as specific to a cultural group rather than to Islam, though this qualitative finding needs further substantive research.[46]

45 Tehmina Kazi, interview with author, London, January 14, 2013.
46 Change Institute, *Summary Report, supra*, at 6.

Today, in some closed Muslim communities in the UK, core messages of fundamentalism have become mainstreamed. A 2016 survey commissioned by Channel 4 suggests that while a large majority of British Muslims feel a strong sense of belonging to Britain (86%), a chasm develops between those Muslims who were surveyed and the wider population on attitudes to liberal values on issues such as gender equality, homosexuality and issues relating to freedom of expression. It also reveals significant differences on attitudes to violence and terrorism.

For example, only 34% of those surveyed said they would inform the police if they thought someone they knew was getting involved with people who support terrorism in Syria. Only 32% would condemn those who take part in violence against people mocking the Prophet. On more personal issues, 23% support the introduction of Shari'a law, 31% think it's acceptable for a man to have more than one wife, and 39% agree that "wives should always obey their husbands". And 52% do not believe that homosexuality should be legal in Britain.[47]

Fundamentalism goes hand in hand with segregation, which is a significant issue in the UK. In 2016, an independent government report by Dame Louse Casey made headlines by stating something that is public knowledge: minorities are segregated.

The report said that as diversity has increased in the United Kingdom, another dynamic has become clear. People from minority groups have become both more dispersed and in some cases more concentrated and segregated. And people of Pakistani and Bangladeshi ethnicity tend to live in more residentially segregated communities compared to other ethnic minority groups. In many areas, these concentrations are growing at the ward level.[48]

Segregation is compounded by the pattern of marriages taking place. The report states that high levels of transnational marriage may have undermined the rates of integration in some communities. In other words, marriage partners, both men and women, are imported from outside the country: people who

47 N.N. (April 11, 2016), "C4 survey and documentary reveals What British Muslims Really Think", Channel 4, http://www.channel4.com/info/press/news/c4-survey-and-documentary-reveals-what-british-muslims-really-think. For the full results of the survey, conducted between 25 April and 31 May 2015, see N.N. (April 11, 2016), "ICM Muslims Survey for Channel 4", ICM Unlimited Polling, https://www.icmunlimited.com/wp-content/uploads/2016/04/Mulims-full-suite-data-plus-topline.pdf.

48 L. Casey, *The Casey Review: A review into opportunity and integration*, Department for Communities and Local Government, UK Government, December 2016, at 10ff, available at: https://www.gov.uk/government/uploads/system/uploads/attachment_data/file/575973/The_Casey_Review_Report.pdf.

are not familiar with UK traditions and the way of life. As native-born people marry foreign-born partners, they create the phenomenon of '*first generation in every generation*' in which children in each new generation grow up with one foreign-born parent. This seems particularly prevalent in South Asian communities. The writers of the report "were told on one visit to a northern town that all except one of the Asian Councillors had married a wife from Pakistan. And in a cohort study at the Bradford Royal Infirmary, 80% of babies of Pakistani ethnicity in the area had at least one parent born outside the UK".[49]

The Casey report argues that the demographic structure of schools mirrors the segregation described above; more than 50% of ethnic minority students are in schools where ethnic minorities are the majority. This school segregation was highest among students from Pakistani and Bangladeshi ethnic backgrounds, compared to other ethnic groups. Taken together, the report tells us, this high concentration of ethnic minority children in residential areas and in schools increases the likelihood that they will grow up without meeting or better understanding people from different backgrounds.[50]

It is not surprising that a Survey conducted by YouGov-Cambridge Centre for Public Opinion Research in March 2015 survey and cited by the Casey report found that more than 55% of the general public agreed that 'there was a fundamental clash between Islam and the values of British society'. On the other hand, 46% of British Muslims felt that 'being a Muslim in Britain was difficult due to prejudice against Islam'. In addition, the polling indicated a growing sense of grievance among sections of the Muslim population, and a stronger sense of identification with the 'plight' of the *Ummah*, the global Muslim community.[51]

3 The Political Dimension: Islamism and the Introduction of Islamic Law in the UK

There is a political dimension that is often ignored when discussing the issue: those 'Muslims' in the West who call for the introduction of legal pluralism and the use of Islamic law are often affiliated with forms of Islamism, societal or/and political. Some Western academics and politicians take their

49 *Ibid.*, at 9.

50 *Ibid.*, at 11.

51 J. Rogers de Waal, "GB Tracker: Islam and British Values" (Cambridge Centre for Public Opinion Research, March 2015), available at: https://yougov.co.uk/topics/politics/articles-reports/2016/02/19/tracker-islam-and-british-values, cited in L. Casey, at 11–12.

calls at face value, in the process ignoring the political agenda of Islamism and its totalitarian nature.

'There is a disconnect!' Gita Sahgal told me. She is the Indian-born British director of the Centre for Secular Space in London and the founder of Women against Fundamentalism. People in Britain working on security issues, and fighting extremism, are not concerned about shari'a courts. But, she explained, the two issues are connected.

The two are connected in three ways: through membership, ideology and co-optation. First, consider membership. The key is that many members of the shari'a courts belong to the various movements promoting societal and political Islamism. Several activists and experts on extremism argue that the two types of Islamism played a central role in the creation and work of Islamic courts in the UK.

Maryeam Namazi, Director of One Law for All, is an Iranian-born human rights activist and one of the leading voices lobbying for the end of shari'a courts in Britain. She described the programmatic nature of this connection to Islamism:

> It is not [that] a group of Muslims came together and said 'oh, we want to have shari'a courts as a form of mediation'. If you look at the shari'a courts themselves, the people who are running the courts, they have links with the Islamic movement [...]. But also a lot of them are linked with the Muslim Brotherhood and Jamaat-e-Islami; they have this link.[52]

Rashad Ali, the expert on extremism I quoted earlier, also mentioned this aspect, in a matter of fact way. Just like Gita Saghal and Maryam Namazie, he highlighted the link and gave the following example:

> I think in some respects you will find that the shari'a Council in Birmingham, in the Central Mosque in Birmingham, is a mixture of Jamaat-e-Islami, Maududis and Deobandi scholars who run it. The central mosque is an affiliation of the two groups [...] So I think you do get trends [... and] find transnational [Islamist] movements like the Muslim brotherhood and Jamaat-e-Islami being involved with such movements.[53]

52 Maryam Namazie, interview with author, London, January 19, 2013.
53 Rashad Ali, interview with author, London, January 18, 2013.

My research supports this observation. Members of the two types of Islamism, societal and political, often control British shari'a courts. For example, according to its website, the Islamic Shari'a Council in Leyton was founded by several organisations that have known affiliations with political and societal Islamism: Jamaat-e-Islami (UK Islamic Mission), Muslim Brotherhood (Muslim Welfare House), and global Wahhabi Islam (Muslim World League).[54] Some of those working in the council as 'judges' belong to Salafi Islam (such as Haitham Al Haddad) and to Ahl Al Hadith,[55] the Salafis of South Asia (such as Dr Suhaib Hasan).

Second, consider ideology. Those working in the shari'a courts often display the ideological and political features of Islamism, an aspect I illustrated earlier in this chapter when I discussed the two forms of Islamism. These features include the emphasis on creating an Islamic state through incremental steps, on implementing shari'a, on jihad against enemies of Islam, and on the division of the world into two camps, believers and non-believers. Controlling women and their behaviour through a patriarchal and archaic interpretation of Islam is another common feature.

Dr Usama Hasan, who in 2012 authored the Quilliam Foundation's response to the Baroness Cox Arbitration and Mediation Services (Equality) Bill, specifically mentioned the problem of extremism in relation to the shari'a councils: he referred to the ways that extremist clerics sitting in the UK shari'a councils make women's lives hard. He commented on this aspect in a follow-up interview:

> Yes, there are certainly people with strong Islamist ideas [sitting in the shari'a councils], but you know Islamist ideas have infected Muslims worldwide, so that is no surprise. So, yes, there will be people who have these vague notions of the Islamic state, shari'a and the caliphate and jihad and all this stuff.[56]

54 "Welcome to the Islamic Shari'a Council," accessed September 15, 2023, available at: http://www.islamic-sharia.org/.

55 Literally the people of the prophetic narrations, this is another revivalist movement that grew out of India in the nineteenth century (1870s). They are Salafis but are known as Ahl Al Hadith in South Asia and since the 1960s have maintained close ties with the Saudi religious establishment. For more information see E. Manea, *Women and shari'a law supra,* at 151–152.

56 Usama Hasan, interview with author, August 2013.

This ideological feature, which he described as fundamentalist in nature, affects the way 'they look at certain issues in terms of resistance to reform', specifically in relation to gender relations. It explains why it will be difficult to reform the shari'a councils. Indeed, the attitude is of a literalist adherence to the strict, restrictive parochial worldview of women and insistence on their treatment as minors:

> [These extremist clerics] will say, a woman can never marry on her own accord, she can never divorce on her own accord, she can never have equal inheritance with men, let alone more than men. And they are all basing this on a literalist interpretation of the Qur'an, which is one characteristic of fundamentalism in my understanding.[57]

Third, consider co-optation. Islamists have co-opted the idea of weak legal pluralism to suit their own political agenda. The shari'a courts 'certainly grew out of an ideological' Islamist agenda:[58] the first council, created in the UK in 1982, was the Islamic Shari'a Council in Leyton and it has clear connections with transnational Islamist groups, both societal and political.

Over time, however, and because of the Islamisation in British Muslim communities, as Rashid Ali explains, some of these courts have become a venue for resolving 'practical issues' for some individuals with specific religious beliefs who need 'to have issues resolved' in ways that fit their dogma, and so 'councils sometimes serve as a place for fatwa, serve as a place to help them fulfil their own religious needs'.[59]

Given the problems and discrimination women face in the shari'a courts, some Muslim religious scholars, such as Dr Usama Hasan, try to extend help to women and assist them in getting what they need: a religious divorce.

That said, the Islamist co-optation of shari'a courts takes several shapes. One is what Tahmina Saleem, co-founder of Inspire, the British Muslim women's organisation, describes as framing the use of these shari'a councils as obligatory and presenting a de-contextualised patriarchal interpretation of Islamic law as the standard that should be used:

> I do see a relationship between Islam being used for political purposes and shari'a councils within the UK. I would describe the relationship being presented as 'obligatory', meaning that the existence of these

57 *Ibid.*

58 Rashad Ali, interview with author, January 2013.

59 *Ibid.*

> councils is presented as fulfilling fundamental religious needs within Muslim communities that are not being met elsewhere within the British context. Many of these shari'a councils are supported by conservative bodies, such as affiliates of Jamaat-e-Islam and the Muslim Brothers, both of which promote patriarchal, narrowly defined, roles for women. These roles are based on de-contextualised interpretations of shari'a that are irrelevant to the UK today. Yet these interpretations are promoted as the defining standard by which all other standards are secondary including Western legal notions of women's human rights.[60]

Co-optation takes the form of defending shari'a courts regardless of their shortcomings, and arguing that for Muslim communities, 'implementation of shari'a' is a 'religious necessity'. This presentation precludes any mention that the necessity is linked to the political agenda of Islamism, and that such courts do not meet the general needs of diverse communities of Islamic heritage. Dr Usama Hasan put it this way:

> But it is also true that the Islamists co-opt this whole project as part of their own, and that is also why the Islamist groups in this country have tended to defend the shari'a councils no matter what whenever there have been criticisms. They rallied around the shari'a councils because [of] this desire to implement shari'a [...] And the wider society can see that, they can see the Islamists active and talking about shari'a a lot, and they see the shari'a councils trying to implement a kind of form of shari'a within family law and family situation, and they often put the two together because in their mind they are linked. And yes, there is that link. [61]

The Islamists co-opt weak legal pluralism on two levels. The first level is the transnational institutional arms of political Islamism. The global institutional arms of societal and/or political Islamism often propagate the idea of a separate legal system based on shari'a for the 'Muslim minority'. The issue is often framed in a way that portrays it as a religious demand that should be respected under the banner of freedom of religion.

This example illustrates my point. The European Council for Fatwa and Research (ECFR) is an influential, private institution based in Dublin, Ireland. It was founded in March 1997 in London on the initiative of the Federation

60 Tahmina Saleem, written answers to author's questions, email exchange, August 14, 2014.

61 Usama Hasan, interview with author, August 2013.

of Islamic Organisations in Europe (FIOE). It often refers to itself on English-language Islamist websites as 'the first and the most important fatwa-reference and research institute in Europe'; 'which have shaped and helped the European Muslim community to live in conformity with their Islamic values in non-Islamic environment'.[62]

Once the council was established, the first recommendations of its two inaugural regular sessions fostered an Islamist worldview that defines identity by religious affiliation and observance. It also ignores the nationalities of migrants of Islamic heritage, and calls on them to follow Islamic law in their lifestyle and seek to recognise Islamic law in their family matters.

Hence, it called on Muslims 'to preserve their Islamic identity and religious personality, follow what the Lord has commanded in what he allowed and forbade' in their 'worship and dealings'. It also demanded that they 'work hard' to get the states where they live to recognise 'Islam as a religion, and […] Muslims as a religious minority like other religious minorities'. This recognition would include 'full enjoyment of their rights, and ability to regulate their personal status such as marriage, divorce and inheritance' according to Islamic law.[63]

A key fact is often missing in the presentation of these recommendations: this council and the federation that created it are all international arms of the Muslim Brotherhood. The ECFR is headed by Sheikh Yusuf al-Qaradawi, the Chairman of the International Union of Muslim Scholars, and a well-known global spiritual leader of the Muslim Brotherhood movement. He has often used his television show on the Aljazeera and Qatar TV channels to support and spread Islamist causes worldwide. He has also fostered the idea of Islam, or more accurately Islamism, conquering Europe gradually without resorting to the sword. For example, he said this on one TV show:

> The peaceful conquest has foundations in this religion, and therefore I expect that Islam will conquer Europe without resorting to the sword or fighting. It will do so by means of *da'wa* [proselytising] and ideology. Europe is miserable with materialism, with the philosophy of promiscuity, and with the immoral considerations that rule the world,

62 See Sheikh Dr. K. Hanafy (Assistant Secretary), "The European Council for Fatwa and Research: Renewed leadership, renewed hopes", European Council for Fatwa and Research, (December 16, 2018), available at: https://www.e-cfr.org/blog/2018/12/16/european-council-fatwa-research/.

63 European Council for Fatwa and Research, *Resolutions and Fatwas* [*edicts*] *of the European Council for Fatwa and Research*, in Arabic (Cairo, Islamic House for Distribution and Publication, 2002), at 19.

> considerations of self-interest and self-indulgence. It is high time Europe woke up and found a way out from this. Europe will find no lifesaver or lifeboat other than Islam. Islam will save Europe from the raging materialism from which it suffers. The promiscuity, which permits men to marry men and women to marry women, is horrifying. All religions condemn this. [Islam] is capable of granting Europe and the entire West the world to come, without denying them this world. It can grant them faith without denying them science. It can grant them truth, without denying them power. It can connect them to the heavens, without tearing them away from the earth. It can grant them spirit, without denying them matter. The message of Islam is a message of global balance, and therefore, I believe the next conquest will be conducted through *da'wa*. But, of course, the Muslims must start acting in order to conquer this world. [64]

Moreover, the *Online Muslim Brothers Encyclopaedia*, published in Arabic, identifies the FIOE, the council's parent organisation, as 'the European wing of the global Muslim Brothers movement'.[65]

This political affiliation is simply absent from the English website of the FIOE. Instead, it defines itself as a 'cultural organisation' – one with hundreds of member organisations spread across 28 European States'. It also portrays itself as the 'largest Islamic organisation on the European level'. Whether this reflects reality is open to discussion; it is certainly well funded and highly organised. What is important, though, is that this organisation is a political organisation, one that works as an arm of the global political Islamism movement.[66]

In pluralistic Western democracies the two organisations are certainly entitled to their opinions regarding Islamic law in the West. The problem I see is with the way they present their demands as Islamic, ordained by Islam, and hence religious demands of the Muslim minority. In fact, what they call for are political demands of a political ideology: Islamism. They never openly acknowledge this link.

The second level at which they co-opt weak legal pluralism is through the national-level organisations of political Islamism. These organisations and

64 Sheik Yousuf Al-Qaradhawi, 'Islam's "Conquest of Rome" will save Europe from its subjugation to materialism and promiscuity', *Qatar TV*, July 28, 2007. The TV clip, no. 1592, translated and posted by *MERI TV, The Middle East Media Research Institute*, is available at: http://www.memritv.org/clip/en/1592.htm..

65 Ikhwan Wiki, Federation of Islamic Organisations in Europe, in Arabic, accessed July 01, 2015, http://goo.gl/u57S2R.

66 *Ibid.*

associations working at the national level in Europe and North America often endorse the application of weak legal pluralism for the Muslim community.

For example, in the UK, the Muslim Council of Britain (MCB), with its clear links to Jamaat-e-Islami, has been at the forefront in attempts to 'mainstream' shari'a courts and to introduce Islamic law in family affairs, as 'religiously mandated arbitration panels'. It reiterated this point in its latest paper, on the 2015 general election.[67] Again, similar to the strategy of the transnational institutional arms of political Islamism, the MCB presents its Islamist perspective as 'British Muslims' perspectives at the 2015 General Election – the title of its paper. It fosters the separation of Muslims by promoting the notion that British Muslims have specific needs that can only be fulfilled via special treatment for them, including sanctioning the work of the shari'a councils.[68]

Most importantly, it politicises any critique of these courts as a 'critique of Islam' and an expression of 'Islamophobia'. Baroness Cox is one target of such accusations.

Baroness Cox was one of the first members of Parliament to alert the public to the problem of the quasi-legal systems working in the UK and how they affect women negatively. When she first published her 2011 bill, mentioned earlier, which seeks to amend the arbitration law of 1996 and make 'criminal and family law matters not arbitrable',[69] the MCB issued a statement criticising it and insisting that the shari'a councils operate under the concept of 'consent'. Khurshid Drabu, an adviser on constitutional affairs to the MCB, commented on the bill in an interview with the *Guardian*:

> Bills of this kind don't help anybody. They don't appear to understand that we live in a free country where people can make free choices. Yet again, it appears to be a total misunderstanding of the concept that underpins these arbitration councils. Shari'a councils operate under consent. If there is a woman who suffers as a result of a decision by one of these councils a woman is free to go to the British courts. [70]

67 Muslim Council of Britain (MCB), *Fairness not Favours: British Muslims' Perspectives at the 2015 General Election* (London: MCB, 2015), at 11, available at: http://www.mcb.org.uk/wp-content/uploads/2015/03/fairnessnotfavours-MCB.pdf.

68 *Ibid.*

69 Arbitration and Mediation Services (Equality Bill), Baroness Cox, June 07, 2011, National Archive, Part 2, Article 4, at 3.

70 K. McVeigh and A. Hill, "Bill limiting sharia law is motivated by "concern for Muslim women"", *The Guardian*, June 08, 2011, accessed May 26, 2015, available at: http://www.theguardian.com/law/2011/jun/08/sharia-bill-lords-muslim-women.

Never mind that 'consent' in a closed community is often framed by structures of power and patriarchy that render the 'freedom' to go to the British courts excruciatingly unrealistic. The MCB went on to pick on Baroness Cox and her personality in a tactic that Islamists often use in response to any critique of their agenda, or of extremism, or of the negative consequences of applying Islamic law. They simply brand the person or group and the government as 'Islamophobic'.

Dr Usama Hasan, known for being a pious scholar critical of extremism and Islamism, recalls what happened:

> They brought separate grievances around baroness Cox's work itself. Because she has worked in Sudan for example on behalf of the Christian communities there, [...], she was painted as a caped crusader, who is attacking Islam and Muslims mainly because of her work in Sudan and [...] other areas on behalf of Christians. And they [...] turned that into a political issue.
>
> They tend to label anybody who does raise these issues as Islamophobic. If you criticise anything Muslims do, or any interpretation of shari'a or Islam like that, the standard response 'oh this is Islamophobic and you cannot do this'. I have been accused of being Islamophobic for talking about extremism, so that is how it is.[71]

These three elements – membership, ideology and co-optation – highlight the political dimension of the issue. Ignoring it will not make it go away. It does have implications, not only for the fight against terrorism and extremism, but also for the cohesion of society and the successful integration into British society of diverse migrants of Muslim heritage. Islamists are making use of a theoretical discussion promoted by an essentialist paradigm to achieve political goals in what one may call a 'cultural jihad': one that aims to Islamicise migrants of Muslim heritage according to tenets of societal and political Islamism, and to separate them from their wider societies and gradually 'conquer the West', to use the words of Sheikh Yusuf al-Qaradawi.

Many Western politicians and academics are hesitant to voice their concerns over this political dimension for fear of being labelled 'racist' or worse, 'Islamophobic'. Those shaped by an essentialist's paradigm on the other hand, either ignore this dimension of weak legal pluralism or do not consider it valid in the first place.

---

71 Usama Hasan, interview with author, August 2013.

The same can be said about the perception regarding the consequences for human rights and women's rights of introducing this system in Western legal systems.[72] Two attitudes prevail: either people belittle these concerns or they consider them part of a natural process, one that will ultimately lead to a moderation of the 'conservative reading of Islam'. Female scholars, activists, and organisations of Muslim heritage beg to differ. In fact, in Islamic countries the discourse is going in the other direction: moving away from family laws with a religious basis to laws that respect concepts of gender equality and justice.

4 The Type of Islamic Law Implemented in UK Sharia Councils and Muslim Arbitration Tribunal

There are different approaches to defining shari'a, Islamic law. One approach distinguishes between shari'a as the 'expression of the universal principles of Islam' and shari'a as fiqh: the 'doctrinal traditions developed by jurists over centuries'. Another approach would avoid defining shari'a in legally philosophical terms and would focus more on studying the sources that are understood to constitute the corpus of shari'a, especially on the work of pre-modern jurists, work which is so central to the study of Islamic law in the twentieth century. The approach I adopt here, which is closer to the second one mentioned above, defines shari'a by the way it is being implemented in Islamic states and within Muslim family laws: a selection from the corpus of legal opinions of jurists developed over the course of Islamic history, especially between the seventh and tenth centuries. Looking at Islamic law from this perspective will highlight its problematic nature, for we are not considering its theoretical potential to provide justice. What we are in fact looking at is its actual implementation and hence its obvious limitations and how it contravenes modern concepts of human rights. What matters is how it is being interpreted and used today, not how it could be used a century from now.

In the world view of classical Islamic law, woman is part of a hierarchical social structure dominated by the man at the top; and as a legal person the woman is controlled before her marriage by her male guardian and after marriage by her husband. The rules regarding marriageable age and guardianship make child marriages and forced marriages possible, and rules on divorce and maintenance rights discriminate against the wife.

---

72 E. Manea, *Women and Shari'a Law supra,* at 120–121.

This reflects on the type of provisions applied in family affairs. Classical Islamic law does not envision marriage and family relations as an equal partnership between man and woman. In the paragraphs below I summarise the common provisions regarding marriage and divorce.

4.1 *Marriage*

- *Age of marriage:* A Muslim man or a woman must be of sound mind and must have attained puberty to be considered legally eligible for marriage. In classical Islamic law, puberty occurs with the physical signs of maturity such as the emission of semen for boys and menstruation for girls.[73]
- *Guardianship:* In contracting a marriage, male guardianship is necessary. The established interpretations of Islamic jurisprudence schools insist that a woman cannot marry without the consent of her male guardian. A guardian handles all kinds of affairs for both his male and female wards, including contracting marriage. When the ward is a male, the guardianship ceases when the boy reaches puberty. For a girl, however, a guardian has the power to impose a marriage on a virgin girl without her knowledge or consent.[74] If she contracts a marriage without her guardian's consent, the marriage is not valid. If she was divorced, her consent, in addition to that of the guardian, is necessary to contract the marriage.
  The one crucial exception to this rule in Sunni Islam occurs in the Hanafite school of jurisprudence (dominant in south and central Asian states); it is also present in Shi'a jurisprudence.[75] Guardianship is required when the girl is not of age, that is, has not yet reached puberty. But once she reaches puberty, she is allowed to contract her marriage without her guardian's consent.[76] However, under Hanafite jurisprudence, if the guardian is not satisfied with her choice of husband, he has the right to demand that marriage be annulled on the basis of lack of *kafaa:* social equality. The

73 For more on this subject see A. Büchler and C. Schlatter, "Marriage age in Islamic and contemporary Muslim family laws: A comparative survey", (2013) 1 *Electronic Journal of Islamic and Middle Eastern Law* 37–74.

74 E. Manea, *Ich will nicht mehr schweigen: Der Islam, der Westen und die Menschenrechte* (Freiburg, Herder Verlag, 2009), at 34.

75 In Sunni Islam, there are four main schools of jurisprudence named after their founders. These are Hanafi, Maliki, Shafi'i, Hanbali. In Shia Islam, there are three: Twelvers, Ismailis, and Zaydis.

76 Some of the Twelver Shi'a jurists added the condition that for a woman to enjoy this right, she should previously have been married. For more details on the jurisprudences positions on guardianship see W.B. Hallaq, *Shari'a: Theory, Practice and Transformations* (Cambridge, Cambridge University Press, 2007), at 274–276.

concept of *kafaa*, literally suitability, gives the guardian the right to dissolve and annul a marriage, if he considers the groom/husband not to be fit or suitable.

- *Polygamy:* A Muslim man may be married up to four wives at the same time but a Muslim woman can only be married to one man at a time. A Muslim man may marry a Christian or a Jewish woman, but a Muslim woman may not marry a non-Muslim man.

4.2 *Divorce*

- A Muslim man may divorce his wife, or any of his wives, by unilateral repudiation, *talaq*, without having to give any reasons or justify his action to any person or authority. When he divorces his wife by uttering the word three times, the divorce is considered irrevocable: *bain*. In order to return to him, she must first marry a different man and get a divorce from the new husband.
- A Muslim woman can obtain a divorce in three ways: a) by gaining the consent of her husband; b) by getting a judicial decree for limited specific grounds/harms; or 3) by *khula*. This means a divorce sanctioned by a judge, but she must give up her financial rights to gain it.
- A woman divorced by her husband must observe a waiting period (*iddah*), normally lasting three months. During this period she cannot marry another man.
- A divorce in which the word is uttered fewer than three times is revocable (*raji'i*). So even if a woman gets a divorce, her husband may change his mind. During the waiting period, he has the right to return her to his household against her will and he need not sign another marriage contract. One reference on *fiqh* (Muslim Jurisprudence) explained this rule this way: 'until the period of *iddah* has elapsed, the repudiation is revocable (*raji'i*), and the husband may resume conjugal relations with his wife, if he be so inclined, by a revocation of the repudiation. This he can do whether she be willing or not'.[77]

4.3 *Obedience, Maintenance, and Beating*

- Obedience is considered a duty of the wife. A wife should be obedient to her husband insofar as his commands are legally allowed and are ordained as duties of marriage. If a wife is disobedient, she loses her right to maintenance. According to Hanafi jurisprudence, a wife is considered disobedient

---

77 A. Shukri, *Muhammedan Law of Marriage and Divorce, supra,* at 97.

if she leaves their home without the consent of her husband or without a lawful excuse. Other schools of jurisprudence, however, say that even if she stays at home, she will not be entitled to maintenance if she refuses sexual intercourse.[78] A husband may beat his wife if she is disobedient. The husband can resort to several measures when his wife disobeys him, the last of which is the most severe: beating her. If the woman obeys him, then he should stop using these measures.[79]

4.4 *Maintenance after Divorce*

- Maintenance for a divorced wife ceases after the *iddah* period, the 3-month waiting period after the divorce.
- After a divorce, the wife is only entitled to the sum of money set in the marriage contract: the *muakhar.*

4.5 *Inheritance*

- A Muslim woman receives less than the share of a Muslim man when both parties have an equal degree of relationship to the deceased person. Hence, a sister inherits from her father half of what her brother inherits. A Muslim husband inherits half of what his wife leaves, provided that she did not have a son. If she does, then the husband inherits a quarter. A Muslim wife inherits a quarter of her husband's estate if he has no son. If he has a son, then she inherits an eighth.[80]
- Being of a different religion is a total bar to inheritance. Thus a Muslim may neither inherit from, nor leave an inheritance to, a non-Muslim.[81]

4.6 *Custody of Children*

- After a divorce, the custody of a child is entrusted to either the mother or father, depending on the child's age and sex. Younger children tend to be placed in the mother's care and the father takes over custody when the child reaches a given age. However, shari'a makes a distinction between custody and guardianship: the father is the guardian of the child after separation

78 *Ibid.*, at 81; D. Pearl, *A Textbook on Muslim Law* (London, Croom Helm, 1979), at 65.

79 E. Manea, *Ich will nicht mehr schweigen, supra,* at 141–143.

80 Imam M.Abu Zahrah, *Ahkam Al Tirkat wa al Mawari'ith – Provisions for Legacies and Inheritances,* in Arabic (Beirut, Dar Al Fikr Al Arabi, 1963), at 122, 131; A. An-Na'im, *Toward an Islamic Reformation, supra,* at 176.

81 A. An-Na'im, *Ibid.*, at 176.

even if the mother is granted the right to custody up to a certain age, after which custody reverts to the father.[82]
- If the mother decides to remarry she automatically loses her right to custody.

4.7 *Testimony*

The testimony of two women equals that of one man. Originally this rule was meant for financial affairs; but the jurists expanded the rule and made it a general rule. This overview leads us to the question: What type of Islamic law is being implemented within Britain's shari'a courts? The short answer is: the classical Islamic law with all its contradictions and discrimination.

From the perspective of Britain's sharia courts, what they are applying is not only *fiqh*, the jurists' traditions. They are applying what they think of literally as God's Law, the law of Allah. Hence, depending on the type of shari'a court applying this law, it can either seek a fundamentalist interpretation of *fiqh*, or it can try to make the lives of women easier by seeking the most lenient interpretation. But the mindset is framed by the perception that shari'a is God's law and therefore better than any other secular law. The mindset is also shaped by the acceptance of the rules I mentioned above, that regulate marriage, divorce, polygamy, guardianship, inheritance, etc., anything related to family affairs and women's position within the family. They accept these rules and do not question them. Hence during my interviews with five 'judges', including a female member of a Sharia council, they reflected their perception that this *is what Islam commands, this is what God commands, and we are following God's law.*

Within this mindset, the jurists' traditions somehow seem to become sacred in these judges' minds; they reflect a 'divine wisdom' that transcends our understanding. Naturally this leads them to apply the classical Islamic law to the letter, picking and choosing as they want from within that pool of traditions.

Consider the issue of the proper age for marriage. Sheikh Siddiqi of the Muslim Arbitration Tribunal is clear regarding this issue.

> Sheikh Siddiqi: In my view, puberty is the right age. But puberty is the minimum age; then the next criterion is the decision of the guardian, he has to make the decision. Because in some societies, 12- or 13-year-old women, girls, they are more or less fully fledged women, they are fully functional, and you in Western societies, [...] are having babies, they are

82 C. Mallat, *Introduction to Middle Eastern Law* (Oxford, Oxford University Press, 2007), at 357.

> having sex, so they are fully grown and fully mature; there are some 12-year-olds that are not in that condition, they are very weak, they are not fully functional as women, and they do not want to get married. So it is the job of the *wali,* the guardian, to ensure that the girl is protected and the girl is not subjected to a marriage in this situation where her personal circumstances do not allow this marriage to take place.

Again, we see classical Islamic jurisprudence being used as a point of reference in these courts.

The guardianship issue clearly illustrates this point. As we saw above, Sheikh Siddiqi considers that the guardian knows best for his ward. Dr Mohammad Shahoot Kharfan, of the Muslim Welfare House, demands that the bride and the groom and the guardian be present at the wedding ceremony. But to contract the marriage, the guardian has to approve. One example he gave me was of a woman in her thirties who wanted to marry. Dr Kharfan asked for her guardian to contract the marriage. When she told him he lives in another country, he called him to get his approval and to ask him to delegate his right of guardianship to another person, a male of course. When I asked Dr Kharfan if her voice was not enough, his answer was matter-of-fact: 'the guardian is present, the guardian is present', meaning, we have a guardian here, and he will decide.

By the same token, Hanafi jurisprudence allows the guardian to annul the marriage of his female ward against her will, if he is not satisfied with her choice of the groom,[83] and the people I interviewed consider this provision valid. In fact, it has been used and applied in the Islamic Shari'a Council, Leyton, and the Birmingham Islamic Shari'a Council of the Central Mosque. As I said before, the latter is considered to be supportive of women's needs.

5 Conclusion

There is a problem. That is at least something that the British government recognises. How to solve it, though, seems to elude the policy makers.

The recognition that the soft parallel legal system existing in Britain poses a problem was in fact due to persistence efforts and awareness campaigns by

83 Incompatibility according to the Hanafi Jurisprudence is often related to the groom's lack of religiosity or social incompatibility. Other reasons include cast and colour. Whereas the first set of reasons are accepted by religious scholars, they reject the reasons related to cast and colour.

women's rights groups (which included groups and individuals of Muslim heritage).

In June 2015 a coalition of 200 women's rights and secular campaigners, in addition to several reputable NGOs, alarmed at the increasing influence of shari'a courts over the lives of citizens of Muslim heritage, called for the UK government to stick to its pre-election promises to hold an inquiry into shari'a courts.[84]

The bold call in 2015 stands in contrast to the silence that shrouded the issue in the 1980s and 1990s. In fact as recently as 2005 some women's and human rights groups were reluctant to scrutinise the effects of the shari'a courts for fear of interfering in the religious domain of minorities. The issue was considered 'sensitive'.

The sensitivity was related to a culture of 'looking the other way' – part of the multicultural maxim of group difference and the collective cultural rights of others. As the fascination with multiculturalism as a state policy started to wane, the sensitivity shifted to a fear of providing the far right with fuel for its xenophobic agenda.

At first, addressing the problem was not an option. The combination of cultural sensitivity and fear of the xenophobic agenda has proved to be very powerful. But UK women's organisations began to become aware of the problem in the early 2000s. A woman's rights advocate I interviewed told me that these organisations' own experiences with women led to a growing concern that the services offered by faith groups might not be operating for the best interests of those women and might not be supporting their human rights.[85]

The faith groups this woman mentioned included Hindus, Jews, Christians, and Muslims. Some of these faith groups, I was told, were working within the UK human rights framework, but others were not. The concerns were not only related to Muslim arbitration – which has been receiving the bulk of criticism – but extended to other forms of arbitration, such as the Jewish Beth Din tribunals.

---

84 N.N. "Nearly 200 Signatories Call to Dismantle Parallel Legal Systems", Press Release, *Southhall Black Sisters*, June 15 2015, accessed September 02, 2023, https://southallblacksisters.org.uk/news/nearly-200-signatories-call-to-dismantle-parallel-legal-systems/; E. Batha, "Britain must ban Sharia 'Kangaroo Courts', say Activists", *Reuters*, June 15 2015, accessed September 19, 2023, available at: https://www.reuters.com/article/us-britain-sharia-court-idUSKBN0OV2EX20150615.

85 Interviewee 2, anonymous women's rights advocate, interview with author, London, January 16, 2013. This person was not authorised to speak by the organisation and thus asked to remain anonymous.

As a result, some women's organisations started to launch a wider critical discussion of the government's faith-based approach. For example, Southall Black Sisters (SBS) showed that contrary to the popular view often promoted by state and religious leaders, the women they interviewed (a qualitative sample from South Asian or African-Caribbean backgrounds) do not feel the need to be 'deferential' to religious leaders, nor do they want some form of religious laws. In fact, the SBS stated that once they were assured anonymity and felt safe to express themselves, these women 'have no problems in critiquing the idea of religious laws including sharia'.[86]

Women's views were tied directly to their negative experiences in religious institutions and at the hands of religious leaders: experiences of sexist and misogynistic discrimination, corruption and petty politics. Women expressed the view that religious institutions are corrupt and unaccountable places; they are divided over differences and fighting rival factions of trustees seeking to assert their authority and/or interest in financial gain. Divisions and discrimination based on religion, class and caste are common within these institutions. The lack of transparency and accountability of religious institutions only increased women's general distrust of faith-based organisations. These women have also raised cases of sexual abuse; some recounted cases where religious authorities had abused their positions of power and tried to sexually abuse the very women who turned to them for help.[87]

This awareness was combined with recognition of how social pressure was, and remains, an integral feature of the mechanism that allows shari'a councils and tribunals to function, especially when they are embedded within closed communities. Contravening the norms in a closed community leads to 'ostracism and isolation and so many things that are not necessarily direct threats but can make your life hell', Maryam Namazie (a British Iranian human rights activist and director of the organization One Law for All) told me.[88] If a woman does not dare to take off her veil (for fear of social ostracism and reprisal) in Tower Hamelt in London, Coventry in Birmingham, Little Horton in Bradford, or in some communities in Leicester, how is she supposed to insist on not turning to one of these courts or resist the bullying that takes place in them?

The more the women's organisations and advocates became aware of the problematic nature of these religious courts and their consequences, the more

86 P. Patel and U. Sen, *Cohesion, Faith and Gender: A Report on the Impact of the Cohesion and Faith-based Approach on Black and Minority Women in Ealing* (London, Southall Black Sisters, 2010), at 60, available at: http://comodino.peacelink.org/tdt/docs/1933.pdf.

87 *Ibid*, at 58–63.

88 Maryam Namazie, interview with author, January 2013.

they also recognised its political dimensions. In fact, these women were the first to loudly alert the public that Islamists were promoting the implementation of shari'a law and a political agenda that is inherently discriminatory and totalitarian. The issue is not only about conservative clerics and imams, who are using the law in ways they have always known about. The issue is most significantly political, as several clerics and imams, working in these forums, affiliated with Islamist organisations or neo fundamentalist movements.[89]

These efforts, in addition to the rising tide of religious extremism, were instrumental in UK government decision to hold an inquiry into shari'a courts. The inquiry which started in 2016 was conducted in two forms: 1) An independent review "into sharia law, specifically within sharia councils in England and Wales. The review's terms of reference focused on whether sharia law is being misused or applied in a way that is incompatible with the domestic law in England and Wales, and in particular whether there were discriminatory practices against women who use sharia councils."[90] 2) A Home Affairs Committee inquiry into Sharia councils operating in the UK. The Committee was to examine "how Sharia councils operate in practice, their work resolving family and divorce disputes and their relationship with the British legal system". [91]

The outcome was disappointing to those demanding an end to this parallel legal system. The first inquiry published its recommendation in 2018. It demanded a necessary amendment to the Marriage Act 1949 and the Matrimonial Causes Act 1973, which ensures that civil marriages are conducted, before or at the same time as the Islamic marriage ceremony. However, it called for a regulation of these sharia councils, hence, legally integrating them in the UK legal system.[92] The government accepted the first recommendation while rejecting the second.

The second inquiry was closed in an absurd silence. A statement published on its website, which was removed later, stated: "Due to the general election

89 Gita Sahgal, former head of Amnesty International's Gender Unit and a vocal campaigner against oppression of women in particular by religious fundamentalists, interview with author, London, January 2013 24; Usama Hasan, interview with author, *supra*.

90 "The independent review into the application of sharia law in England and Wales", Presented to Parliament by the Secretary of State for the Home Department, (February 2018), at3.

91 "Sharia Councils Inquiry Launched", UK Parliament Website, available at: https://committees.parliament.uk/committee/83/home-affairs-committee/news/100712/160623-new-inquiry-sharia-councils/

92 N.N., "The independent review into the application of sharia law in England and Wales" *supra* (February 2018), at 17, 19.

on 8 June 2017 the Committee has now closed this inquiry. Following the dissolution of Parliament on 3 May 2017, all Select Committees cease to exist until after the general election. If an inquiry on this subject is held in the future, the Committee may refer to the evidence already gathered as part of this inquiry."[93]

Again, the issue is considered 'sensitive' and that sensitivity shapes to a great extent a policy makers' reluctant attitude of dealing with such a 'difficult topic'. Confronting this silence, British media has been playing an important role in revealing the difficult reality of the on-going discrimination against women and the toxic consequences of segregated communities. Two programs have demonstrated the pressing need for serious policy measures.

The first was the November 2017 Chanel 4 documentary 'The Truth about Muslim Marriage'.[94] It conducted a survey of 1000 Muslim women across Britain, revealing that while 78 per cent of those questioned wanted their marriage to be legally valid under British law, nearly two thirds (61%) only had a religious marriage, meaning that their marriage is not legally recognised. These women are often left without protection when seeking divorce and forced to resort to the Shari'a councils. The program called for a change of the marriage act that makes civil marriage mandatory for Muslim women.

The problem of unregistered Muslim marriages was specifically mentioned in 2018 by the Secretary of State for the Home Department when presenting the results of "The independent review into the application of sharia law in England and Wales" to Parliament. In her presentation, she stated that "a key finding was that a significant number of Muslim couples fail to civilly register their religious marriages and therefore some Muslim women have no option of obtaining a civil divorce".[95]

The second program was the January 2018 Panorama with the title White Fright Divided Britain – Blackburn.[96] Blackburn was named in the Casey Report

93 "Sharia Councils Inquiry", UK Parliament Website, available at: https://www.parliament.uk/business/committees/committees-a-z/commons-select/home-affairs-committee/inquiries/parliament-2015/inquiry6/.

94 N.N., "New Channel 4 survey reveals The Truth About Muslim Marriage", November 27, 2017, accessed September 20, 2023, https://www.channel4.com/press/news/new-channel-4-survey-reveals-truth-about-muslim-marriage. This author was a scientific advisor to the production team of the documentary.

95 N.N., "The independent review into the application of sharia law in England and Wales", Presented to Parliament by the Secretary of State for the Home Department by Command of Her Majesty, (February 2018), at 5, available at: https://assets.publishing.service.gov.uk/government/uploads/system/uploads/attachment_data/file/678478/6.4152_HO_CPFG_Report_into_Sharia_Law_in_the_UK_WEB.pdf#page=10.

96 BBC), "Panorama: White Fright Divided Britain – Blackburn," January 22, 2018, available at: http://www.bbc.co.uk/programmes/b09pz718.

on Integration as one of the most segregated towns in Britain. The program was following on another documentary conducted ten years ago by Panorama on the town. At that time, the town was becoming segregated along ethnic and religious lines. Ten years later Panorama has returned and found a town that is even more divided. Some parts of Blackburn were almost entirely Muslim Asian. Other parts were only lived in by white residents. This social segregation has been described as a national crisis. Again, a group based policies of multiculturalism led to an absence of integration.

Dame Louise Casey, who was interviewed in the program, said the town is not a single issue, it mirrors a national issue: "we are living with the consequences of not managing migration effectively, ..., and I think we have a divided country".[97]

The connection between closed communities and religious extremism was only touched fleetly in the program. No mention was made of the parallel legal system.

Chuka Umunna, an MP and the Chair for Parliamentary group on Social Integration, insisted in the program that the Casey Report was "being ignored – put on the shelf in the 'too hot', 'too difficult to handle' box. But the longer we park this, the more dangerous the atmosphere and environment will become".[98]

The government finally reacted with its March 2018 Integrated Communities Strategy Green Paper.[99] It acknowledged the challenges facing Britain ranging from school segregation, residential segregation, extremism and racism, and cultural practices and attitudes that hamper integration. It also recognised that these circumstances disproportionately affect women and girls. It proposed several measures including an amendment to the religious marriage act that makes civil marriage before or during a religious marriage mandatory. Imams, who fail to ensure the civil registration, will face legal consequences. Introducing a minimum age requirement for spouse visas to help prevent forced marriages is also suggested as a measure. Although the paper is still open to consultation and revision, a sense of recognition has finally dawned on UK policy makers.

This recognition should be combined with concrete policy measures. I suggest that the UK government consider four policy recommendations:

---

97 *Ibid.*, starting at 14.05 minutes.

98 *Ibid.*, starting at 14.38 minutes.

99 UK Government, "Integrated Communities Strategy Green Paper", (March 2018), available at: https://www.gov.uk/government/uploads/system/uploads/attachment_data/file/690819/Integrated_Communities_Strategy_green_paper.pdf.

1. Make it mandatory to have a civil marriage before contracting any religious marriage; and implement this ruling firmly and consequently.
2. Launch a nationwide campaign to register all Islamic marriages. This will ultimately reveal many polygamous marriages. The women who are parties to these marriages, and their children, should be protected. But that protection should not entail recognising polygamy as a form of marriage, as some essentialist legal scholars are arguing.
3. Attach to the British court system a unit (with local branches nationwide) that is authorised to automatically issue an Islamic divorce after the civil divorce has been issued: a decree absolute. In many Islamic countries, the religious authorities recognise a civil divorce as religiously valid; the situation should be the same in the UK.
4. Launch a nationwide campaign that reaches women within closed communities to inform them about their rights, the importance and protection of civil marriage, the need to register their marriage and how the law functions in the UK.

Bibliography

Books

Abu Zahrah, Imam M., *Ahkam Al Tirkat wa al Mawari'ith – Provisions for Legacies and Inheritances,* in Arabic (Beirut, Dar Al Fikr Al Arabi, 1963).

An-Na'im, A. A., *Toward Islamic Reformation: Civil Liberties, Human Rights, and International Law* (Syracuse, NY, Syracuse University Press, 1990).

Barbalet, J. et al, *Religion and the State: a Comparative Sociology* (London, Anthem Press, 2013).

Bono, S., *Muslim Women and Shari'ah Councils: Transcending the Boundaries of Community and Law* (London, Palgrave Macmillan, 2012).

Divino, L., *The New Muslim Brotherhood in the West* (New York, Columbia University Press, 2010).

Dupret, B. *et al* (eds.), *Legal Pluralism in the Arab World* (The Hague, Kluwer Law International, 1999).

Dworkin, R. *Law's Empire*, (Cambridge, Belknap Press of Harvard University Press, 1986).

Grillo, R. *et al* (eds.), *Legal Practice and Cultural Diversity* (Surrey, Ashgate, 2009).

Hallaq, W. B., *Shari'a: Theory, Practice and Transformations* (Cambridge, Cambridge University Press, 2007).

Heininger, B., *Ehrenmord und Emanzipation: Die Geschlechterfrage in Ritualen von Parallelgesellschaften* (Berlin, LIT Verlag, 2009).

Kemper, M. and M. Reinkowski (eds.), *Rechtspluralismus in der islamischen Welt: Gewohnheitsrecht zwischen Staat und Gesellschaft* (Berlin, Walter de Gruyter, 2005).

Kepel, G., *Allah in the West: Islamic Movements in America and Europe* (Cambridge, UK, Polity Press, 1997).

Kour, Z. H., *The History of Aden 1839–1872* (London, Frank Kass, 1981).

MacEoin, D., *Sharia Law or 'One Law for All'?* (London, CIVITAS: Institute for the Study of Civil Society, 2009).

Malik, K., *From Fatwa to Jihad: the Rushdie Affair and its Aftermath* (Brooklyn, NY, Melville House Publishing, 2009).

Mallat, C., *Introduction to Middle Eastern Law* (Oxford, Oxford University Press, 2007).

Manea, E., *Women and Shari'a Law, The Impact of Legal Pluralism in the UK*, (London, I.B. Tauris, 2016).

Manea, E., *The Arab State and Women's Rights: the Trap of the Authoritarian Governance*, (London, Routledge, 2011).

Manea, E., *Ich will nicht mehr schweigen: Der Islam, der Westen und die Menschenrechte* (Freiburg, Herder Verlag, 2009).

Manea, E., *Regional Politics in the Gulf* (London, Saqi Books, 2005).

Menski, W., *Comparative Law in a Global Context: the Legal Systems of Asia and Africa*, Second Edition (Cambridge, Cambridge University Press, 2006).

Molyneux, M., *State Policies and the Position of Women Workers in the People's Democratic Republic of Yemen, 1967–1977* (Geneva, International Labour Office, 1982).

Page, D., *Prelude to Partition: the Indian Muslims and the Imperial System of Control (1920–1932)* (Delhi, Oxford University Press, 1982).

Pearl, D., *A Textbook on Muslim Law* (London, Croom Helm, 1979).

Pieragostini, K., *Britain, Aden and South Arabia: Abandoning Empire* (New York, St. Martin's Press, 1991).

Prasad Saksena, K., *Muslim Law as Administered in India and Pakistan*, 4th edition (Lucknow, Eastern Book Company, 1963).

Rawls, J., *A Theory of Justice* Revised Edition (Cambridge, Belknap Press of Harvard University Press, 2005).

Shah, P., *Legal Pluralism in Conflict: Coping with Cultural Diversity in Law* (London, Glasshouse Press, 2005).

Schiffauer, W., *Parallelgesellschaften* (Bielefeld, transcript Verlag, 2008).

Shukri, A., *Muhammedan Law of Marriage and Divorce* (New York, Ams Press, 1996).

Woodman, G, "The Idea of Legal Pluralism" in B. Dupret *et al* (eds.), *Legal Pluralism in the Arab World* (The Hague, Kluwer Law International, 1999).

Yilmaz, I., *Muslim Laws, Politics and Society in Modern Nations States: Dynamic Legal Pluralism in England, Turkey and Pakistan* (Surrey: Ashgate Publishing Limited, 2005).

Yilmaz, I., *Muslim Laws*; B. Dupret *et al* (eds.), *Legal Pluralism in the Arab World* (The Hague, Kluwer Law International, 1999).

Zahlan Said, R., *The Making of the Modern Gulf States: Kuwait, Bahrain, Qatar, the United Arab Emirates and Oman* (London, Unwin Hyman, 1989).

Periodicals, Reports, Documentaries and Speeches

Arbitration and Mediation Services (Equality Bill), Baroness Cox, (7th June 2011), National Archive, Part 2, Article 4.

BBC, "Panorama: White Fright Divided Britain – Blackburn," January 22, 2018, accessed September 19, 2023, http://www.bbc.co.uk/programmes/b09pz718.

Büchler, A. and C. Schlatter, "Marriage age in Islamic and Contemporary Muslim Family Laws: a Comparative Survey", (2013) 1 *Electronic Journal of Islamic and Middle Eastern Law*.

Casey, L., (Dame), *The Casey Review: a Review into Opportunity and Integration*, Department for Communities and Local Government, UK Government, (Dec 2016), available at: https://www.gov.uk/government/uploads/system/uploads/attachment_data/file/575973/The_Casey_Review_Report.pdf.

Change Institute, *Summary Report: Understanding Muslim Ethnic Communities* (London, Change Institute, Department for Communities and Local Government, April 2009).

Donnelly, J., "Cultural Relativism and Universal Human Rights", (1984) 4 *Human Rights Quarterly*.

Faksh, M. A., "The Alawi Community of Syria: a New Dominant Political Force", (1984) 20(2) *Middle Eastern Studies*.

Griffiths, J., "What is Legal Pluralism?", (1986) 32(24) *Journal of Legal Pluralism*.

Haqqani, H., *Pakistan: between Mosque and Military* (Washington, DC, Carnegie Endowment for International Peace, 2010).

Kaschuba, W., "Ethnische Parallelgesllschaften: Zur kulturellen Konstruktion des Fremden in der europäischen Migration", (2007) 1 *Zeitschrift für Volkskunde*.

Manea, E., "In the Name of Culture and Religion: the Political Function of Blasphemy in Islamic States", (2016) 27(1) *Islam and Christian–Muslim Relations*.

Mirza, M. *et al*, "Living Apart Together: British Muslims and the Paradox of Multiculturalism", *Policy Exchange Report* (2007).

Muslim Council of Britain (MCB), *Fairness not Favours: British Muslims' Perspectives at the 2015 General Election* (London, MCB, 2015), at 11, available at: http://www.mcb.org.uk/wp-content/uploads/2015/03/fairnessnotfavours-MCB.pdf.

N.N. "Nearly 200 Signatories Call to Dismantle Parallel Legal Systems", Press Release, *Southhall Black Sisters*, June 15, 2015, accessed September 02, 2023, available at: https://southallblacksisters.org.uk/news/nearly-200-signatories-call-to-dismantle-parallel-legal-systems/.

N.N. "The Independent Review into the Application of Sharia Law in England and Wales", Presented to Parliament by the Secretary of State for the Home Department, (February 2018), at 3.

N.N., "New Channel 4 Survey Reveals the Truth about Muslim Marriage", November 27, 2017, accessed September 20, 2023, https://www.channel4.com/press/news/new-channel-4-survey-reveals-truth-about-muslim-marriage. For transparency, this author was a scientific advisor to the production team of the documentary.

N.N. "ICM Muslims Survey for Channel 4", *ICM Unlimited Polling*, April 11, 2016, available at: https://www.icmunlimited.com/wp-content/uploads/2016/04/Mulims-full-suite-data-plus-topline.pdf.

Patel, P. and U. Sen, *Cohesion, Faith and Gender: A Report on the Impact of the Cohesion and Faith-based Approach on Black and Minority Women in Ealing* (London, Southall Black Sisters, 2010), at 60, a vailable at: http://comodino.peacelink.org/tdt/docs/1933.pdf.F.

Roudi-Fahimi, F. and I., Shaimaa, *Ending Child Marriage in the Arab Region* (Washington, DC, Population Reference Bureau, 2013).

Thatcher, M., "My kind of Tory Party", *Daily Telegraph*, January 20, 1975, accessed July 02, 2015, http://www.margaretthatcher.org/document/102600 (accessed July 02, 2015).

Thatcher, M., Speech at St Lawrence Jewry, March 4, 1981, accessed July 01, 2015, available at: http://www.margaretthatcher.org/document/104587.

United Nations Development Program, *Arab Human Development Report 2005: 'Towards the Rise of Women in the Arab World'* (New York, United Nations Publications, 2006).

UK Government, "Integrated Communities Strategy Green Paper" (March 2018), available at: https://www.gov.uk/government/uploads/system/uploads/attachment_data/file/690819/Integrated_Communities_Strategy_green_paper.pdf.

Women Living Under Muslim Laws (WLUML), *Knowing our Rights: Women, Family, Laws and Customs in the Muslim World* (London, WLUML, 2006).

Yilmaz, I., "The Challenge of Post-modern Legality and Muslim Legal Pluralism in England", (2002) xxvii(2) *Journal of Ethnic and Migration Studies*.

Websites and Newspapers

Al-Qaradhawi, Y., "Islam's "Conquest of Rome" will save Europe from Its Subjugation to Materialism and Promiscuity", *Qatar TV*, July 28, 2007, The TV clip, no. 1592, translated and posted by *MERI TV, The Middle East Media Research Institute*, accessed July 01, 2015, http://www.memritv.org/clip/en/1592.htm.

Bangladesh Genocide Archive, *War Crimes File – a Documentary by Twenty Twenty Television*, accessed July 01, 2015, http://www.genocidebangladesh.org/war-crimes-file-a-documentary-by-twenty-twenty-television/ ().

Brown, C., "Let us Adopt Islamic Family Law to Curb Extremists, Muslims Tell Kelly', *The Independent*, August 15, 2006, accessed July 15, 2015, http://www.independent.co.uk/news/uk/politics/let-us-adopt-islamic-family-law-to-curb-extremists-muslims-tell-kelly-411954.html.

Emma B., "Britain must ban Sharia 'Kangaroo Courts', say Activists", *Reuters*, June 15, 2015, accessed September 02, 2023, https://www.reuters.com/article/us-britain-sharia-court-idUSKBN0OV2EX20150615.

Encyclopedia Britannica Online, s.v. "Ottoman Empire", accessed September 02, 2023, https://www.britannica.com/place/Ottoman-Empire.

European Council for Fatwa and Research, *Resolutions and Fatwas* [*edicts*] *of the European Council for Fatwa and Research*, in Arabic (Cairo, Islamic House for Distribution and Publication, 2002).

Ikhwan Wiki, Federation of Islamic Organisations in Europe, in Arabic, accessed July 01, 2015, http://goo.gl/u57S2R ().

McVeigh, K. and A. Hill, "Bill Limiting Sharia Law is Motivated by "Concern for Muslim Women"", *The Guardian*, June 08, 2011, Accessed May 26, 2015, http://www.theguardian.com/law/2011/jun/08/sharia-bill-lords-muslim-women.

Office for National Statistics (ONS), "01 request: Statistics of the Muslim population in the UK for 2011, 2012, 2013" (London, ONS, May 16, 2013).

Sheikh Dr. Khaled Hanafy (Assistant Secretary) (December 16, 2018), "The European Council for Fatwa and Research: Renewed leadership, renewed hopes", *European Council for Fatwa and Research*, accessed September 02, 2023, https://www.e-cfr.org/blog/2018/12/16/european-council-fatwa-research/.

"Sharia Councils Inquiry", UK Parliament Website, available at: https://www.parliament.uk/business/committees/committees-a-z/commons-select/home-affairs-committee/inquiries/parliament-2015/inquiry6/.

"Sharia Councils Inquiry Launched", UK Parliament Website, available at: https://committees.parliament.uk/committee/83/home-affairs-committee/news/100712/160623-new-inquiry-sharia-councils.

Wolfgang K., "Wie Fremde gemacht werden", *der Tagesspiegel*, January 14, 2007, accessed September 02, 2023, https://www.tagesspiegel.de/meinung/wie-fremde-gemacht-werden-1435909.html.

CHAPTER 3

The System of Bilateral Legislation Tested by 'Neo' Religious Groups: The Case of Italy

Francesco Alicino

1 Introduction

The Italian religious landscape has become increasingly more diversified over the past few decades. This diversification is caused not only by the proliferation of different confessions into the region, but also due to the increased presence of three new categories: unaffiliated believers; believers who, although they remain faithful to their denominational religion, adopt forms of personal spirituality; and nonreligious people who assert patent claims against the public role of religions. These phenomena fostered Italy's transition from a weak pluralism to a new diverse identity.[1]

Italy's new religious pluralism is certainly less varied than the multicultural societies of other European States, like Germany, France, or the UK. However, Italy's current identity is even stronger when compared to the situation the country experienced until few decades ago. As such, Italy's growth in religious diversity has impacted on the role of legislations resulting from the bilateral Churches-State relations, as stated in Articles 7.2 and 8.3 of the 1948 Constitution, what scholars typically refer to as 'bilateralism principle' (*principio di bilateralità pattizia*).

The bilateralism principle now appears to be trapped in its own past. The principle's out-of-date nature is challenging not only for 'neo' minority religious and non-religious organizations, such as Islam(s) and militant atheisms but also appears problematic for the Catholic Church. This was illustrated by the judicial rulings on the 1984 Villa Madama, an agreement that, following the historical path marked out by the 1929 Lateran Pacts, represents the prototype of the principle of bilateralism and the related methods.[2]

---

1 S. Ferrari, "Religion Between Liberty and Equality", (2016) 4(2) *Journal of Law, Religion and State* 179–193.

2 N. Colaianni, *Diritto pubblico delle religioni. Eguaglianza e differenze nello Stato costituzionale* (Bologna, il Mulino 2012), at 120–137; F. Alicino, "The Place of *Minority* Religions and the Strategy of Major Denominations. The Case of Italy", (2017) *Rivista AIC*, at 1–20, accessed 27 August 2023, https://www.rivistaaic.it/images/rivista/pdf/2_2017_Alicino.pdf.

 | DOI:10.1163/9789004446816_005

In the first part of this article, I will focus on the traditional aspects of the State-confessions relationship system, under which the Catholic Church and few other denominations have played a vital role. I will analyse how the bilateralism principle performs in Italy's current religious pluralism, with the rising presence of 'other' communities – other than Judeo-Christian traditional ones – that, not by accident, are considered as new *nomoi* groups.[3] This will allow me to analyse the impact Italy's new religious landscape has had on the traditional rules, which have regulated the relationship between the State and the Catholic Church.

I will try to demonstrate how the bilateralism principle can be used when referring to traditional Judeo-Christian denominations. On the contrary, it can hardly be considered for other minority groups, other than the Judeo-Christian traditional ones. Furthermore, the bilateralism principle does not fit in easily with the current Italian society, which, due to immigration and globalization, is no longer a monocultural society.

2 The Roots of the Bilateralism Principle

The Catholic Church has historically occupied a key place in Italy's State-confessions legal system. Until the second half of 1800, Rome was the core of the Papal State and the pope was both head of the Church and a temporal king who passed laws, collected taxes, and maintained an army. The Church's temporal power ended on 20 September 1870, when the Italian army bombarded Porta Pia, one of the city's old gates, and entered through a breach, which later was historically known as "the breach of Porta Pia" (*la breccia di Porta Pia*). Depending on one's political perspective, the breach of Porta Pia was either the capture of Rome or its liberation. This event also explains the so-called "Roman question" (*la questione romana*) based on the disputes and conflicts between the new-born State and the Holy See.[4] The Catholic Church displayed little desire to compromise with the newly formed State, especially

3 For the notion of *nomoi* groups see A. Shachar, "The puzzle of Interlocking Power Hierarchies: Sharing the Pieces of Jurisdictional Authority", (2000) 35 *Harvard Civil Rights – Civil liberties Law Review* 394.

4 F. Margiotta Broglio, "Dalla questione romana al superamento dei Patti lateranensi", in General Director of President of the Council of Ministers (ed.), *La revisione del Concordato. Un accordo di libertà* (Roma, Istituto Poligrafico e Zecca dello Stato, 1986), at 19.

since Italian nationalism and the movement of *Risorgimento* (Rising Again) was readily identified with liberalism, anti-clericalism and revolution.[5]

Nevertheless, Italy has maintained Catholicism as its national religion. This was corroborated in Article 1 of the 1848 Constitution (known as *Statuto albertino*), stating that Catholicism was "the only State religion" and that other existing creeds had to be "tolerated in conformity with laws." The implementation of these principles, and the subsequent socio-cultural environment, made the relations between the Catholic Church and the new state progressively less tense. Just after the Fascists took the power, they paved the way for the historical turning point of 1929, when Benito Mussolini in the name of the Italian Government signed with the Holy See the Lateran Pacts (hereafter 1929 Pacts).[6] According to these Pacts, Italy recognized and reaffirmed the principle established in Article 1 of the 1848 *Statuto albertino*. This granted the Catholic Church access to benefits and privileges in important sectors of Italian society, such as education, family, marriage, and fiscal regime.[7] After the Second World War, the 1929 Pacts launched a specific method-principle of Church-State bilateral collaboration[8] that also extended to other denominations.[9] This was made possible due to Articles 7.2 and 8.3 of the 1948 republican Constitution intentionally emphasised the deeply-rooted bonds between Italy and Catholicism.

Article 7 establishes the mutual independence and sovereignty of both the State and the Roman Catholic Church. Albeit less strong, this principle is also affirmed in Article 8.2 of the Constitution, which guarantees the free organization of minority religions, what the same provision significantly

5 F. Margiotta Broglio, *Italia e Santa Sede dalla grande guerra alla conciliazione* (Roma-Bari, Laterza, 1966); R. Pertici, *Chiesa e Stato in Italia. Dalla Grande Guerra al nuovo Concordato. Dibattiti storici in Parlamento* (Bologna, il Mulino, 2009).

6 The Italian State ratified these Pacts through the 810/1929 law, *Esecuzione del Trattato, dei quattro allegati annessi e del Concordato, sottoscritti in Roma, fra la Santa Sede e l'Italia, l'11 febbraio 1929*, in the *Italian Official gazette*, 5 June 1929, No. 130. See also the King's decree 851/1929, *Norme per la escuzione della Convenzione finanziaria con la Santa Sede*, in the *Italian Official gazette*, 5 June 1929, No. 130.

7 A. Ferrari, "The Italian Accommodations. Liberal State and Religious freedom in the 'Long Century'", in L. Derocher, C. Gélinas, S. Lebel-Grenier and P.C. Noël (eds.), *L'État canadien et la diversité culturelle et religieuse 1800–1914* (Québec, Presses de l'Université du Québec, 2009), at 143–153.

8 P. Floris, "Laicità e collaborazione a livello locale. Gli equilibri tra fonti centrali e periferiche nella disciplina del fenomeno religioso", (2010) *Stato, Chiese e pluralismo confessionale*, accessed 28 January 2021, https://statoechiese.it/contributi/laicita-e-collaborazione-a-livello-locale-gli-equilibri-tra-fonti-centrali.

9 C. Cardia, "Concordato, intese, laicità dello Stato", (2004) 1 *Quaderni di diritto e politica ecclesiastica* 30; N. Colaianni, *Confessioni religiose e intese* (Bari, Cacucci, 1990), at 97.

defines as "denominations other than Catholicism" (*confessioni diverse dalla Cattolica*). At the same time, Article 7.2 declares that the Lateran Pacts governs the relationships between the State and the Catholic Church. However, Article 7.2 also claims that any change to the Lateran Pacts, when accepted by both parties, does not require the procedure of Article 138 in regulating constitutional amendments. This entails that when there is a bilateral agreement, a legislative (not constitutional) act is sufficient in order to amend the 1929 Pacts. Both the 1929 Pacts and Article 7.2 are thus seen as legal prototypes of the bilateralism principle, which is also incorporated into Article 8.3 of the Constitution. Accordingly, only legislative acts can regulate the relationships between minority religions and the State.[10] However, these acts must be based on *intese*, meaning 'understandings' between the State and religions other than Catholicism.[11] In other terms, once the Italian Government and the representatives of a given religion have signed an agreement (Article 7.2 related to Catholic Church) or an *intesa* (Article 8.3 referring to denominations other than Catholicism), these two documents need to be ratified (for the agreement) or approved (for the *intesa*) by specific legislative acts of the Parliament.

On the 18th of February 1984, under Article 7.2 of the Constitution the Holy See signed its agreement with the State, also known as Villa Madama agreement. This agreement nearly changed the entire content of the 1929 Lateran Pacts, except for the the first part called Treaty. In 1985, the Villa Madama agreement was ratified by the Parliament with the 1985 law (no. 121), which is an atypical legislation, meaning it can be amended only on the basis of a new State-Church agreement. Italian Government also signed the first *intese* with the Waldensian Church in 1985. Since then, the State authorities have engaged other understandings following Article 8.3, eleven of which have been approved by the Parliament until now. As mentioned above, both the Villa Madama agreement and the *intese* can be changed via bilateral State-confessions legislations.[12] It implicates that some aspects of the legal status

10 G. Bouchard, "Concordato e intese, ovvero un pluralismo imperfetto", (2004) 1 *Quaderni di diritto e politica ecclesiastica*, 70–71; G.B. Varnier, "La prospettiva pattizia", in V. Parlato and G.B. Varnier (eds.), *Principio pattizio e realtà religiose minoritarie* (Torino, Giappichelli, 1995), at 8–13.

11 G. Casuscelli, "La rappresentanza e l'intesa", in A. Ferrari (ed.), *Islam in Europa/Islam in Italia tra diritto e società* (Bologna, Il Mulino, 2008), at 304.

12 M. Ventura, *Creduli e increduli. Il declino di Stato e Chiesa come questione di fede* (Torino, Einaudi, 2014), at 30; S. Ferrari, "Il Concordato salvato dagli infedeli", in V. Tozzi (ed.), *Studi per la sistemazione delle fonti in materia ecclesiastica* (Salerno, Edisud, 1993), at 127.

of the Catholic Church and some few other denominations, those with *intese*, cannot be altered without considering the voices of their representatives.[13]

3 The Theory and the Practice of Bilateralism Principle

In theory, the bilateralism principle protects religious groups from being overpowered by the State's unilateral laws. Due to the highly general nature of unilateral laws, these legislations are reluctant to meet the requirements for specific religions. In contrast, bilateral legislations have a more consistent implementation of the constitutional principle of equality, which implies the rights to be different and equally free before the law. Bilateral legislation promotes new rules that aim to combine respect for general constitutional obligations and attention to specific religious claims.[14]

An example of this is seen in Article 8 of the Villa Madama agreement. Article 8 regulates the so-called *matrimonio concordatario*, under which a Catholic marriage is valid in the eyes of the State law and the Ecclesiastical Tribunal's sentence of annulment could be effective in the Italian Republic by the judgement of a State competent Court of Appeal.[15] This is also the case of Article 9 of the 1984 agreement, according to which every student

13 It is interesting to note that the Italian Constitution provides similar legal instruments in the field of relationship between the central State and the Regions and between the Regions and foreign States as well as the relationship between the Regions and local authorities of other States. In this sense, it is important to consider Article 116 of the Constitution, under which "[a]dditional special forms and conditions of autonomy, related to the areas specified in Article 117 (paragraph three and paragraph two) [...] may be attributed to [...] Regions by State Law, upon the initiative of the Region concerned, after consultation with the local authorities, in compliance with the principles set forth in Article 119. Said law is approved by both Houses of Parliament with the absolute majority of their members, on the basis of an understanding (*intesa*) between the State and the Region concerned". See also Article 117.4, under which "[u]nderstandings (*intese*) between a Region and other Regions that aim at improving the performance of regional functions and that may also envisage the establishment of joint bodies shall be ratified by regional law. In the areas falling within their responsibilities, Regions may conclude understandings (*intese*) with foreign States and local authorities of other States in the cases and according to the forms laid down by State legislation."

14 B. Barry, *Culture and equality* (Cambridge, Polity Press, 2001); S. Bedi, "What is so special about religion? The dilemma of the religious exemption", (2007) 15 *The Journal of Political Philosophy* 235–249; M. Festenstein, *Negotiating diversity: Culture, deliberation, trust* (Cambridge, Polity Press, 2005); M. Minow, "Should religious groups be exempt from civil rights laws?", (2007) 48 *Boston College Law Review* 781–849.

15 Article 8 of the 1984 Villa Madama agreement.

at any level of public education can choose to attend 1 hour per week the teaching of Catholic religion.[16] Moreover, Article 10 refers to the Catholic University of the Sacred Heart, which is private University legally recognised by the Italian Minister of Education: this article states that the nominations of teaching staff of the Catholic University of the Sacred Heart are subject to the ecclesiastical authority's approval, on the basis of a candidate's religious profile.[17] In general, the bilateral legislations allow Catholic religious ministers and religious representatives to enter prison, hospitals, nursing home and rehab centres without special authorization from public authorities. Along with these rules, religious ministers of minority confessions, those that have signed *intese* with the State,[18] can enjoy similar rights and

16 In the last few years about 88% of the Italian students have chosen to attend this teaching. See C. Giorda, "Religious Diversity in Italy and the Impact on Education: The History of a Failure", (2015) 17(1) *New diversities* 77–93; R. Mazzola, "La religion á l'école en Italie: état des lieux et évolutions", in J. P. Willaime (ed.), *Le défi de l'enseignement des faits religieux à l'ecole* (Paris, Riveneuve, 2014), at 103–120. It is important to note that almost all *intese* that have been signed until now (except from the one with Jewish community) have rules concerning teaching on the religious phenomenon. These provisions aim at providing confessions other than Catholicism with lessons managed by these organizations, in order to give pupils a general knowledge on their own religious teachings. The fact is that these rules have hardly ever been used in public schools.

17 C. Cardia, *Manuale di diritto ecclesiastico* (Bologna, il Mulino, 1996), at 309.

18 See the following legislative acts: *Law 11 August 1984, No. 449* (approving the *intesa* with the Waldensian Church of Italy, which was originally signed on 21 February 1984); *Law 22 November 1988, No. 516* (approving the *intesa* with Christian Churches of the Seventh-Day Adventists, which was originally signed on 29 December 1986); *Law 22 November 1988, No. 517* (approving the *intesa* with Assemblies of God in Italy, which was originally signed on 29 December 1986); *Law 8 March 1989, No. 101*, (approving the *intesa* with the Union of Jewish Communities in Italy, which was originally signed on 27 February 1987); *Law 12 April1995, No. 116* (approving the *intesa* with the Christian Evangelical-Baptist Union in Italy, which was originally signed on 29 March 1993); *Law 29 November 1995, No. 520*, (approving the *intesa* with the Lutheran Church, which was originally signed on 20 April 1993); *Law30 July 2012, No. 216* (approving the *intesa* with the Greek Orthodox Metropolis of Italy, which was originally signed 4 April 2007); *Law 30 July2012, No. 127* (approving the *intesa* with the Church of Jesus Christ of Latter-Day Saints, which was originally signed on 4 April 2007); *Law 30 July 2012, No. 128* (approving the *intesa* with the Apostolic Church in Italy, which was originally signed on 4 April 2007); *Law 31 December 2012, No. 245* (approving the *intesa* with the Italian Buddhist Union, which was originally signed on 4 April 2007); *Law 31 December 2012, No. 246* (approving the *intesa* with the Italian Hindu Union, which was originally signed on 4 April 2007); *Law 28 June 2016, No. 130* (approving the *intesa* with the Italian Institute of Soka Gakkai, which was originally signed on 27 June 2015). See also the *intesa* with the Association *Chiesa d'Inghilterra* (Church of England) that was signed on 30 July 2019 and approved by Law 20 December 2021, No. 240, *Norme per la regolazione dei rapporti tra lo Stato e l'Associazione "Chiesa d'Inghilterra", in attuazione dell'articolo 8, terzo comma, della Costituzione.*

prerogatives.[19]

Other significant examples refer to the national fiscal system, in particular to Article 47 of the 222/1985 law (which is connected to the Villa Madama agreement) and the similar rules incorporated on the laws approving the *intese*. According to these provisions, all taxpayers can choose how to allocate 0.008 of the entire Italian income taxes (called *IRPEF*) to one of the following institutions: the State, the Catholic Church, and one of the minority religions that have signed an *intesa*.[20] The fund (i.e. the overall amount of 0,008 of the *IRPEF*) is divided proportionally based on the choices the taxpayers made when submitting their income tax return statement. This division does not consider those taxpayers who do not sign for any of the mentioned institution. Since the beginning, the system of 0,008 of the *IRPEF* has seen only a minority of taxpayers (about 40% of the all the Italian taxpayers) who have made a choice. Until now the majority (about 80%) of this minority have signed in favour of the Catholic Church. Due to the formatting of the *IRPEF*, even the taxpayers who do not choose the Catholic Church will end up funding a religious organization, according to the selection made by those who do sign in favour of religious group or the State.[21] Moreover, most of Italian taxpayers do not understand how the system of 0,008 of the *IRPEF* really works.[22]

In sum, the bilateralism principle underscores the importance of religious denominations in society and, as such, it seems suitable to govern the religious diversity in the framework of a democratic, pluralistic legal system.

Bilateralism is even more relevant in the light of the principle of *laicità* (secularity), which is not expressly enshrined in the 1948 Constitution. Yet, this has not prevented the Constitutional Court from specifying that, on the basis of a series of constitutional provisions,[23] secularity is one of the supreme principles

19 F. Alicino, "Italy Tested by New Religious Diversity: Religion in the Italian Prison System" in A. Zwilling and J. Martínez-Ariño (eds.), *Religion and Prison in Europe* (Cham, Springer, 2020) at 219–236.

20 The only exception is the *intesa* with the Church of Jesus Christ of Latter-Day Saints. See *supra* footnote 18.

21 F. Alicino, "Un referendum sull'otto per mille? Riflessioni sulle fonti", (2013) 33 *Stato, Chiese e pluralismo confessionale*, accessed 2 February 2023, https://www.statoechiese.it/contributi/un-referendum-sullotto-per-mille-riflessioni-sulle-fonti.

22 Criticism against this system have been affirmed by the Italian Audit Office (*Corte dei Conti*). See *Corte dei Conti, Sezione centrale di controllo sulla gestione delle Amministrazioni dello Stato, Destinazione e gestione dell'8 per mille dell'IRPEF: le azioni intraprese a seguito delle deliberazioni della Corte dei Conti*, 2016, available at: https://www.corteconti.it.

23 Namely Articles 2 (under which "[t]he Italian Republic recognizes and guarantees the inviolable rights of the person, both as an individual and in the social groups where human personality is expressed. The Republic expects that the fundamental duties of political,

(*principi supremi*)[24] of the Italian legal order.[25] *Laicità* does not imply indifference towards religions, rather, it acknowledges the special status of denominational religions while also affirming the equidistance and impartiality of the State.[26] In other words, Italian secularism has a positive attitude towards confessions, whose importance is precisely delineated through the principle and the method of bilateralism.

Nevertheless, we can notice that the coexistence between the supreme principle of secularism and the method-principle of bilateral legislations is complicated by at least four problems. First, the system of bilateral State-Churches relationship presupposes a clear distinction between the Catholic Church and other confessions, which risks undermining the status of the latter ones. Second, the bilateralism principle concerning minority religions presupposes a relatively comprehensive religious institution capable of representing a denomination at the national level: this requirement has proved to be challenging for a number of religious organisations, such as those related to Islam.[27] Third, the system of the bilateral legislations seems attractive to some

---

economic and social solidarity be fulfilled"), 3 (regulating the principle of equality); 7 (concerning the relation between the State and the Catholic Church), 8 (1st para.: "[a]ll religious denominations are equally free before the law"; 2nd para.: "[d]enominations other than Catholicism have the right to self-organization according to their own statutes, provided these do not conflict with Italian law"), 19 ("[a]nyone is entitled to freely profess their religious belief in any form, individually or with others, and to promote them and celebrate rites in public or in private, provided they are not offensive to public morality"), and 20 ("[n]o special limitation or tax burden may be imposed on the establishment, legal capacity or activities of any organization on the ground of its religious nature or its religious or confessional aims") of the 1948 Constitution.

24 F. Finocchiaro, "Principi supremi, ordine pubblico italiano e (auspicata) parità tra divorzio e nullità canonica del matrimonio", in F. Cipriani (ed.) *Matrimonio concordatario e tutela giurisdizionale* (Napoli, ESI, 1992), at 67.

25 See *Corte costituzionale*, especially the following decisions: No. 203/1989; No. 259/1990; No. 13/1991; No. 195/1993; No. 421/1993; No. 334/1996; No. 329/1997; No. 508/2000; No. 327/2002.

26 A. Oddi, "Il principio di laicità nella giurisprudenza costituzionale", in R. Bin, G. Brunelli, A. Pugiotto, P. Veronesi (eds.), *Laicità crocefissa?* (Torino, Giappichelli, 200), at 241; S. Lariccia, "Problemi in temi dello Stato e delle istituzioni civili", in *Scritti in memoria di Livio Paladin* (Napoli, Jovene, 2004), at 1251; S. Sicardi, "Il principio di laicità nella giurisprudenza della Corte costituzionale (e rispetto alle posizioni dei giudici comuni)", (2007) *associazionedeicostituzionalisti.it.*, accessed 2 February 2023, https://www.associazionedeicostituzionalisti.it/old_sites/sito_AIC_2003-2010/materiali/convegni/200611foggia/sicardi1.html x.

27 When one compared Islam to religions that have long been present in Italy and considering its problematic history (which currently implies the emergence of transnational fundamentalism and terrorism), this religious minority highlights the most striking aspects of the country's neo cultural-religious pluralism: it indicates and signals the pluralisation

confessional organisations while creating unfavourable distinctions for others, including non-religious ones.[28] Four, there is no formal procedure of using *intese* under Article 8.3 of the 1948 Constitution; this can turn the discretionary power of the Government into unreasonable and discriminatory distinctions between denominations with *intese* and those without *intese*.[29]

4 Square the Circle

The Italian bilateralism principle has not only created a clear differentiation between the Catholic Church and religions other than Catholicism but it has also been characterised by e the so-called "copy & paste" phenomenon (*intese fotocopia*). Meaning, the Italian bilateralism principle is characterized by the substantial similarity of all *intese* which have been signed by minority religions

---

of Italian society. Islam has in other words become the discursive substitute for religious and cultural pluralism, which implies other sensitive matters that, in a way or another, are correlated to this religion: gender roles, clothing codes, family models, the relationship between religion and politics, the role of religions within a democratic system, the rights and duties of the major religion, the rights and duties of religious minorities. So, in the light of these issues, Islam has become the most extreme example of 'other' religions, other than traditional ones. See S. Allievi, "Immigration, Religious Diversity and Recognition of Differences: The Italian way to Multiculturalism", (2014) 21(6) *Identities* 724–737. C. Decaro Bonella, "Le questioni aperte: contesti e metodo", in C. Decaro Bonella (ed.), *Tradizioni religiose e tradizioni costituzionali. L'islam e l'Occidente* (Roma, Carocci, 2013), at 34–34. The most relevant Muslim organizations existing in Italy are: the Italian Islamic Confederation (CII); the Islamic Cultural Centre of Italy (CICI); the Union of Islamic Communities and Organizations of Italy (UCOII); the Italian Islamic Religious Community (COREIS); the Union of Muslim Albanians in Italy (UAMI); the Association of Muslim Women in Italy (ADMI); the Cheikh Ahmadou Bamba Association; the Association of Somali Mothers and Children; the Islamic Association of Imams and Religious Leaders; the Pakistani Islamic Association 'Muhammadiah'. All these organizations in 2017 signed the *National Pact for an Italian Islam, expression of an open and integrated community, adhering to the values and principles of the Italian legal system* (see *infra*). It is interesting to note that, in accordance with the 1929 Law, no. 1159, only the the Islamic Cultural Centre of Italy has been recognised as a religious legal entity (see *Decreto del Presidente della Repubblica 21 dicembre 1974, n. 712, Riconoscimento della personalita' giuridica dell'ente "Centro islamico culturale d'Italia"*).

28 The notion of 'religious nones' indicates the category of people who select 'no religion' when surveyed about their religious affiliations. It refers to lack of organizational affiliation rather than lack of personal belief. In origin this expression was used in the US Now it is commonly used throughout the world. See J. Thiessen and S. Wilkins-Laflamme, "Becoming a Religious None: Irreligious Socialization and Disaffiliation", (2017) 5 (1) *Journal for the Scientific Study of Religion* 64–82.

29 See *Corte costituzionale,* No. 52/2016.

so far.[30] This has led to the creation of a 'common legislation' that, as such, is far from being considered general law: it is common to all religious denominations that have signed an understanding, but it cannot be applied to other creeds.[31] As a matter of fact, religions without *intese* are subject to the 1929 law (no. 1159). Having been approved during the Fascist regime, this law is not always congruent with constitutional provisions. For example, according to the 1929 law, the Minister of Interior will take into consideration the characteristics of the denomination or religious entity that claims recognition. Thus, the Minister of Interior can take into account: 1) the number of the claimants' members and how widespread they are in the Country; 2) the compatibility between the claimants' statute and the main principles of the Italian legal system; 3) the aim of the denomination that claims to be recognised by the State, an aim that has to be 'prevalently' of religion and worship. In contrast, religious groups possessing an understanding with the State are no longer subject to the 1929 law whose rules are entirely replaced by those, more favourable, of legislative acts approving *intese*.[32]

These difficulties are even more evident in the light of the Italian principles of secularity, which can certainly favour religion, but it cannot favour one religion over another. That is true not only with reference to the comparison between the Catholic Church but with all other religious denominations. Evidence of this can be seen when comparing the minority religions that have signed an *intesa* and those groups that do not possess an understanding with the State.[33] Thus, instead of implementing the freedom of religion and the

30 See "Le intese con le confessioni religiose", accessed 2 February 2023, http://presidenza.governo.it/USRI/confessioni/intese_indice.html.

31 V. Crisafulli, "voce Fonti del diritto (dir. cost.)", (1968) XII *Enciclopedia del diritto* XII 948; F. Carnelutti, *Teoria generale del diritto* (Roma, Soc. ed. del Foro italiano, 1951), at 35; M. Ricca, *Legge e Intesa con le confessioni religiose: sul dualismo tipicità-atipicità nella dinamica delle fonti* (Torino, Giappichelli, 1996), at 35; B. Randazzo, *Diversi ed eguali. Le confessioni religiose davanti alla legge* (Milano, Giuffrè, 2008), at 55.

32 On this aspect see R. Zaccaria, S. Domianello, A. Ferrari, P. Floris and R. Mazzola (eds.), *La legge che non c'è. Proposta per una legge sulla libertà religiosa* (Bologna, il Mulino, 2019). In particular see the following articles: P. Floris, "le istanze di libertà collettiva e istituzionale", at 145–190, and F. Alicino, "I problemi pratici e attuali della libertà religiosa", at 235–246.

33 V. Tozzi, "Le confessioni religiose senza intesa non esistono" in R. Mazzola *et al*, *Aequitas sive Deus. Studi in onore di Rinaldo Bertolino* (Torino, Giappichelli, 2011), at 1033–1042; G. Casuscelli, "La rappresentanza e l'intesa", in A. Ferrari (ed.), *Islam in Europa/Islam in Italia tra diritto e società* (Bologna, il Mulino, 2008), at 285–322; N. Colaianni, *Diritto pubblico delle religioni. Eguaglianza e differenze nello Stato costituzionale* (Bologna, il Mulino, 2012), at 68; F. Finocchiaro, *Diritto ecclesiastico*, updated by Adrea Bettetini and Gaetano Lo Castro (Bologna, Bologna, Zanichelli, 2012), at 120; A. Bettetini, "Commento

right to be equally free on the grounds of religious faith, the bilateralism principle has become the source of privileges, which are accessible only to a limited number of denominations. In other words, the practice of bilateral legislation seems to be in contrast not only with the Italian Constitution, but also with the constraints deriving from the supranational obligations, such as those related to the European Convention of Human Rights (ECHR).

Under this aspect, it is worth noting that the 1984 Villa Madama agreement between the Catholic Church and the State (which, as said before, amended and replaced the 1929 Lateran Pacts, except for one part) is assimilable to an international treaty.[34] However, this does not make it a legal binding source of constitutional rank.[35] As the Constitutional Court affirmed in 1989,

> [t]he thesis according to which international treaties that are introduced into the Italian legal system by ordinary legislation would assume constitutional or a higher rank has never been shared by the jurisprudence of the Court of Cassation, nor by this Court.[36]

In fact, the norms of international treaty, including those concerning the 1984 Villa Madama agreement between the State and the Catholic Church, do not fall into Article 10.1 of the Constitution regulating "the generally recognized principles of international law".

While the Lateran Pact are mentioned in Article 7.2 of the Constitution,[37] but it is evident that this Article should be understood as a fixed-referral law (*norma di rinvio fisso*). That means Article 7.2 of the Constitution makes "a precisely identified reference to the Pacts stipulated and entered into force in

all'art. 20 Cost.", in B. Raffaele, A. Celotto and M. Olivetti (eds.), *Commentario alla Costituzione* (Torino, UTET, 2006) at 441–448; M. Ricca, "Art. 20 della Costituzione ed enti religiosi: anamnesi e prognosi di una norma non inutile", in *Studi in onore di Francesco Finocchiaro* (Padova, CEDAM, 2000), at 1557–1580; P. Di Marzio, *L'art. 20 della Costituzione. Interpretazione analitica e sistematica* (Torino, Giappichelli, 1999); S. Fiorentino, "Gli enti ecclesiastici e il divieto di discriminazione", in G. Casuscelli (ed.), *Nozioni di diritto ecclesiastico* (Torino, Giappichelli, 2006), at 57–68.

34 See the following *Corte costituzionale*'s decisions: No. 348/2007; No. 349/2007; No. 73/2001; No. 15/1996; No. 168/1994; No. 323/1989, No 153/1987; No. 96/1982; No. 188/1980; No. 48/1979, No. 104/1969; No. 32/1960; No. 323/1989.

35 A. Cassese, "Art. 10," in Giuseppe Branca (ed.), *Commentario della Costituzione* (Bologna-Roma, Zanichelli-Il foro italiano, 1977), at 485.

36 *Corte costituzionale*, No. 323/1989 (translation mine).

37 Article 7.2 of the Constitution stated that the relations between the State and the Catholic Church "are regulated by the Lateran pacts. Amendments to such Pacts which are accepted by both parties shall not require the procedure of constitutional amendments".

1929".[38] Given the fact that these Pacts were almost entirely replaced with the 1984 Villa Madama agreement and this kind of agreement is assimilable to an international treaty, the Villa Madama agreement's rules cannot fall into the scope of Article 7.2 of the Constitution.[39] As the constitutional jurisprudence clearly implies, the rules of the 1984 agreement between the State and the Catholic Church are actually protected under article 117.1 of the Constitution, as constructed by the constitutional revision of 2001 (no. 3). Under this revision,

> [l]egislative powers shall be vested in the State and the Regions in compliance with the Constitution and with the constraints deriving from EU legislation and international obligations.[40]

This implies that if the provisions of the 1929 Lateran Pacts were considered as part of the Constitution (meaning these provisions could compete with other constitutional rules),[41] the provisions of the 1984 Villa Madama agreement do not have a constitutional status. In other words, the provisions of Villa Madama agreement are subject to all norms of the Constitution and can only compete with ordinary legislations.[42] Furthermore, if this is true for the provisions of 1984 Villa Madama agreement, it is even more evident with the laws based on *intese*, those concerning the relationship between the State and religions other than Catholicism.

In addition, we must take into account the content of Article 117.1, which clearly establishes that the Italian legislative powers shall be vested in compliance with not only the Constitution, but also with "the constraints deriving from EU and international obligations". As a result, the products of bilateralism (Churches-State) legislations are now subject not only to the Constitution, but also to the provisions of ECHR, including those referring to freedom of religion

38 *Corte costituzionale,* No. 16/1978.

39 They were replaced with the only exception of the first part formally called Treaty, which does not really concern religious matters, in the strict sense of the terms; it gives Vatican its own City-State.

40 C. Colaianni, "Il sistema delle fonti costituzionali del diritto ecclesiastico al tempo dell'emergenza (e oltre?)" (2020), *Rivista AIC* 4, accessed 5 February 2021, https://www.rivistaaic.it/images/rivista/pdf/4_2020_9_Colaianni.pdf.

41 For this reason, the 1929 Lateran Pacts had a constitutional status, meaning their rules were constitutional rule subordinate only to the supreme principles of the legal constitutional order (*principi supremi dell'ordine costituzionale*). On the supreme principles of the constitutional order see *Corte Costituzionale,* No. 30/1971.

42 N. Colaianni, *Diritto pubblico delle religioni: Eguaglianza e differenze nello Stato costituzionale* (Bologna, il Mulino, 2012), at 153–174.

(Article 9 ECHR) and the prohibition of "discrimination on any ground such as … religion" (Article 14 ECHR).[43]

This point of discussion becomes even more pertinent when we look into the jurisprudence of the European Court of Human Rights (ECtHR), holding that the Convention does not require a Member State to create a particular legal framework in order to grant religious communities a special status. Yet a State which has created such a status through specific bilateral State-Churches legislations must comply with its duty of neutrality and impartiality. In particular, the State should ensure that any group has a fair opportunity to apply for this status and that the criteria established are in accordance with the principles of proportionality and non-discrimination.[44] This signifies that when Member States rule (via bilateralism method) in favor of some individuals and organizations, these States must demonstrate with reasonable arguments why it is necessary to exclude other persons or other organizations from the scope of application of those special status and privileges. In brief, when not supported by both valid aims and objective justifications, the exclusion of certain religious groups identifies a form of unreasonable discriminations under the European Convention of Human Rights.[45]

In conclusion, this information illustrates that under the current unprecedented pluralism, the Italian principle of bilateralism has become increasingly more complicated and difficult to administer within the State. The result has caused the current intense scrutinization of the Italy's State-Church legislations. That is even more evident in the light of the case of atheistic associations alongside rigorous legal actions. These disputes have indeed raised concerns over the system of State-religions relationship related to Article 7.2 (concerning the relations between the Catholic Church and the State) and 8.3 (related to the relation between the State and minority religions) of the Constitution.

5 The Bilateralism Principle and the Italian Atheism

In the past decades, Italian atheism and agnosticism have experienced a significant evolution, from a purely individual dimension to a rampant militant

43 On this aspect see: *Corte costituzionale*, Nos. 348–349/2007; *Corte costituzionale*, No. 311/2009; *Corte costituzionale*, No. 317/2009; *Corte costituzionale*, No. 1/2011.

44 ECtHR, *Savez crkava "Riječ života" and others v. Croatia*, 9 December 2010, Appl. No. 7798/08; ECtHR (Grand Chamber), *İzzettin Doğan and others v. Turkey*, 26 April 2016, Appl. no. 62649/10.

45 *Ibid.*

activism. As such, the group has called into question the moral ascendancy of religion and the importance of religion as a feature in civic belonging and national identity. Italian atheists have demanded the outlawing of many practices related to the privileged position of religions (particularly the Catholic Church) in public life. Atheist groups have highlighted several indicators that position Catholic Church as a powerful figure in Italian society, such as the display of the crucifix in classrooms, the legal impossibility of renouncing one's baptism,[46] the teaching of religion in classes, and the system of 0.008 of the *IRPEF* (a tax applied to every person's income). Associations of nonreligious people argue that while they enjoy many rights as individuals, it is difficult for them to identify within the State's law as a group. Atheist groups argue that Italy's legal system excludes them from achieving a sense of belonging in the State, and eliminates the possibility of ever achieving a constitutional identity of Italian citizenry.[47]

Consequently, many non-religious groups have sued the State authorities on several occasions and have challenged the State's activities on religious issues, including the bilateralism principle. In this specific matter, the Italian militant atheism wants to confront these problems directly. In 1996, the Italian Union of Rationalist Atheists and Agnostics (UAAR) requested the Italian Government to initiate negotiations to sign an *intesa* with the State.[48] This request was rejected by the President of the Council of Ministers because the UAAR was not eligible candidate in the national list of confessional beliefs. The President went on to affirm that the refusal to accept an association's request to launch negotiations could not be subject to judicial review, as this would violate the sphere of constitutional powers vested in the Government.[49] However, UAAR decided to bring the case before the judges, which has resulted in a long legal battle, marked by several judicial decisions.

46 See the 'Debaptism Certificate,' available at: https://www.uaar.it/laicita/sbattezzo/, whose procedure has been partially validated by the Italian Data Protection Authority (*Garante per la protezione dei dati personali*), https://www.garanteprivacy.it/web/guest/home/docweb/-/docweb-display/docweb/1090502 See also the Italian Bishops' Conference (CEI), *Decreto Generale. Disposizioni per la tutela del diritto alla buona fama e alla riservatezza. Prot. n. 1285/99, art. 2, par. 9.*

47 F. Garelli, "Flexible Catholicism, Religion and the Church: The Italian Case", (2014) 4 *Religions*, at 1–13.

48 F. Alicino, *La legislazione sulla base di intesa. I test delle religioni "altre" e degli ateismi* (Bari, Cacucci, 2013), at 218.

49 See the President of the Council of Ministers of the Italian Republic, 1996. *Atto protocollato DAGL 1/2.5/4430/23 e comunicato all'UAAR con lettera datata 20 febbraio 1996.* See also *Consiglio di Stato, Parere 29 ottobre 1997, n. 3048.*

Many of these decisions have been issued by both administrative and ordinary Courts, namely the Regional Administrative Court, the Council of the State, and[50] the Italian supreme Court (known as *Corte di Cassazione*, the highest level of the Italian judicial system). In 2013, the Supreme Court upheld that the original goal of the *intese* is to make the constitutional right of religious freedom better implemented, more widely valued, and universally appreciated.[51] The Supreme Court also affirmed that, under the above-mentioned phenomenon of "copy & paste" understandings, the instrument of the *intesa* has been transformed into a sort of legislative framework, which is accessible only for few minority religions at the exclusion of all other groups.[52] For this reason, the decision to initiate negotiations could not be left to the absolute discretion of the Government: negotiations should be considered as a corollary of the equal freedoms guaranteed to all religious faiths. It follows that the Government's refusal to launch the negotiations cannot be considered as a political act. It should instead be qualified as a legal document subject to judicial review.[53]

The Italian Constitutional Court (ICC) intervened in the case in 2016, adopting the opposite approach: *intese* are no longer bound to equal freedom of all beliefs before the law.[54] According to ICC, the significance of the provision under Article 8.3 of the Constitution consists in the extension of the bilateralism principle-method from the Catholic Church to non-Catholic faiths. This is possible only where the method reflects the common intentions of both religious minorities and the Government not only to conclude an agreement, but also to initiate negotiations.[55] As far as the supreme principle of secularity is concerned, ICC clarified that it certainly implies impartiality and equidistance with regard to each religious faith as well as the right to profess religious belief. Nevertheless, ICC also concluded that the *intesa* does not involve these aspects.

In other words, the 2016 constitutional decision stated that the general principle of secularism and the general rights to profess religious belief are actually protected by other constitutional rules,[56] including those related to Article 19 (in conjunction with Articles 2, 3 and 8.1) of the Constitution.[57] However, it

50 TAR Lazio (sede di Roma), judgement of 5 November -31 December 2008, No. 12539; Consiglio di Stato, judgment of 18 November 2011, No. 6083.

51 Corte di cassazione, Sez. Un. civ., judgment of 28 June 2013, No. 16305.

52 *Ibid.*

53 *Ibid.*

54 Corte costituzionale, No. 52/2016.

55 *Ibid.*

56 In particular, those of Articles 3, 8.1, 8.2, 19 and 20 of the Constitution.

57 Corte costituzionale, No. 52/2016.

remains that the Italian government holds a broad margin of discretion not only to decide whether an organization can be defined as a religion and are eligible for the benefits of bilateral legislation, but also whether to initiate a negotiation with any religious group in order to conclude an *intesa*. In brief, in regard to the implementation of Article 8.3 of the Constitution and the relative instrument of *intese*, the Government has autonomous power.[58]

It is important to note that ICC supported the 2016 decision by a significant *obiter dictum*. In a statement, ICC commented;

> the changing and unpredictable reality of national and international political relations, which may lead the Government to conclude that it is not appropriate to allow an association that requests it to launch negotiations. When confronted with this considerable variety of situations, the Government is vested with a broad discretion.[59]

Strangely enough, the *dictum* has little to do with the Italian atheism and more to do with the confessional organisations that would subscribe an *intesa* in the future. This is important not only for UAAR case-law, but also for the entire Italian system of State-Churches relationship.

In other terms, the 2016 constitutional decision in general and the *obiter dictum* in particular uncover other important aspects of today's new pluralism in Italy, which can be fully understood when considering the presence of 'new' religious creeds, such as those made up of Muslims.

C The Bilateralism Principle and Islam

The religious changes seen within Italian society within the past decades are not caused by the presence of Islamic groups. Given the specificity of the groups (especially when compared to religions that have long been present in Italy) and its problematic interconnected issues (which also implies the emergence of transnational fundamentalism and terrorism), Muslim communities nevertheless highlight the most striking facets of the Italian neo pluralism: these communities indicate and signal the fast tendency to foster plurality

58 F. Alicino, "La bilateralità pattizia Stato-confessioni dopo la sentenza n. 52/2016 della Corte costituzionale", *Osservatorio sulle fonti* 2016, 2, accessed 5 February 2023, https://www.osservatoriosullefonti.it/mobile-note-e-commenti/note-e-commenti-n-2-2016/1021-osf-2-2016-alicino.

59 Corte costituzionale, No. 52/2016, para. 5.2, *conclusion on points of law* (translation mine).

within society.[60] For this reason, Islam has become the discursive substitute for religious and cultural pluralism, which implies other sensitive matters that somehow are correlated to this religion: gender roles, clothing codes, family models, the relationship between religion and politics.[61]

From a legal point of view, it is important to remember the content of the 1948 Constitution, which states that community with religious aims can operate within the Italian legal system. Religious communities can do so without authorization or prior registration. From this point of view, the only limit is based on the protection of public order and common decency. In theory, this gives Muslim groups the opportunity to choose among various types of legal capacity, including those referring to confessional organizations.[62] Yet in practice, they have been regulated by the general legislation concerning association in its double version, recognised and non-recognised associations. More specifically, many Muslim organizations constitute themselves as 'non-recognized associations,'[63] which is the simplest model of association. It is true that this kind of associations does not provide control from the State's authorities; but it is also true that their legal capacity within the public space is reduced to basic, limited services. Muslim organizations can also choose the form of 'recognized associations,' which provides legal personality through registration at the local Prefecture; however, this legal capacity is not comparable to other confessions.[64] In sum, not only the legal capacities of recognized and non-recognised associations are incomparable with those related to confessions with *intese*. These kinds of associations also prevent Muslim organizations to be legally recognised by reasons of their religious under the 1159/1929 law.[65]

---

60 S. Allievi, "Immigration, Religious Diversity and Recognition of Differences: The Italian way to Multiculturalism", (2014) 21(6) *Identities* 724–737; F. Pastore, "Immigration in Italy Today. A community out of Balance: Nationality Law and Migration Politics in the History of Post-Unification Italy", (2004) 9(1) *Journal of Modern Italian Studies*, at 27–48.

61 F. Alicino, "The Italian Legal System and Imams: A difficult Relationship", in M. Hashas *et al.* (eds.), *Imams in Western Europe. Developments, Transformations, and Institutional Challenges* (Amsterdam, Amsterdam University Press, 2018), at 359–380.

62 L. Paladin, "voce *Ordine pubblico*", (1965) *Noviss. Digesto it.*, XII, at 130.

63 Article 36–38 of the Italian Civil Code.

64 Articles 14–35 of the Civil Code and the 2000 decree of the President of Italian Republic (no. 361).

65 See A. Ferrari, 'Libertà religiosa e nuove presenze confessionali (ortodossi e islamici): tra cieca deregulation e super-specialità, ovvero del difficile spazio per la differenza religiosa', in *Stato, Chiese e pluralismo confessionale*, 2011, at 13, accessed 2 February 2023, https://riviste.unimi.it/index.php/statoechiese/article/view/1213. See also S. Allievi, *Islam italiano. Viaggio nella seconda religione del Paese* (Torino, Einaudi, 2003).

In fact, some Muslim organizations have tried to engage forms of cooperation with the Government in order to sign an *intesa*. In 1990, two years after its establishment, the Union of Islamic Communities and Organizations in Italy (UCOII) publicly stated their intentions by issuing a draft *intesa*-understanding and sending it to the Italian government. Similar attempts have been made by other Islamic organizations, such as the Association of Italian Muslims (1994) and the Islamic Italian Community (1996).[66] Yet their efforts have not been taken into consideration by public authorities who, instead of using Article 8.3 of the Constitution or the 1159/1929 law, have chosen other solutions.

For example, in 2005 the Italian Minister of the Interior established the Consultative Council for Islam in Italy (*Consulta per l'Islam italiano*).[67] This Council issued documents that aimed at reaffirming the values of a secular State and religious freedom as well as encouraging the creation of a federation of Islamic groups. In this context Charter of values for the integration and citizenship (*Carta dei valori per l'integrazione e la cittadinanza*) was approved under the decree of the Minister of the Interior. The Charter was conceived as the basis for a future understanding between the State and Islam(s).[68] The Italian Committee for Islam suggested that if imams should subscribe to the Charter, they had to do so in accordance with the 1159/1929 law which had to be accompanied by a circular of the Minister of the Interior.[69] Likewise, the Minister of the Interior established in 2010 a Committee for Islam in Italy (*Comitato per l'Islam Italiano*) which was made up of 19 members, including not only Muslim representatives but also non-Muslim academic experts on Islam and even anti-Muslim prominent figures in journalism. This choice was

66 L. Musselli, *A proposito di una recente proposta di bozza d'intesa con l'Islam*, (1997) *Il Diritto ecclesiastico*, I, 295; M. Tedeschi, "Verso un'intesa tra la Repubblica italiana e la Comunità islamica in Italia?", (1996) *Il diritto di famiglia*, at 1574; A. Cilardo, *Diritto islamico, diritto occidentale: ambiguità semantica*, in V. Tozzi and G. Macrì (eds.), *Europa e Islam. Ridiscutere i fondamenti della disciplina delle libertà religiose* (Soveria Mannelli, Rubbettino, 2009), at 94.

67 S. Ferrari, *La consulta islamica*, in ISMU, *Dodicesimo rapporto sulle migrazioni 2006* (FrancoAngeli, Milano 2007), at 249–263.

68 See C. Cardia, *Introduzione alla Carta dei valori della cittadinanza e dell'integrazione*, in Ministero dell'Interno, *Carta dei valori della cittadinanza e dell'integrazione*, (s.i.d.) (2008), at 8; N. Colaianni, "Alla ricerca di una politica del diritto sui rapporti con l'Islam (Carta dei valori e Dichiarazione di intenti)", (2009) *Stato, Chiese e pluralismo confessionale*, available at: https://riviste.unimi.it/index.php/statoechiese/article/view/2856 (accessed 5 February 2023).

69 See *Parere del Comitato per l'Islam Italiano, Parere su Imam e formazione*, 31 May 2011, at 6, available at: https://www.coreis.it/documenti-ufficiali/comitato-per-islam-italiano-parere-su-imam-e-formazione/.

clearly intended to soften the vague attempt of representativeness of the 2005 Consultative Council.

A few years later (March 2012) the Minister for Cooperation and Integration created a "Permanent Conference on Religions, Culture and Integration (CRCI)," where representatives of Muslim organisations and experts on Islam and on other religions were properly represented. However, the CRCI was essentially conceived as a space for meetings and seminars rather than a consultative body. In 2015, it was the turn of another Council for an Italian Islam, consisting of university professors and experts, who set up a common agenda with representatives of the major national Muslim associations in Italy.[70] In 2016, the Council elaborated a document, which was delivered on the 1st of February, 2017[71] called the "National Pact for an Italian Islam expression of an open community, integrated and adhering to the values and principles of State laws".[72]

The content of hese documents helps us to gain a better appreciation of how organizations are trying to find new legislative avenues, by promoting collaborations between the State and Muslim groups. A similar approach has been followed at the local level, where consultative forums with representatives of

---

70 Namely: the Islamic Cultural Centre of Italy (CICI); the Union of Islamic Communities and Organizations of Italy (UCOII); the Italian Islamic Religious Community (COREIS); the Union of Muslim Albanians in Italy (UAMI); the Association of Muslim Women in Italy (ADMI); the Cheikh Ahmadou Bamba Association; the Association of Somali Mothers and Children; the Islamic Association of Imams and Religious Leaders; the Pakistani Islamic Association 'Muhammadiah'.

71 P. Naso, "For Italian Islam", (January-February 2017) *Intercultural dialogue* 1, at 4.

72 This Pact is divided into three parts: the first one refers to the constitutional principles and regulations concerning religious freedom; the second and third contain two 'decalogues' engaging representatives of Muslim communities and the Interior Ministry to support the establishment of Italian Islam that, among other things, should contribute in the prevention and the contrast against religion-inspired radicalization. More specifically, the Pact should serve to start process of legal organization of Muslim communities, in accordance with the constitutional rules, including those related to freedom of religion. The Pact also aims at promoting the preliminary conditions to start negotiations related to Article 8.3 of the Constitution as well as to train "imams and religious leaders who can also act as effective mediators to ensure full implementation of the civil principles of coexistence, State secularism, legality and equality of rights between men and women". Furthermore, the Pact supports organization that ensure the utmost transparency in the funds received from Italy or abroad and that deliver the Friday sermons into Italian. See Patto nazionale per un Islam Italiano, accessed 28 January 2023, https://www.prefettura.it/cremona/contenuti/Patto_nazionale_per_un_islam_italiano-6670488.htm#:~:text=Il%20Ministro%20dell%27Interno%20in,islamiche%20presenti%20nel%20territorio%20italiano.

Muslim communities and experts in religion have been established.[73] This is the case of the so-called mini-understandings (*mini intese*) between branches of the public administration and minority religions that do not have an *intesa* yet.[74] For example, along with the agreement between the Department of Penitentiary Administration (DAP), the Jehovah's Witnesses and some Protestant Churches, the DAP and UCOII signed a Protocol on 5 November 2015, which was replied on 8 January 2020 and extended to the Italian Islamic Conference (IIC) on October of the same year. These new protocols allowed religious ministers to enter prisons.[75]

These protocols reaffirm that instead of relying on bilateral legislation related to Article 8.3 of the Constitution and the relative instruments of *intese*, public actors and religious leaders can explore other solutions, like those performed during the pandemic outbreak of Covid-19. The attention focuses on the "Protocol concerning the resumption of public Masses", which was signed on 7 May 2020 by the President of the Council of Ministers Giuseppe Conte, the Ministry of the Interior Luciana Lamorgese and the CEI's President Cardinal Gualtiero Bassetti.[76] Few days later very similar (copy&paste) documents were

---

73 On February 2016 the City of Florence and a local Muslim community also signed a Pact for integration and citizenship. In the same period, the City of Turin and twenty local Islamic organizations signed the "Pact of shared values" (*il patto di condivisione*) approved in the context of Turin Islamic Forum.

74 F. Alicino, *La legislazione sulla base di intese. I test delle religioni "altre" e degli ateismi* (Bari, Cacucci, 2013), at 73–80.

75 These Protocols allow imams to offer spiritual assistance to Muslim inmates detained in Italian prisons. UCOII and IIC will provide prison administration with a list of people who "perform the functions of imam in Italy" and who are "interested in guiding prayers and worship within prisons nationwide." The list will also specify at which mosque or prayer room each imam normally performs his worship. Imams will have to indicate their preference for three provinces where they would be willing to lead prayers for inmates. See M. Belli, "Religione in carcere: intesa tra Dap e Comunità Islamiche", (5 June 2020) *gNews*, accessed 28 January 2021, https://www.gnewsonline.it/religione-in-carcere-intesa-tra-dap-e-comunita-islamiche/. See also at "La Confederazione Islamica Italiana-Firma L'Accordo Con Il D.A.P- Ministero della Giustizia", 19 October 2020, accessed 28 January 2021, https://it.italiatelegraph.com/news-40724; S. Angeletti, "L'accesso dei ministri di culto islamici negli istituti di detenzione, tra antichi problemi e prospettive di riforma. L'esperienza del Protocollo tra Dipartimento dell'Amministrazione penitenziaria e UCOII", (2018) 24 *Stato, Chiese e pluralismo confessionale*, accessed 28 January 2021, https://riviste.unimi.it/index.php/statoechiese/article/view/10331.

76 The document states that Masses for the public would resume on May 18 but under strict conditions. Its clauses say that religious ministers determine the maximum number of people who can fit in a church while staying at least one meter apart. If there is demand, additional masses would be held, rather than allowing more people into the church for one service. The faithful would have to wear masks in church. Priests celebrate most of the

signed by other representatives of religions, including those referring to group without *intese* or even not formally recognized as religious denominations, such as the case of many Muslims communities.[77] It is worth remarking that these Protocols fall into neither Articles 7.1 (related to the relations between the Catholic Church and the State) nor Article 8.3 (referring to the relations between the state and religions other than Catholicism) of the Constitution, which means that these protocols have nothing to do with the bilateralism principle. On the contrary, they are part of the unilateral law regulating public administrative procedure according to which associations or committees (that have concrete interest for the defense of legally important situations and that could be prejudiced by the measure taken by public authorities) have the right to intervene during rulemaking proceedings.[78] The administrative nature of the 2020 Protocols is also confirmed by the fact that they were approved by the Technical Scientific Committee[79] before going to the State's authorities and the religious representatives for their signature.[80]

Apart from the confusion over their possible or perceived legal effects, all those documents stress the ability of the bilateralism principle to govern the Italian existing pluralism. They could in fact be interpreted as its failure or as signal for its lack of capacity, perseverance and goal commitment; which is

Mass without masks but they will have to wear one, as well as gloves, when they distribute the eucharist. The Protocol also states that choirs is banned, holy water fonts remain dry, and the traditional exchange of a sign of peace, usually in the form of a handshake, is eliminated. The collection, in which a basket is passed around for offerings of money, is replaced by containers where the faithful can make contributions. All rooms and objects used will be sanitized at the end of each ceremony. See The Italian Government, "Protocollo circa la ripresa delle celebrazioni con il popolo", available at: http://www.governo.it/sites/new.governo.it/files/Protocollo_CEI_GOVERNO_20200507.PDF.

77 See the Italian Government, *Protocollo con le Comunità Islamiche*, available at: https://www.interno.gov.it/sites/default/files/2020.05.14_protocollo_comunita_islamiche.pdf.

78 Law 7 August 1990 no. 241, "Nuove norme sul procedimento amministrativo," OGIR 192 (18 August 1990). See Giovanni Cimbalo, "Il papa e la sfida della pandemia," in (2020) 15 *Stato, Chiese e pluralismo confessionale*, at 9, accessed 5 February 2021, https://www.giovannicimbalo.it/wp-content/uploads/2020/05/Cimbalo.M_Il_Papa.pdf.

79 This is an advisory board of experts supporting the Head of the Civil Protection Department. See the Ordinance of the Head of the Civil Protection Department No. 663 of April 18, 2020, available at: https://www.protezionecivile.gov.it/it/normativa/decreto-del-capo-dipartimento-n--371-del-5-febbraio-2020--istituzione-del-comitato-scientifico/.

80 See the above mentioned *Protocollo circa la ripresa delle celebrazioni con il popolo*, where it is stated that "during the meeting of 6 May 2020 the Technical-Scientific Committee has analysed and approved this 'Protocol concerning the resumption of public Masses'" (*il Comitato Tecnico-Scientifico, nella seduta del 6 maggio 2020, ha esaminato e approvato il presente 'Protocollo circa la ripresa delle celebrazioni con il popolo'*) (translation mine).

also visible in relation to the implementation of the 1984 Catholic Church-State agreement's provisions concerning marriage and public instruction.

7 Catholic Marriage and Public Instruction

Based on Article 8 of the 1984 Catholic Villa Madama Church-State agreement agreement (which replaced the 1929 Lateran Pacts), a marriage contracts made in accordance with the Canon law has civil effects when registered in the State's registry office. The application for registration is made in writing by the Catholic priest, no more than five days from wedding date. Article 8 also states that the sentence of annulment of a marriage pronounced by ecclesiastical tribunals is, at the request of the parties or one of them, effective in the Italian (civil-secular) State by the judgement of the competent Court of Appeal. This is possible when certain conditions have been ascertained. In particular, the ecclesiastic sentences must be enforced by the Italian Courts of Appeal in accordance with Canon Law. However, the concrete element of the case shall not be re-examined by these Courts which, on the other hand, should make provisional economic measures in favour of one of the spouses: these measures are valid until the final decision of the State Court takes place.[81]

It is interesting to note that with the 1984 agreement the Holy See wanted to reaffirm the "immutable value of Catholic doctrine on marriage as a fundamental principle of society".[82] It supposes that, according to the Holy See, the State marriage laws and their interpretation must respect as far as possible the Catholic doctrine. This explains why the 1984 agreement sustains that the Italian Courts of Appeal should consider the specificity of the Church's legal system governing the bond of matrimony, which had its origin therein.[83] It also clarifies why after the 1984 agreement entered into force most of the Italian Courts of Appeal continued to use the logic of the 1929 Lateran Pact, under which the religious effects of the ecclesiastical judgements turned almost automatically into civil effects. In fact, for several years after 1984 the role of the Courts of Appeal was minimized to 'approve' canonical sentences as if nothing had changed since the 1929, when the disputes concerning nullity of religious marriage were reserved to the exclusive competence of the Church's

81 L. Bellanova *et al.*, *Nullità dei matrimoni e tribunali ecclesiastici. Giudizio di delibazione e conseguenze sui processi di separazione e divorzio* (Padova, CEDAM, 2010), at 201–265.

82 Article 8.3 of the 1984 Villa Madama agreement.

83 No. 3(b) of the Additional Protocol of the 1984 Villa Madama agreement.

Tribunals.[84] However, since 2000, both an increasingly pluralistic society and a more secular interpretation of fundamental rights undermined the principle of bilateralism. The most evident sign was the judgment of *Pellegrini v. Italy* delivered on 20 July 2001, when ECtHR held that there had been a violation of the European Convention of Human Rights.[85]

The case regarded the union between Mrs. Pellegrini and Mr. Gigliozzi in 1962. Under the 1929 Lateran Pacts, their religious ceremony was valid in the eyes of the State law. On 23 February 1987 Mrs. Pellegrini petitioned the Rome District Court for judicial separation, which granted her petition and ordered Mr. Gigliozzi to pay her alimony. However, Mrs Pellegrini was summoned to appear before the Regional Ecclesiastical Court of Rome "to answer questions in her matrimonial case". She unaware of this case until the Court informed that her husband had sought to have an ecclesiastical nullification of their union on the ground of consanguinity, since Mrs. Pellegrini's mother and Mr. Gigliozzi's father were cousins. In a judgment delivered on 10 December 1987, the Ecclesiastical Court annulled the marriage following the *praetermissis solemnitatibus processus ordinarii* which under Article 1688 of the Code of Canon Law, consists in a summary procedure: this article can be used when it is clear from an agreed document that there is a canonical ground for annulling a marriage.[86] Although Mrs. Pellegrini petitioned Court's decision, the Court of Romana Rota upheld the decision on the 13th of April 1988.[87] Four years later, the Italian Court of Appeal in Florence declared the ecclesiastical judgment enforceable. In order to produce an appeal before the Italian Supreme Court (*Corte di Cassazione*), Mrs. Pellegrini requested the Ecclesiastical Court to give her a copy of the documents filed in the annulment proceedings. The Ecclesiastical Court refused to grant her request on the ground that the parties could receive only the operative provisions of the judgment, which they claimed would be "sufficient to allow them to exercise their defense rights". On 21 June 1995, the Supreme Court dismissed the appeal without ruling on the fact that the Court of Appeal did not examine the ecclesiastical proceedings.

Consequently, Mrs. Pellegrini applied to ECtHR, which readily noted that the Vatican had not ratified the Convention and the application had been lodged against Italy. For this reason, the ECtHR's task consisted not in

84 Article 34 of the Concordat of the 1929 Lateran Pacts.

85 Application no. 30882/96.

86 *Actorius Libellius, Sessio II, Judiciale examen DN.AE «M.G.», Conventa, (Romae, die Decembris 1987, h. 9,00).*

87 *Sentenza Rota Romana*, in C. Mirabelli *et al.*, *La sentenza della Corte dei diritti dell'Uomo del 20 luglio 2001* (Milano, Giuffrè, 2004), at 367–371.

examining whether the proceedings before the Ecclesiastical Courts complied with Article 6 of the Convention, but whether the Italian Courts, before authorizing enforcement of the canonical decision, adequately controlled that the relevant proceedings fulfilled the guarantees of Article 6 ECHR. In this manner, ECtHR revealed that the case referred to a violation of the Convention on account of the failure of the Italian Courts to ensure that the applicant had had a fair hearing during the ecclesiastical proceedings. In particular, these proceedings had not respected the adversarial principle, as the Mrs. Pellegrini was not informed in detail about the petition for declaration of nullity filed by her husband.[88]

Due to this case's proceedings, the ECtHR's *Pellegrini* decision opened a new frontier in the Italian jurisprudence concerning religious marriage. So much so that a few years later Italy's Supreme Court managed to follow the same path, calling for a more rigorous application of the State public order in this matter.[89] Accordingly, through a series of ruling the Supreme Court not only refused to enforce the ecclesiastical judgment for reasons related to the rights of defense. The Italian judges also stated that it is not possible to recognize and incorporate the effect of the ecclesiastical annulments when a couple had been living for more than three years in a marital relationship; what in the Italian legal system is known as *convivenza* (coexistence).[90]

88 ECtHR, *Pellegrini v. Italy*, *supra*, para. 44.

89 G. Casuscelli, 'Delibazione e ordine pubblico: le violazioni dell'Accordo "che apporta modificazioni al Concordato lateranense"', (2014) *Stato, Chiese e pluralismo confessionale*, accessed 28 January 2021, https://riviste.unimi.it/index.php/statoechiese/article/view/4307); F. Alicino, "Delibazione di sentenza ecclesiastica di nullità e limiti di ordine pubblico interno. Le ultime indicazioni delle Sezioni Unite", (2008) 1–2 *Il Diritto ecclesiastico*, at 309–329; J. Pasquali Cerioli, "La "maggiore disponibilità" nei confronti del diritto canonico matrimoniale: una formula "ellittica" al vaglio dell'evoluzione dell'ordine pubblico", (2008) 1 *Diritto e religioni*, at 348. On the domestic public order see: M.C. Folliero, "Cassazione e delibazione matrimoniale: il lungo addio", (2000) 1 *Il Diritto ecclesiastico*, at 772.; G. Dalla Torre, *Lezioni di diritto ecclesiastico* (Torino, Giappichelli, 2007), at 180; C. Marino, *La delibazione delle sentenze ecclesiastiche di nullità matrimoniale nel sistema di diritto internazionale e processuale* (Milano, Giuffrè, 2005), at 22; A. Licastro, "Il riconoscimento delle sentenze ecclesiastiche matrimoniali e le nuove forme di cooperazione giudiziaria europea", in *Il diritto di famiglia e delle persone*, 2000, at 1262; F. Mosconi, C. Campiglio, *Diritto internazionale privato e processuale. Parte generale e contratti* (Torino, UTET, 2007), at 9; G. Balena, "Le condizioni per la delibazione delle sentenze ecclesiastiche di nullità matrimoniale", (1991) 4 *Riv. dir. proc. civ.*, at 965; C. Cardarello, 'L'ordine pubblico "costituzionale" come limite alla esecutività delle sentenze ecclesiastiche', *Il Diritto ecclesiastico*, 1985, at 98 s.

90 Cass., sez. un. civ., 3 December /17 July 2014, Nos. 16379 and 16380; Cass., sez. un. civ., 18 July 2008, No. 19809; Cass., sez. I civ., 20 January 2011, No. 134; Cass., sez. I civ., 4 June 2012,

This jurisprudence is important because it marks the point of rupture between the ecclesiastical doctrine and the State civil law in the field of marriage. For the Canon law marriage is a sacrament with a lasting commitment of a man and a woman to a lifelong partnership established for the good of each other and the procreation of their children. Under the civil-secular law perspective a marriage is above all a relationship arising from a marital contract.[91] In other words, the ECtHR's *Pellegrini* decision put Article 8 of the 1984 Villa Madam Church-State agreement under a different legal perspective, as the 2009 ECtHR's *Lombardi Vallauri v. Italy* did in relation to the nomination of the professors of the Catholic University of the Sacred Heart.[92] Here, the attention focuses on Article 10.3 of the 1984 Villa Madama agreement stating that, in order to secure that nothing shall be wanting from the moral and religious point of view, those nominations are subject to the *gradimento* (approval) of the Congregation for Catholic Education, an institution of the Holy See.

In 2009, a case was brought forward regarding Mr. Lombardi Vallauri, a part-time teacher of legal philosophy in 1976 at the Faculty of Law of the Catholic University. When a competition for the post of full-time teacher was advertised for the 1998/99 academic year, he applied. The Congregation for Catholic Education informed the President of the University that some of Mr. Vallauri's views were "in clear opposition to Catholic doctrine" and that, "in the interests of truth and of the well-being of students and the University," Mr. Vallauri should be terminated even from his part-time teaching. The University President wrote to the Dean of the Faculty; the President notifyed the Dean of the Congregation's position. The Faculty Board took note and, in the light of Article 10.3 of the 1984 agreement, decided not to examine Mr. Vallauri's application.[93] The Faculty Board also observed that "no authority in the Republic may rule on the findings of the ecclesiastical authority".

After all domestic judicial remedies were exhausted,[94] Mr. Vallauri applied to ECtHR, which held that, in omitting to explain how the applicant's views could oppose to Catholic doctrine, the Faculty Board had not given adequate reasons for its decision. Thus, the European Court went on to observe that, in

No. 8926; Cass., sez. I civ.: 27 January 2015, Nos. 1495 and 1496; 28 January 2015, No. 1622; 2 February 2015, No. 1788; 9 February 2015, No. 2398.

91 F. Alicino, "L'Insostenibile incertezza della delibazione di sentenza ecclesiastica", (2012) 3 *Quaderni di diritto e politica ecclesiastica* 760–774.

92 ECtHR, *Lombardi Vallauri v. Italy*, 20 October 2009, Appl. No. 39128/05.

93 On this matter see also the 1972 Cordero's case-law, Corte costituzionale, No. 195/1972.

94 Namely two administrative Courts: TAR Lombardia, Sez. II, judgment of 27 October 2001, No. 7027; and Consiglio di Stato, judgment of 18 April 2005, No. 1762.

the interests of the principle of adversarial debate, the Italian Administrative Courts should have addressed the lack of reasons for the Faculty Board decision.[95] Moreover, ECtHR considered that the University’s interest in dispensing teaching based on Catholic doctrine could not extend to impairing the very substance of the procedural guarantees afforded by the Convention. Accordingly, the interference with freedom of expression had not been “necessary in a democratic society”.[96] For the same reason, the Court also held that Mr. Vallauri had not had effective access to a Court and, therefore, his right to a fair trial had been violated.[97]

8 Conclusion

The Catholic Church and some other confessions have sustained the bilateralism principle as it serves to preserve their special status and the privileges in Italian society. The Catholic Church, for example, does so by identifying as the traditional connection between the Italian national identity and the State’s major religion. From this perspective, the State is requested to recognize “the value of the religious culture and the principles of the Catholic Church,” which are considered integral “part of the historical heritage of the Italian people”. These ideas were affirmed in the 1984 Villa Madama agreement, which is the most instructive example of the bilateral legislations, as set by Articles 7.2 of the Constitution. Simultaneously, religious groups that do not possess *intese* also operate with the aim to improve their legal status. In doing so, these groups have also referred to the 1948 Constitution, where it is stated that all religious confessions enjoy equal freedom before the law and that everyone has the right to profess freely their religious faith in any form, individually or in association, to disseminate it and to worship in private or public.[98] In this scenario, the historical roots of the system of State-Churches relationship and the presence of some different conspicuous forms of religious affiliation complicate the role of the bilateral legislations, especially in the light of the requirements of the supreme principle of secularism. While these legislations ensure a potentially greater diversity in the public sphere, they do not necessarily

95 ECtHR, *Lombardi Vallauri v. Italy*, *supra*, para. 69.

96 *Ibid.*, para. 79.

97 P. Bellini, “Libertà della scienza come premessa della libertà di insegnamento”, (2014) *Stato, Chiese e pluralismo confessionale*, accessed 5 February 2023, https://riviste.unimi.it/index.php/statoechiese/article/view/4000.

98 Articles 8 and 19 of the Italian Constitution.

promote the interests of all religious communities, including those that are part of neo-religious landscape. As a result, the way of implementing bilateralism system remains trapped in the past and has caused a weak pluralism landscape in the country. The data illustrated in this paper demonstrate how the bilateralism method makes it difficult to govern the present cultural and religious landscape in Italy.[99]

The bilateralism principle can be perfectly applied when referring to traditional Judeo-Christian denominations,[100] which have long co-existed in Italy.[101] In contrast, this method can hardly be considered for other minority groups, other than the traditional ones. Therefore, the method of bilateral legislations only appears attractive for some religious denominations, while for others it is perceived as a problem. Moreover, these kinds of legislations do not fit in easily with the current Italian society, which no longer identities as monocultural.

Therefore, it is necessary to rethink the Italian method of implementing the collaboration between the State and religious groups by renewing a joint governance approach. The State must collaborate with religious *nomoi* groups, as they equally important for individuals in developing their personality and identity. For the same reason, however, these groups are not important *per se*, unless one wants to support the old organic-nationalistic conceptions, like those supported by the Fascist regime under which the 1929 Lateran Pacts were approved. These Pacts were based on a religious dominant culture and refused the separation between the State and the Catholic Church. For these reasons, the 1929 Pacts legalized discriminations against denominations other than the dominant one.

The Italian State authorities should now pay attention to the legal instruments carrying out the collaboration between State and confessions, including minority ones. With proper use and care, the method of bilateral collaboration should create not only conditions for a suitable State-confessions interaction, but also an acceptable balance between universal principles of liberal constitutionalism and ethnic-cultural-religious differences. In order to do that, one needs to follow the fundamental premises of the principle of equality which, in the light a rational legal system, cannot accept unreasonable distinctions on the ground of religious and non-religious faith.

99 F. Alicino, *La libertà religiosa*, in F. Buffa and M. Giuliana Civinini (eds.), *La Corte di Strasburgo* (Roma, Questione giustizia, 2019), at 458–467.

100 Articles 8.1 and 19 of the Italian Constitution.

101 Article 20 of the Italian Constitution.

Bibliography

Actorius Libellius, Sessio II, Judiciale examen DN.AE «M.G.», Conventa (Romae, die Decembris 1987, h. 9,00).

Alicino, F., "Delibazione di sentenza ecclesiastica di nullità e limiti di ordine pubblico interno. Le ultime indicazioni delle Sezioni Unite", (2008) 1(2) *Il Diritto ecclesiastico*, 309–329.

Alicino, F., "La bilateralità pattizia Stato-confessioni dopo la sentenza n. 52/2016 della Corte costituzionale", *Osservatorio sulle fonti* 2016, 2. accesed 5 February 2023, https://www.osservatoriosullefonti.it/mobile-note-e-commenti/note-e-commenti-n-2-2016/1021-osf-2-2016-alicino.

Alicino, F., *La legislazione sulla base di intese. I test delle religioni "altre" e degli ateismi* (Bari, Cacucci, 2013).

Alicino, F., *La libertà religiosa*, in F. Buffa and M. Giuliana Civinini (eds.), *La Corte di Strasburgo* (Roma, Questione giustizia, 2019).

Alicino, F., "L'Insostenibile incertezza della delibazione di sentenza ecclesiastica", (2012) 3 *Quaderni di diritto e politica ecclesiastica* 760–774.

Alicino, F., "Italy Tested by New Religious Diversity: Religion in the Italian Prison System" in A. Zwilling and J. Martínez-Ariño (eds.), *Religion and Prison in Europe* (Cham, Springer, 2020).

Alicino, F., "The Italian Legal System and Imams: a Difficult Relationship" in M. Hashas *et al.* (eds.), *Imams in Western Europe. Developments, Transformations, and Institutional Challenges* (Amsterdam, Amsterdam University Press, 2018).

Alicino, F., "The Place of *Minority* Religions and the Strategy of Major Denominations. The Case of Italy", (2017) *Rivista AIC* 1–20, accessed 28 January 2021, https://www.rivistaaic.it/images/rivista/pdf/2_2017_Alicino.pdf

Alicino, F., "Un referendum sull'otto per mille? Riflessioni sulle fonti", (2013) 33 *Stato, Chiese e pluralismo confessionale* accessed 2 February 2021, https://www.statoechiese.it/contributi/un-referendum-sullotto-per-mille-riflessioni-sulle-fonti.

Allievi, S., "Immigration, Religious Diversity and Recognition of Differences: the Italian way to Multiculturalism", (2014) 21(6) *Identities* 724–737.

Barry, B., *Culture and Equality* (Cambridge, Polity Press, 2001).

Bedi, S., "What is so special about religion? The dilemma of the religious exemption", (2007) 15 *The Journal of Political Philosophy* 235–249.

Bellanova, L. *et al.*, *Nullità dei matrimoni e tribunali ecclesiastici. Giudizio di delibazione e conseguenze sui processi di separazione e divorzio* (Padova, CEDAM, 2010).

Bellini, P., "Libertà della scienza come premessa della libertà di insegnamento", (2014) *Stato, Chiese e pluralismo confessionale*, accessed 5 February 2021, https://riviste.unimi.it/index.php/statoechiese/article/view/4000.

Bettetini, A., "Commento all'art. 20 Cost." in B. Raffaele *et al.* (eds.), *Commentario alla Costituzione* (Torino. UTET, 2006).

Bouchard, G., "Concordato e intese, ovvero un pluralismo imperfetto", (2004) *Quaderni di diritto e politica ecclesiastica* 70–71.

Casuscelli, G., "Delibazione e ordine pubblico: le violazioni dell'Accordo che apporta modificazioni al Concordato lateranense", (2014) *Stato, Chiese e pluralismo confessionale* accessed 28 January 2021, https://riviste.unimi.it/index.php/statoechiese/article/view/4307.

Cardia, C., "Concordato, intese, laicità dello Stato", (2004) 1 *Quaderni di diritto e politica ecclesiastica*.

Cardia, C., *Manuale di diritto ecclesiastico* (Bologna, il Mulino, 1996).

Carnelutti, F., *Teoria generale del diritto* (Roma, Soc. ed. del Foro italiano, 1951).

Cassese, A., "Art. 10" in Giuseppe Branca (ed.), *Commentario della Costituzione* (Bologna-Roma, Zanichelli-Il foro italiano, 1977).

Casuscelli, G., "La rappresentanza e l'intesa" in Alessandro Ferrari (ed.), *Islam in Europa/Islam in Italia tra diritto e società* (Bologna, il Mulino, 2008).

Cilardo, A., "Diritto islamico, diritto occidentale: ambiguità semantica" in V. Tozzi and G. Macrì (eds.), *Europa e Islam. Ridiscutere i fondamenti della disciplina delle libertà religiose* (Soveria Mannelli, Rubbettino, 2009)

Cimbalo, G., "Il papa e la sfida della pandemia", (2020) *Stato, Chiese e pluralismo confessionale* accessed 5 February 2021, https://riviste.unimi.it/index.php/statoechiese/article/view/13416.

Colaianni, C., "Il sistema delle fonti costituzionali del diritto ecclesiastico al tempo dell'emergenza (e oltre?)", (2020) 4 *Rivista AIC* accessed 5 February 2021, https://www.rivistaaic.it/images/rivista/pdf/4_2020_9_Colaianni.pdf.

Colaianni, N., *Confessioni religiose e intese* (Bari, Cacucci, 1990).

Colaianni, N., *Diritto pubblico delle religioni. Eguaglianza e differenze nello Stato costituzionale* (Bologna, il Mulino, 2012).

Crisafulli, V., "voce Fonti del diritto (dir. cost.)", (1968) XII *Enciclopedia del diritto* 948.

Di Marzio, P., *L'art. 20 della Costituzione. Interpretazione analitica e sistematica* (Torino, Giappichelli, 1999).

Ferrari, A., "The Italian Accommodations. Liberal State and Religious freedom in the 'Long Century'" in L. Derocher *et al.* (eds.), *L'État canadien et la diversité culturelle et religieuse 1800–1914* (Québec, Presses de l'Université du Québec, 2009).

Ferrari, S., "Il Concordato salvato dagli infedeli" in V. Tozzi (ed.), *Studi per la sistemazione delle fonti in materia ecclesiastica* (Salerno, Edisud, 1993).

Ferrari, S., "Religion between Liberty and Equality", (2016) 4(2) *Journal of Law, Religion and State* 179–193.

Ferrari, S., "La consulta islamica" in ISMU, *Dodicesimo rapporto sulle migrazioni 2006* (FrancoAngeli, Milano 2007).

Festenstein, M., *Negotiating diversity: Culture, deliberation, trust* (Cambridge, Polity Press, 2005).

Finocchiaro, F., *Diritto ecclesiastico*, updated by Adrea Bettetini and Gaetano Lo Castro (Bologna, Bologna, Zanichelli, 2012).

Finocchiaro, F., "Principi supremi, ordine pubblico italiano e (auspicata) parità tra divorzio e nullità canonica del matrimonio" in F. Cipriani (ed.) *Matrimonio concordatario e tutela giurisdizionale* (Napoli, ESI, 1992).

Fiorentino, S., "Gli enti ecclesiastici e il divieto di discriminazione" in G. Casuscelli (ed.), *Nozioni di diritto ecclesiastico* (Torino, Giappichelli, 2006).

Floris, P., "Laicità e collaborazione a livello locale. Gli equilibri tra fonti centrali e periferiche nella disciplina del fenomeno religioso", (2010) *Stato, Chiese e pluralismo confessionale*, accessed 28 January 2021, https://statoechiese.it/contributi/laicita-e-dimensione-pubblica-del-fattore-religioso-stato-attuale-e-p.

Garelli, F., "Flexible Catholicism, Religion and the Church: the Italian Case", (2014) 4 *Religions* 1–13.

Lariccia, S., "Problemi in temi dello Stato e delle istituzioni civili" in *Scritti in memoria di Livio Paladin* (Napoli, Jovene, 2004).

Margiotta Broglio, F., "Dalla questione romana al superamento dei Patti lateranensi" in General Director of President of the Council of Ministers, *La revisione del Concordato. Un accordo di libertà* (Roma, Istituto Poligrafico e Zecca dello Stato, 1986).

Margiotta Broglio, F., *Italia e Santa Sede dalla grande guerra alla conciliazione* (Roma-Bari, Laterza, 1966).

Minow, M., "Should religious groups be exempt from civil rights laws?", (2007) 48 *Boston College Law Review* 781–849.

Mirabelli, C. *et al.*, *La sentenza della Corte dei diritti dell'Uomo del 20 luglio 2001* (Milano, Giuffrè, 2004).

Musselli, L., "A proposito di una recente proposta di bozza d'intesa con l'Islam", (1997) I *Il Diritto ecclesiastico* 295.

Naso, P., "For Italian Islam", (2017) *Intercultural Dialogue*, January-February 1–4.

Oddi, A., "Il principio di 'laicità' nella giurisprudenza costituzionale" in R. Bin*et al.* (eds.), *Laicità crocefissa?* (Torino, Giappichelli. 2005).

Paladin, L., "Voce Ordine pubblico", (1965) XII *Noviss. Digesto it.* 130.

Pasquali Cerioli, J., "La 'maggiore disponibilità' nei confronti del diritto canonico matrimoniale: una formula 'ellittica' al vaglio dell'evoluzione dell'ordine pubblico", (2008) 1 *Diritto e religioni* 348.

Pastore, F., "Immigration in Italy Today. a Community out of Balance: Nationality Law and Migration Politics in the History of Post-Unification Italy", (2004) 9(1) *Journal of Modern Italian Studies* 27–48.

Pertici, R., *Chiesa e Stato in Italia. Dalla Grande Guerra al nuovo Concordato. Dibattiti storici in Parlamento* (Bologna, il Mulino, 2009).

Randazzo, B., *Diversi ed eguali. Le confessioni religiose davanti alla legge* (Milano, Giuffrè, 2008).

Ricca, M., "Art. 20 della Costituzione ed enti religiosi: anamnesi e prognosi di una norma non inutile" in *Studi in onore di Francesco Finocchiaro* (Padova, CEDAM, 2000).

Ricca, M., *Legge e Intesa con le confessioni religiose: sul dualismo tipicità-atipicità nella dinamica delle fonti* (Torino, Giappichelli, 1996).

Sicardi, S., "Il principio di laicità nella giurisprudenza della Corte costituzionale (e rispetto alle posizioni dei giudici comuni)", (2007) *associazionedeicostituzionalisti.it* accessed 2 February 2021, https://www.associazionedeicostituzionalisti.it/old_sites/sito_AIC_2003-2010/materiali/convegni/200611foggia/sicardi1.html.

Tedeschi, M., "Verso un'intesa tra la Repubblica italiana e la Comunità islamica in Italia?", (1996) *Il diritto di famiglia* 1574.

Tozzi, V., "Le confessioni religiose senza intesa non esistono" in Mazzola, R. et al., *Aequitas sive Deus. Studi in onore di Rinaldo Bertolino* (Torino, Giappichelli, 2011).

Varnier, G.B., "La prospettiva pattizia" in V. Parlato and G.B. Varnier (eds.), *Principio pattizio e realtà religiose minoritarie* (Torino, Giappichelli, 1995).

Ventura, M., *Creduli e increduli. Il declino di Stato e Chiesa come questione di fede* (Torino, Einaudi, 2014).

CHAPTER 4

The Three Junctions of the Italian 'Islamic Policy'

Alessandro Ferrari

1 The Three Junctions of the 'Muslim Question' in Italy

Compared to the debates, legislative interventions, and jurisprudential interventions that the 'Islamic question' has spurred in other EU countries, the 'Islamic question' seems to have caused a deep freeze of action in the Italian political and legislative system that neither the phase of the so-called Islamic terrorism nor the reflexive parenthesis following the first phase of the fight against the Covid-19 pandemic have really defrosted. It is true that this freezing effects not only the 'Islamic question', but many other issues that would typically require political intervention. At the same time, this stalemate may not be the worst prospect for 'Italian Muslims', given the hectic outcomes of proactive 'Islamic policies' in other European countries (e.g. France and Austriajust to stay in 'Western Europe') and, the wider continental securitarian regression of protections for religious freedom. However, the hibernation of the Italian 'Muslim question' condenses and accentuates the character of what seems to be a constant in the country over the last forty years, that is, the period following the February 1984 reform of the 1929 Concordat with the Catholic Church, and the stipulation of the first agreement (*intesa*) with a religious confession other than Catholic, in the same month and year.[1] More specifically, this period has been defined by the constant of secularisation without an intentional laicisation, i.e. of a profound social transformation of the Italian religious panorama without any explicit political organic governance of the phenomenon.[2] This constant exists not only because of a fortunate lack of a jurisdictionalism anxious to control and direct from above what are and must remain free social transformations, but also because there is the problematic lack of a policy

1 According to the third paragraph of art. 8 of the Italian Constitution the relations between denominations other than Catholicism and the State "are regulated by law, based on *agreements* with their respective representatives".

2 See E.o Pace, "Achilles and the tortoise. A society monopolized by Catholicism faced with an unexpected religious pluralism", (2013) 60 (3) *Social Compass* 315–331 and J. Baubérot, 'Sécularisation, laïcité, laïcisation', (2013) 2 (90) *Empan* 31–38 and *Laïcité 1905–2005, Entre passion et raison* (Paris, Seuil 2004).

 | DOI:10.1163/9789004446816_006

aimed concretely and effectively implementing the principle of *laicità*, understood by the Constitutional Court as the "supreme constitutional principle" of confessional and cultural pluralism in the frame of the distinction between distinct orders.[3] The lack of policy comes from the inability of the political class to metabolize the profound changes in the country's cultural and religious demographics and to directly address them through a constitutional policy of fundamental rights. Instead, they have dumped them on the shoulders of civil society. In this sense, the hibernation of the 'Muslim question' signals the difficulty for Italy in moving from being a *nation-state* founded on the natural reproduction of Catholic values as the basis of its unity to a *state-nation* able to combine its history with an ever-changing identity and the integrating function of constitutional rights within a multilevel frame.

Without any intention of addressing here these general issues or the main difficulties in the management of the 'Muslim question',[4] I will limit myself to outlining only three junctions, at which an Italian political decision-maker, hopefully inspired by constitutional principles, must eventually indicate a direction to follow. The first junction concerns the relationship between the different Muslim universalisms. Given the attraction of the 'Catholic paradigm' and the myth of unitary Islamic representation, the question is how to reconcile a directly state-centric Islamic universalism (seen in Moroccan Islam for instance) with one a more directly theocentric model like that of the broad Muslim Brotherhood. The second junction concerns the process of recognition of Islam(s) in Italy. A policy-maker must decide how to remove the redundant political discretion and ambiguous bureaucratic red tape on which such recognition depends. Finally, the third junction, which is reached after overcoming the other two, leads to the question of whether the problems of recognition are not in fact better overcome without – rather than with – the right to religious freedom.

2 First Junction: the Question of Universality

September 11th and the recognition of the link between rights and security in globalised societies serve as reminders of the transnational and fluid character

3 N. Colaianni, "Trent'anni di laicità Rileggendo la sentenza n. 203 del 1989 e la successiva giurisprudenza costituzionale", (2020) 21 *Rivista telematica*, 52–66, accessed Septembr 20, 2023, https://riviste.unimi.it/index.php/statoechiese/article/view/14650.

4 A. Ferrari, "Islam in Italy: A Religion Under Construction" in D. Ehlers and H. Glaser (eds.), *State and Religion. Between Conflict and Cooperation* (Baden, Nomos, 2020).

of whatever we call religions. In Italy, the awareness of the universal and international character of Islam and its connection with security has highlighted a change in the orientation previously held towards Muslim universality. For many years the idea was that the legal integration of Islamic communities should be done through a liberal-oriented and conscience-based right to religious freedom, attentive to the need of 'Italian Muslims' and, so, promoter of a strict national 'Italian Islam': plural Islam, but strictly Italian in the singular, had been the motto of the pre-11 September years.[5] On the contrary, after that date, the awareness of the intertwining of the national and international levels and the realisation that this same transnationality was necessary to combat terrorism and radicalisation also pushed Italy to look at the right to religious freedom in a different way, putting the securitarian dimension before that of individual consciences. This new perception has fostered a metabolisation of the links between Muslim communities in Italy and foreign entities depending on the impact these links could have on the security of the country. At the same time, this metabolization is not one-way but produces an osmotic process. On one side, the Italian authorities have mitigated their prejudice towards Muslim internationality and become used to a more complex reading of the 'Italian Islam'. On the other side, Muslim leadership, both at home and abroad, have become more attentive in highlighting their effective Italian roots. In recent years, this osmosis has been highlighted by the special cooperation between the Italian Government and the Moroccan-Saudi Mosque of Rome.[6] A cooperation that reveals the ease of recognition of the inter-state Muslim internationality thanks to the benefits of the verticality of State Islam (of which the Rome Mosque is an expression) that allows the Italian state to trace back, albeit with the tortuousness due to the many apparatuses involved, to a unified political and religious Muslim summit. Disjointly involved in this process of metabolization of Muslim transnationality, for the Italian government, were above all the Ministry for University and Research and the Home Ministry. Between 2019–2021, the former has funded a temporary university cooperation program (PriMed – PRevention and Interaction in the MEDiterranean area) where the universities of the Kingdom of Morocco have been the most involved. Additionally, there were initiatives originally planned on Italian territory, and which has included a training program for imams and murshidats in collaboration with both the Rome Mosque and its territorial offshoot, the Italian

5 C. Cardia and G. Dalla Torre, *Comunità islamiche in Italia. Identità e forme giuridiche* (Torino, Giappichelli, 2015).

6 M. Bombardieri, "Mappatura dell'associazionismo islamico in Italia" in A. Angelucci *et al.* (eds.), *Islam e integrazione in Italia* (Venezia, Marsilio 2014).

Islamic Confederation. The Home Ministry, while ceremonially attentive to what remains the only national Muslim organisation formally recognised as a 'cult entity', has encouraged the Mosque's change of statute and attempt to spread its national articulation, beyond the institutional Roman apparatus. This change (validated in 2019 by the Council of State but still not approved by the Government as the law requires) is necessary for the Mosque if it wants to better exploit the potential of Italian law on religious freedom and to try to reach the *intesa* (agreement) with the State and receive the substantial public funding that comes with it.[7] On the one hand, the implementation of the new statute would emphasise the Mosque's religious specialisation through both a highly symbolic change of name from Cultural Institute to Religious Institute and the (at least) removal of the foreign OIC ambassadors from its board. On the other hand, the search for a more widespread territorial rooting makes the Mosque the director of the constitution of an ancillary associative network, the Italian Islamic Confederation, which gathers not only Moroccan but also other Muslims such as some Bangladeshi associations, which are on the margins of institutional dialogue and on the sidelines in the competition for the leadership of Italian Islam.

This willingness of the Italian State to recognise the inter-state dimension of Islamic universality could be seen as a consequence of the stalemate of integration policies and the reluctance to widen, also through the reform of the citizenship law, the meshes of Italian civil society.[8] The 'closing of the door of citizenship' has hindered the building of a younger Muslim leadership more capable of resisting foreign pressures thanks to their Italian citizenship.[9] However, it would be reductive to interpret this first metabolisation of religious transnationality as the consequence of a mere externalisation of an 'Islamic question' incapable of becoming a 'national question'. The metabolisation of transnationality, also in its inter-state dimension is rather part of a more complex building of transnational and transcultural identities. The challenge now is to broaden recognition towards other forms of Muslim universality, including non-state forms. In fact, the state-centric universalism represented by the Mosque of Rome and its network is not only traversed by many

7 M. Ventura, *Religion and Law in Italy* (Alphen aan den Rijn, Wolters Kluwer, 2013). For further information, see A. Ferrari, *Religious Freedom in Italy. An Incomplete Paradigm* (Berlin, De Gruyter 2023).

8 S. Forlati, ""Ius soli", "ius culturae" e diritto internazionale", (2019) 1 *Diritti umani e diritto internazionale* 69–84.

9 R. Ricucci, "Religione e politica nell'islam territoriale: Differenze tra le prime e le seconde generazioni", (2014) 66 *Quaderni di sociologia* 73–99.

internal dynamics and does not constitute a completely homogeneous reality, but it stands alongside, intersects, and opposes other universalisms of a theocentric nature, insofar as they are not directly the expression of or mediated by one or more nation-states. This is especially the case of the Union of Islamic Communities in Italy (hereinafter referred to as the UCOII), the historic opponent of the Mosque of Rome and made up of a network of associations that it would be reductive to continue to pigeonhole into an essentialised 'Muslim Brotherhood'.

These different universalities create a tough competition for 'representation' and inevitably force the Italian government to take a stand. On the one hand, this competition could be used, according to the adage of *divide et impera*, as an energy whose consumption continues the hibernation of the question. On the other hand, it could lead to a preference for only one of the competitors, probably the more state-centric one. After all, contemporary times have seen the rise of jurisdictionalist practices which, having been curbed on the Northern Mediterranean shore over the last two centuries, are coming back into the limelight on both sides because of the rising of security concerns. Moreover, the focus on the role of foreign states is not only a 'Muslim exception'. The role played by Russia, India and the United States in the process of legal integration and recognition of (Russian) Orthodox, Hindu and Mormon communities has been significant. The State-centric option is also indirectly endorsed by the *intesa* between the State and the Church of England, in whose Preamble the Italian Republic has explicitly acknowledged the role of "Defender of the Faith and Supreme Governor of the Church of England" played by the "Sovereign of the United Kingdom".[10]

Nevertheless, a state-centric political option has to be legitimized in light of the constitutional principles provided for the exercise of religious freedom and, despite many misconceptions and misleading political rationales, the state cannot completely ignore the confessional-centric (and not state-centric) lens through which Italian legal system prompts policy makers to look at Islam. This 'confessional focus' constitutes a constraint for governments wishing to address the 'Islamic question', but also a lever that can encourage an opening towards non-state universalities and an osmosis between different cultural and legal traditions. Consequently, the junction for Italian political decision-makers in front of the Moroccan state-centric universality is represented by the need to harmonise the traditional Euro-Western religious-confessional

10 F. Colombo, "L'intesa tra la Repubblica italiana e la Chiesa d'Inghilterra. Un'analisi genealogica", (2019) 11 *Rivista telematica* 18–35, accessed September 20, 2023, https://riviste.unimi.it/index.php/statoechiese/article/view/13578.

lens and their principle of distinction between secular and religious orders with the *bay'a*, the indissoluble 'social contract' between Moroccan citizen-believers and their King-Commander of the Believers. The chosen answer given to this dilemma, either by pretending to be like the Anglican model, or by emphasising first the pre-(modern) state, 'confessional' character of Moroccan Islam linked to the Malikite legal school, or by ignoring it altogether, does not produce the same consequences. The invention of some form of answer to this problem constitutes the necessary precondition for benefiting from the bilateralism envisaged by the Constitution between the Italian State and, precisely, specific 'religious confessions' as stated in the third paragraph of the art. 8 of the Italian Constitution. At the same time, while this answer requires creativity on the part of the interpreters and political decision-makers, to encourage, simulate or fabricate the 'confessionalisation' of Italian Islam, it also requires from Morocco the willingness to trigger processes that could end up favoring an institutional recognition of a plural articulation of 'Italian Islam' inclusive also of associations/confessions composed (also) of Moroccans, but outside of the circuit coordinated by the Mosque of Rome and the institutions of the Moroccan Kingdom. In this regard, the impression is that the prospect of 'confessionalisation', which requires the constitution of an Italian 'confessional representation', ends up producing greater autonomy of Italian Moroccans with respect to their North-African country. Thus, the confessional filter through which even inter-state universality must pass could make the full metabolisation of theocentric universalities inevitable. If this were true, one might also wonder whether this outcome is not viewed with some concern by the Mosque of Rome itself that has not yet have found sufficiently reassuring responses to the same questions that are facing the state counterpart and which does not seem so concerned about the delay (fours years now) in government recognition of its new (confessional) statute. Indeed, in the most recent Italian experience, as in the case, for example, of the legal integration of the Orthodox, Pentecostals, Evangelicals and Buddhists, the metabolization of universality has always produced the recognition of a plurality of 'confessional' entities referring to the same religious tradition. This is also the case with the two *intese* signed with Buddhists and the multiple *intese* with Protestant and Evangelical denominations. A plurality that would undoubtedly be strengthened if one wanted to meet the needs of a religious universality justified 'only' by a specific state affiliation. Thus, unsurprisingly, plurality was also the path suggested by the "National Pact for an Italian Islam" of February 2017 in response to the issue of Muslim pluralism and universality. By renouncing its devotion to the sole hypothesis of the construction of a unitary representation of Muslims in Italy, the "Pact", for the first time, opened up to Muslim pluralism, also recognising a possible institutional translation through the constitution of more "religious confessions" and, therefore, at least in hypothesis, of more 'Muslim *intese*' with the state.[11]

The ways of relating and linking national and transnational levels therefore constitute a central junction in the process of the 'recognition' of Islam in Italy. On the one hand, as we have seen, the need to harmonise a state-centred universalism with the categories of Euro-Western right to religious freedom favours an osmosis functional to the emergence of plural confessional identities. On the other hand, this same need for accommodation poses to the States of the Southern Mediterranean shore – and in particular to Morocco – the question of metabolizing a pluralism of choices of conscience and religion of their citizens 'in diaspora' and therefore also the possibility of a plurality of confessional choices by believers who have also retained the citizenship of a 'Muslim' state, thus admitting, in Europe, that plurality of options increasingly demanded by Arab civil societies. In this case, once again, the right to religious freedom would fulfil, in a new geopolitical space, its function as the 'first freedom'.

3 Second Junction: the Question of Recognition

As we have seen, the issue of universality is inextricably linked to the issue of the institutional recognition of Islamic associations in Italy, an issue that has immobilised political decision-makers for the last twenty years and has become increasingly problematic. With the increased connection between religious freedom and security – and the consequent erosion of the link between religious freedom and freedom of conscience – the role of recognition has also grown exponentially and, with it, the weight of political discretion and the demand for loyalty and reliability from Muslim interlocutors.[12] In Italy, the issue of the recognition of Muslim associations has taken on a pathological dimension, once again highlighting the dysfunctionality of a model of religious freedom based on the fiction of trust in impartial and pluralism-oriented political-administrative action. Public recognition by means of administrative procedures with a high degree of political discretion has become a necessary condition for non-Catholic religious associations not only to obtain the

11 A. Ferrari, "Il Governo Giallo-Verde" di fronte all'islam: l'eredità della XVII legislatura", (2018) 3 *Diritto, Immigrazione e Cittadinanza* 1–24.

12 C. Joppke, "Religion and Loyalty in a Non-Laic Regime", (2016) 1 *Quaderni di diritto e politica ecclesiastica* 85–98.

advantages deriving from an *intesa* with the State, but also to be able to be a legal entity. A dubious interpretation by the Council of State, reiterated since 2009, prevents religious associations from gaining access to legal personality under the Civil Code, which thus becomes only reserved for associations without religious purposes. In this way, the special and highly political-discretionary public recognition procedure envisaged back in 1929–1930, in the so-called legislation on 'admitted cults' – becomes the only way for Muslim groups to gain access to formal recognition of their collective identity. Thus, the purposes of religion and worship are at a disadvantage compared to other non-religious purposes, which can easily allow the distinction of the association's assets and the use of more advantageous tax regimes.[13] The 'governance' of Islam thus creates a path that requires the opening of two doors whose keys are both in the discretion of the Council of Ministers. If the latter does not want to open the door of the *intesa*, it will start by keeping the preparatory door of legal recognition as a religious body closed. Needless to say, the only Muslim organisation recognised as a legal religious entity – albeit with the deliberately ambiguous term 'Cultural Institut' – is the Rome Mosque, recognised by the Italian government in 1974 when it was essential to send out signals of friendship to the petro-monarchies. Since then, and at the very time when the Muslim associationism was taking root in the Italian territory – assuming European local characters – there has been nothing more. The many 'Consultative Tables' set up since 2005 at the Ministry of the Interior and renewed for almost twenty years, have brought no concrete results in this field.[14] None of the Muslim associations that have participated in these 'consultations' have so far been added to the Mosque of Rome among the recognized religious bodies. The denial of the recognition of the legal status of the association Comunità Religiosa Islamica (hereinafter referred to as COREIS), which represented almost the entirety of Italian converts, is particularly emblematic. The request for legal recognition made by this association has highlighted the baroque and jurisdictionalist nature of a procedure in which the interplay between different public actors (Ministry of the Interior, Council of State and Council of Ministers) expresses all its political imponderability. An example of this is the ambiguity surrounding the character, compulsory of not, of the advice of the Council of State. After the so-called 'administrative simplification' of 1997, it would no longer be necessary, but the Presidency of the Council has another opinion. For the Presidency,

13 P. Floris, "Le istanze di libertà collettiva e istituzionale" in R. Zaccaria *et al.* (eds.), *La legge che non c'è. Proposta per una legge sulla libertà religiosa in Italia* (Bologna, il Mulino, 2020).

14 A. Angelucci, "Una politica ecclesiastica per l'islam?", (2014) 1 *Quaderni di diritto e politica ecclesiastica* 141–160.

in fact, the advice of the Council of State remains mandatory because, in its eyes, the recognition of the legal personality of a religious association does not simply represent a procedure under the general right to religious freedom aimed at recognizing the existence of a confessional entity finally granted the autonomy of other legal private associations. On the contrary, according to the Presidency of the Council of Ministers, the legal status foreshadows the possibility of a subsequent *intesa* with the State already constituting a specific aspect of the bilateral relationships between the State and a religious denomination regulated by the Article 8 of the Constitution. The effect of this approach is that the unlimited political discretion, which the Constitutional Court, probably with Islam in mind, has recognized for the Government only in relation to the *intese*,[15] ends up being extended in advance to the administrative procedure of recognition of legal personality albeit recognised by the Council of State as being governed by a purely technical-administrative – and not political – discretion. This situation places religious associations on a completely different – and unreasonably discriminatory – level compared to other private associations. A situation that is further aggravated by the fact that the requirements imposed on religious associations by the Ministry of the Interior and the Council of State to obtain this personality have fluctuated over time, producing an unpredictable interpretation of the 1929–1930 legislation. This was the case in relation to the requirement for the presence in the associative statute of the role of 'minister of cult', absent in most religious traditions but necessary for the Council of State. This also occurs both with the requirements relating to the entity of the asset of the association, differently considered case by case and the criterion of "numerosity", which – not required by the law – has been requested by a Home Ministry circular asking to prove the "consistency of believers" rapidly turned by the Council of State into a very different "large consistency of believers" which is persistently and imponderably checked by the police. Consequently, COREIS once received a favourable opinion from the Council of State but suffered the inertia of the Ministry of the Interior and the Presidency of the Council. Then, forced to make a new application, it suffered the interpretation of the Ministry of the Interior that judged its 'numerosity' too small. Thus, a requirement that is neither defined by any norm nor easily ascertainable, also for the absence of any official recording of religious affiliations, becomes the wall, at a discretionary height, against which the expectation for a

15 G. Casuscelli, "La tutela dell'identità delle minoranze religiose deve potersi avvalere di "un giudice e un giudizio" (ancora sulla sentenza della Corte costituzionale n. 52 del 2016)', (2018) 21 *Rivista telematica* 1–31, accessed September 20, 2023, https://riviste.unimi.it/index.php/statoechiese/article/view/10261/0.

legal status can be shattered. The consequence of this situation is that Muslim associations see no other way of bridging the gap between themselves and (generically) private associations than to 'camouflage' their religious identity.[16] Needless to say, when this identity needs to come to the surface, as in the case of a group that applies to the public authorities for the opening of a place of worship or uses its headquarters as a place of worship, various problems arise that the concealment of the religious identity does not help to resolve. This has been very evident in this time of pandemic when the specific exemptions provided for meetings in places recognized as places of worship could not easily be extended to meetings in places not recognized as such.

In 2023, however, both COREIS and UCOII managed to complete the preliminary process for approval of their statutes by getting the green light from both the Ministry of the Interior and the Council of State. All that is now missing is the final step at the Presidency of the Council of Ministries. This is by no means a foregone conclusion. In fact, the change of government, with the arrival of a right-wing majority, makes uncertain the final approval of the statutes of the UCOII, which, despite years of good institutional collaboration and commitment to interreligious dialogue, could now pay for its distance from the state-centeredness of the Mosque of Rome and the jurisdictionalist sensibilities of the new executive.

If it is so difficult for Muslim associations to obtain basic recognition of their religious identity, and so the legal status, it is easy to imagine that an *intesa* still remains a fantasy for all of them. Besides, after the Constitution came into force in 1948, it took thirty-six years for the first *intesa* to be stipulated with the Waldensian Christians (in Italy since the 12th century) and almost forty for the first *intesa* with a non-Christian denomination, the Jews (in Italy since the 3rd or 2nd century of the Common Era). Therefore, new recognitions fifty years after their establishment and their first formal recognition in 1974 (the Mosque of Rome) would not arrive too late for the Italian right to religious freedom, even if it makes the appeal to the common sense of the Keynesian adage on long term inevitable. In any case, in an age when time seems to be passing more quickly, the Italian right to religious freedom offers horizons of stability. Faced with the issue of recognition, Italian institutions have adopted an evasive attitude. On the one hand, Parliament, which for years has been disinterested, with a few of individual exceptions, in the issue of religious freedom, is

16 See A. Ferrari, "Libertà religiosa e nuove presenze confessionali (ortodossi e islamici): tra cieca deregulation e super-specialità, ovvero del difficile spazio per la differenza religiosa", (July 2011) *Rivista telematica* 1–28, accessed September 20, 2023, https://riviste.unimi.it/index.php/statoechiese/article/view/1213.

rather the place where any timid openness towards the recognition of a now plural Italy is an opportunity to unleash, as an automatic response, the barrage of right-wing parties, often part of the government. On the other hand, the government, which does not want 'religious trouble' in its path, has also avoided renewing for four years (2018–2022) the two Commissions at the Presidency of the Council that dealt with *intese* and religious freedom (in 2023 the two commissions were dissolved by the new Government and replaced by one with new members). This has basically left alone the Ministry of the Interior which, since 2005, has been engaging Muslims in various consultations that have produced good documents, good and useful inter-personal relations, but few concrete facts – and formal deeds on the legal recognition front. A turning point seemed to be looming in 2017, when a politically strong Interior Minister convinced the most important Muslims associations (including the Mosque of Rome and UCOII) to sign, as already mentioned, the 'National Pact for an Italian Islam'.[17] The Pact contained twenty commitments made both by the Muslim associations and the Ministry of the Interior, ten on each side, and saw the fight against radicalisation and action for the transparency of internal activities of the former 'exchanged' with the governmental commitment for the political, institutional and cultural recognition of the Muslim presence in Italy. The Pact thus provided a basic unitary paradigm in the relations between Muslim associations and public institutions, without imposing a homologation of identities or excluding a priori a possible diversification of the paths of recognition, aiming rather to make the public administration (the Ministry of the Interior) and the great majority of Muslim associations converge on the fundamental constitutional principles. In addition, in a concordatarian country like Italy, talking about a 'Pact' implies two very symbolic steps. On the one hand, the exit from the jurisdictionalist logic and the recognition of the equal dignity of the signatories, bound by the same constitutional principles. On the other, the encouragement of the progressive confessionalisation of Islam in Italy and, that is, its progressive transformation into a 'religion'. The implementation of the Pact has been good from a social and cultural point of view but scarce in regulatory terms. From a social and cultural point of view, the Pact has been implemented by 'civic' training events for Muslim associative leaders and imams and by specific meetings involving the youth components throughout the country. From a legal point of view, the Pact has started an activity of statutory reorganisation of the main national Muslim associations, but it has not produced a change of pace on the part of the public administration.

17 See Ferrari, "Il "Governo Giallo-Verde" *supra*.

While the public administration promotes and encourages this reorganisation, it does not formally recognise the changes it has called for, passing the responsibility for the stalemate onto one of the other of the state bodies involved.

Although promoted by different governments, the dynamics of recognition show three common constants. The first constant is the identity of the forms: consultative bodies exclusively entrusted to the responsibility and personality of the individual Home Minister with little involvement of the Executive and even less parliamentary connection. The second is a growing 'normalisation' in the definition of the objectives of the dialogue between the Government and Muslim associations, which are focused, at least nominally, on what is becoming the mirage of the signature of one or more *intese*. The third encompasses the difficulty in breaking the glass ceiling of soft law, as a sign of the turbulence linked to the excessive political discretion of the Italian recognition model. However, the difficulty in breaking down the soft law ceiling gives rise to a blind alley that risks producing frustration and delegitimisation in the participants, who may feel like a hamster in its wheel, caged in a pathological repetition.

4 Conclusion. The Third Junction: the Question of the Right to Religious Freedom

As we have seen, the political and institutional recognition of Islamic associations in Italy is held back by the difficulty for the latter to take advantage of all the possibilities guaranteed by the right to religious freedom. In fact, to obtain a status closer to that of the other associations, the Muslim groups renounce seeking a specific recognition and camouflage themselves behind a generically private appearance. One might then wonder whether the problem, more than just the question of excessive political discretion involved does not lie with the right to religious freedom itself, which has become more a problem than a solution. Its Westphalian character would make it resemble the light of a dead star, a relic of a modernity on its wane.

Nevertheless, the understanding of Muslims through the glasses of the right to religious freedom is quite recent. As soon as they arrived in Europe with the first waves of immigration, the first 'European Muslims' were rather seen as workers with their souls left in their countries of origin. It is only with their stable settlement that 'religious glasses' have taken over, but through a pair of differently calibrated lenses. While the universalist constitutional lens sees Muslims as individuals with the fundamental rights granted by the Constitution and international texts, another lens – that of Euro-centric modernity – continues to see individuals as still backward and to be emancipated from their pre-modern beliefs. Sometimes the latter lens gets the upper hand and prevents the other from functioning and, above all, from seeing Muslims in the flesh, mistaken for an essentialised Islam. One might then ask, in the difficulty of obscuring the lens of modernity, whether the radical renunciation of 'religious glasses' themselves would improve the view of European political systems and, thus, also the social and legal condition of Muslims.

In order to avoid the discriminatory consequences of the Eurocentric modernity lens, a few years ago, Silvio Ferrari wisely suggested the need to "de-Islamise" the Islamic question in order to grasp the similarities between this and all other religious experiences whose needs had already been taken into consideration – and often positively satisfied – by the universalistic lens of the European right to religious freedom.[18] The hope was that by downplaying the issue of Muslim exceptionalism, the constitutional lens would have worked better. However, reality has gone beyond de-Islamisation. The impression is that, instead of de-Islamizing the Islamic question, the more radical idea of de-religionising it is gaining prominence among the promoters of better rights for Muslims. The idea is to remove the 'Muslim question' from the ambit of a right to religious freedom hopelessly non-universalist but state-centric and so far incapable of recognising Muslim confessional identities. This is, for example, in Italy, the outcome of the thesis of those who see in the legislation on the so-called Third Sector the egg of Columbus which, by avoiding reference to the special right of religious freedom – and, thus, without having to consult the political – solves once and for all the problems of the more liquid religious groups and those who find it difficult to conform to the demands of an old legislation born in other times and with different objectives from the constitutional ones. In this perspective, the mimicry of the religious identity of Italian Muslim associations would be, in a certain way, an anticipation of a future in which religion would be invisible to law. The problem with this approach is that only Muslims and non-mainstream believers are – and would be – without a specific public voice and invisible to the law and, above all, condemned to a condition of eternal minority compared to those for whom full recognition as a "religion" has already occurred. While most other confessional groups cling to the statutes that the different national histories have reserved for them, thinking of a de-religionisation for the future of Muslims seems more like the recognition of the reciprocal non-universality of the European religious freedom

18 S. Ferrari, "Islam and the European System of Church-State Relations: a (False) Problem?", (2006) I *Derecho y Religión* 87–115.

and Muslim experiences, squeezed between post-modern opt-out relativistic legal approaches and the colonial and racialized boxes of modernity. With Constitutions unchanged because no European nation-state, Italy included, wants to lose the control on 'religion', to renounce the right to religious freedom would only legitimise the exclusion of Muslims from the circuit of institutional recognition, thus condemning them to political marginality. Rather than a night *à la* Schelling, it would perhaps seem better to support the constitutional lens of the right to religious freedom, in Italy entrusted too much to the *ex post* care of the Constitutional Court than to the *ex ante* care of the legislator. The first step in this direction would be to decide to repeal the legislation on religious freedom still dated 1929–1930 and to replace it with a new one that takes better account of the non-institutional, fluid and individual-centered character of contemporary religious experiences limiting the political discretion connected both to recognition and the promotional aspects of the right to religious freedom.[19] In a social context so scourged by the pandemic and in a Mediterranean space where winter prevails over spring, a political statement able to demonstrate that a European country is not obsessed with the veil and a one-way neutrality but rather tries to unveil all the possibilities that constitutional universalism offers to cultural and religious identities could be a good contribution to a more sustainable future.

Bibliography

Angelucci, A.,"Una politica ecclesiastica per l'islam?", (2014) 1 *Quaderni di diritto e politica ecclesiastica*141–160.

Baubérot, J., "Sécularisation, laïcité, laïcisation", (2013) 2(90) *Empan* 31–38.

Baubérot, J., *Laïcité 1905–2005, Entre passion et raison* (Paris, Seuil, 2004)

Bombardieri, M., "Mappatura dell'associazionismo islamico in Italia" in A. Angelucci, M. Bombardieri and D. Tacchini (eds.) *Islam e integrazione in Italia* (Venezia, Marsilio, 2014).

Cantwell Smith, W., *Modern Culture from a Comparative Perspective* (Albany, State University of New York Press, 1997).

Cardia, C. and G. Dalla Torre, *Comunità islamiche in Italia. Identità e forme giuridiche* (Torino, Giappichelli, 2015).

19 R. Zaccaria *et al. La legge che non c'è. Proposta per una legge sulla libertà religiosa in Italia* (Bologna, il Mulino, 2020).

Casuscelli, G.,'"La tutela dell'identità delle minoranze religiose deve potersi avvalere di "un giudice e un giudizio" (ancora sulla sentenza della Corte costituzionale n. 52 del 2016)', (2018) 21 *Rivista telematica* 1–31. (https://www.statoechiese.it).

Colaianni, N., "Trent'anni di laicità Rileggendo la sentenza n. 203 del 1989 e la successiva giurisprudenza costituzionale", (2020) 21 *Rivista telematica* 52–66, accessed Septembr 20, 2023, https://riviste.unimi.it/index.php/statoechiese/article/view/14650. (https://www.statoechiese.it).

Colombo, F., "L'intesa tra la Repubblica italiana e la Chiesa d'Inghilterra. Un'analisi genealogica", (2019) 11 *Rivista telematica* 18–35, accessed September 20, 2023, https://riviste.unimi.it/index.php/statoechiese/article/view/13578

Ferrari, A., "Islam in Italy: A Religion Under Construction" in D. Ehlers and H. Glaser (eds.), *State and Religion. Between Conflict and Cooperation* (Baden, Nomos, 2020).

Ferrari, A., "Il Governo Giallo-Verde" di fronte all'islam: l'eredità della XVII legislatura", (2018) 3 *Diritto, Immigrazione e Cittadinanza* 1–24.

Ferrari, A., *Libertà religiosa in Italia. Un percorso incompiuto* (Roma, Carocci, 2012).

Ferrari, A., "Libertà religiosa e nuove presenze confessionali (ortodossi e islamici): tra cieca deregulation e super-specialità, ovvero del difficile spazio per la differenza religiosa", (July 2011) *Rivista telematica* 1–28, accessed September 20, 2023, https://riviste.unimi.it/index.php/statoechiese/article/view/1213.

Ferrari, S., "Islam and the European System of Church-State Relations: a (False) Problem?", (2006) I *Derecho y Religión* 87–115.

Floris, P., "Le istanze di libertà collettiva e istituzionale" in R. Zaccaria *et al.* (eds.), *La legge che non c'è. Proposta per una legge sulla libertà religiosa in Italia* (Bologna, il Mulino, 2020).

Forlati, S., ""Ius soli", "ius culturae" e diritto internazionale", (2019) 1 *Diritti umani e diritto internazionale* 69–84.

Joppke, C., "Religion and Loyalty in a Non-Laic Regime", (2016) 1 *Quaderni di diritto e politica ecclesiastica'* 85–98.

Pace, E., "Achilles and the tortoise. A society monopolized by Catholicism faced with an unexpected religious pluralism", (2013) 60 (3) *Social Compass* 315–331.

Ricucci, R., "Religione e politica nell'islam territoriale: Differenze tra le prime e le seconde generazioni", (2014) 66 *Quaderni di sociologia* 73–99.

Ventura, M., *Religion and Law in Italy* (Alphen aan den Rijn, Wolters Kluwer, 2013).

Zaccaria, R. *et al., La legge che non c'è. Proposta per una legge sulla libertà religiosa in Italia* (Bologna, il Mulino, 2020).

CHAPTER 5

Religious Diversity in Greece: Recent Developments and the Challenges of the *Molla Sali* Case

Christos Tsevas

Introduction[1]

With the *Molla Sali*[2] judgment, the European Court of Human Rights (hereinafter ECtHR) again provoked reflection on the endless questions of sharia law, religious diversity, and the borders between law and religious rules and between traditional instruments and modern challenges. The idea of finding a balance between those fields is considered the purpose of this contribution. At the same time, new dimensions have opened up for human rights scholarship considering the geographical scope and recent developments stemming from the judgment against Greece and the refugee and migration context in Europe.

Religious minorities as well as refugees and migrants' religious identity shape society's identity, in this case, the identity of Greek society or other European societies, provided that the concept of the societies is evolving and inclusive. Nevertheless, to ensure the latter, more steps need to be taken and more criteria need to be set by the legal framework. Interdisciplinary research and approaches are considered valuable. The present volume and the subjects based on the question between traditional instruments and new challenges are excellent examples of this approach.

The relationship between religious majorities and minorities, their claims, the manner in which they forge the social and cultural environment around them, and the role of the State could be the source of tensions, legal and

---

1 Part of this chapter has been presented in European Academy of Religion Annual Conference in Bologna, March 4–7 2019, available at: https://docs.wixstatic.com/ugd/8f958c_ab9a29d4de6149b2907713ac532591f3.pdf. I wish to express my sincere thanks to Dr. Roberta Medda-Windischer, Kerstin Wonisch, and Peter Glass for taking the time to provide thoughtful comments and feedback on drafts of this contribution. I bear, of course, responsibility for any shortcomings.

2 ECtHR, *Molla Sali v. Greece*, Appl. No. 20452/14, judgment (Grand Chamber), 19 December 2018. See also the judgment of 18 June 2020 on the just satisfaction.

 | DOI:10.1163/9789004446816_007

political disputes, or dialogue between the State and communities. In Greece, as in every European country, such issues are discussed in the public sphere, within dialogue, or based on stereotypes, discrimination, religious hate speech, intolerance, and xenophobia. However, these aspects were not as apparent in Greece as in other European countries, maybe because it was the 2015 humanitarian crisis that made the mixed migration flows visible. In any case, it is evident that even before the refugee crisis of 2015, Greek society included a variety of religious and moral beliefs.

In such a context, we need to add the variable of religious diversity and focus on interpreting the value of pluralism and its types, such as pluralism of measures or legal frameworks. Therefore, we need to wonder: How could the legal framework on freedom of religion be depicted and transplanted into policies?

In other words, in light of emerging challenges in Europe, the overlap between law and religion should not be underestimated in its importance for European human rights law. This contribution's approach considers that the current legal orders (at the Greek, European, and international levels) leave minimal margin for application of sharia law.[3] The structure of this contribution shall not aim to square the circle, as the title of this volume wonders, but to find out if the interaction among the relevant factors and criteria mentioned below, such as religious diversity and neutrality, can safely lead the traditional instruments to new solutions. Therefore, we shall try to ascertain whether the effect of the *Molla Sali* judgment in the human rights dialogue relates to more cases than one, provides solutions to religious diversity in Europe, and sets standards in the European human rights context. Thus, the debate on legal pluralism, as a concept which challenges the European Convention of Human Rights, must be addressed under the framework of religious diversity, reasonable accommodation, and developments in the national context, legal pluralism, and the existence of new religious communities in the migration and refugee context.

3 Y. Ktistakis, *Charia, tribunaux religieux et droit grec* (Istanbul, istos, 2013), at 134; Council of Europe/ECtHR/Research Division, *Article 9 – Application of Islamic law in the domestic legal order*, (2017), Paras. 5, 23, available at: https://www.echr.coe.int/Documents/Research_report_application_islamic_law_ENG.PDF.

1 The Religious Diversity in Greece and Europe

1.1 *Mixed Migration in Europe*

Regarding the religious diversity in Greece and Europe, we need to organize our discussion around two closely interrelated but still separate questions. First, it is the question of the time and place, and second, the policy of the State and the legal responses provided.

At the same time, Greece constitutes a country of transit, of residence, a destination, but also a European country, and member of the EU, Council of Europe, and Organization for Security and Co-operation in Europe. This country's status reveals it is quite familiar with the phenomenon of mixed migration and this is reflected by the numbers of migrants, refugees, and asylum seekers populations in its territory.

During 2015–2016, Greece faced a mixed migration influx of migrants and refugees searching for safety and their proper rights as human beings. Most of those refugees were fleeing conflicts in Syria, Afghanistan, and Iraq. The humanitarian situation was challenging both on the mainland and in the islands. Many refugees sought to cross Greece to reach northern European countries, while there was a rapid rise in the number of people remaining in Greece after the closure of the western Balkans route.[4] Nearly 857.000 refugees and migrants arrived in Greece in 2015; more than 176.000 arrived in 2016, more than 30.000 in 2017, nearly 75.000 in 2018, and 15.669 in 2020.[5] At the end of 2019, Greece was hosting over 186.000 refugees and asylum-seekers, including over 5.000 unaccompanied children, while most persons of concern were coming from Afghanistan, the Syrian Arab Republic, the Democratic Republic of the Congo, and Iran.[6] Hence, integration should seemingly gain importance as a key of ensuring that all those people would build successful lives in their new home, a challenging task in any country but exacerbated in Greece because of its financial difficulties.[7]

---

4 UNHCR, Global Focus – UNHCR Operations Worldwide, Operation: Greece, 2016 Year- End report, available at: https://reporting.unhcr.org/sites/default/files/pdfsummaries/GR2016-Greece-eng.pdf.

5 UNHCR, Operational Portal – Refugee Situations (07 February 2021), available at: https://data2.unhcr.org/en/situations/mediterranean/location/5179.

6 UNHCR, Greece, updated September 2020, available at: https://www.unhcr.org/greece.html.

7 IRC, *Refugees in limbo, Greece crisis briefing*, available at: https://www.rescue.org/country/greece.

A 2021 UNHCR report shows the numbers and the direction of mixed migration routes towards the western and central Mediterranean Sea,[8] easily indicating the different profiles and backgrounds of migrants and refugees entering different parts of Europe. The links between the EU and the mixed migration flows have been at the center of UNHCR's 2021 EU recommendations focusing on solidarity and the creation of more resilient societies.[9]

1.2 *The Identity of Religious Majorities and Minorities*

Greece is a relatively homogeneous country regarding religion, as official statistics show that 95% of its population is Orthodox Christian. At the same time, up to 10% of Greeks may have non-Orthodox beliefs.[10] Muslims are estimated from 300.000 to 400.000, with 100.000 of them in Thrace and 200.000–300.000 as migrants in the urban centers. There are 50.000 Catholics, 46.000 Jehovah's Witnesses, 25.000 Protestants, 5.000 Jews and 700.000 to 1 million Old Calendarists.[11] According to a 2021 statement by the Hellenic Ministry of Foreign Affairs the Muslim minority in Thrace numbers approximately 120,000 members.[12] The populations of these religious minorities depict the importance of their presence and identity in the Greek society. There is a need to mention that, especially, the Muslim community in Thrace has been a vital source of diversity, given the facts of the *Molla Sali* case and the historical, legal and social context. The minority protection after the dissolution of the Ottoman Empire, the populations' exchange between Greece and Turkey and its exemption for the Muslim inhabitants of Western Thrace created a special status. The special status of this religious minority, protected by the Treaty of

8 UNHCR, *Routes towards and Western and Central Mediterranean Sea, UNCHR's Updated Risk Mitigation Strategy and Appeal* (January 2021), available at: https://reporting.unhcr.org/sites/default/files/UNHCR%20Western%20and%20Central%20Mediterranean%20Appeal%202021.pdf.

9 UNHCR, *UNHCR calls for EU to ensure a new chapter for refugee protection* (12 January 2021), accessed 11 February 2021, https://www.unhcr.org/news/press/2021/1/5ffc80f74/unhcr-calls-eu-ensure-new-chapter-refugee-protection.html.

10 L. Molokotos, "Greece – Religious belonging and religious demography – Homogeneousness and evolution", (19 September 2012) *EUREL*, available at: https://eurel.info/spip.php?rubrique274.

11 L. Molokotos and S. Akgönül, "Greece – Other religious and non-religious groups – Religious minorities" (19 September 2012) *EUREL*, available at: https://eurel.info/spip.php?rubrique683&lang=en.

12 MFA, "Statement by the Ministry of Foreign Affairs regarding educational issues of the Muslim Minority", (2 August 2021), available at: https://www.mfa.gr/en/current-affairs/statements-speeches/statement-by-the-ministry-of-foreign-affairs-regarding-educational-issues-of-the-muslim-minority-02082021.html.

Lausanne, justifies the regulation by the state, as described below. However, the lack of more specific official data on the populations of refugees of different religions now residing in Greece must be taken into consideration.

The religious identity of refugees and migrants is a fundamental element to be considered in this religious diversity. The way they shape society's identity impacts the role of the State, regardless of whether the State will follow a neutral path or not based on its system of Church-State relations. Suppose we need to respond to the question of how the legal framework on freedom of religion could be transplanted into policies in such a context. In that case, an answer could be addressing freedom of religion through the relevant integration policies, such as inclusive education, training, and employment opportunities valuing the contribution of migrant communities, as these could be a platform and a first step to work on a religious coexistence. This approach also needs modern perspectives to complement the prism of the traditional instruments, such as religious rules or a traditional interpretation of State law. More specifically, it needs a modern look and in the use of traditional instruments. Thus, every step closer to a more open society might be constructive. As Martha Nussbaum has pointed out, the United States is comfortable with heterogeneity to a greater extent than in Europe, but this difference is part of a more profound difference in ideas of national identity.[13] In our view, Greece and Europe are no exception and the modern look to traditional instruments can be part of the dialogue in this context. In order to give an example, if we consider the legislation and administrative practice considering the veil/headscarf issues, it is evident that the solution of non-imposition and no law enforcement could be a positive aspect, as it has worked till now in Greece. Could this be a model to share? Currently, the response is partially negative given the legal responses on religious issues, such as the headscarf question, in different European countries. While facing religious diversity with various State and society answers, all the solutions must be considered towards new challenges. However, traditional instruments' interpretation and use must be formed accordingly by evolving their content and principles. Otherwise, there is an obstructive resistance to new challenges and persistence to traditional instruments.

Could Greece be an example of how not to regulate such issues through integration in refugee law terms, no matter the level that integration has reached?

13 M. Nussbaum, *The New Religious Intolerance – Overcoming the Politics of Fear in an Anxious Age* (Cambridge – London, The Belknap Press of HUP, 2012), at 13.

Could the approach of non-policy be a policy? The dialogue with new communities should be part of this solution.

2 Recent Developments and Challenges of Religious Neutrality

Before focusing on the *Molla Sali* case, its impact, and its connection to the social context described above, it is crucial to mention two relatively recent developments in the Greek legal framework. They are closely related to the case and its background[14] and the discussion of religious diversity in institutional terms. These developments have not been fully applied, but the discussion on them is interesting for the Greek context, while it is helpful to have in mind the subjects derived from such a dialogue and the State response.

2.1 *The Application of Sharia Law and the National Legal Framework*

First, before the deliberation of the judgment of *Molla Sali* by the European Court of Human Rights, Greece issued Law 4511/2018[15] regarding the amendment of Article 5 of Legislative Act of 24 December 1990 "On Muslim Clerics" ratified by the Sole Article of Law 1920/1991. Greece has passed the 2018 Law to limit the competencies of Islamic courts in the northern region of Thrace that is home to about 100,000 Muslims, giving Muslims the option to take civil cases to Greek courts.[16]

14 D. Anagnostou and A. Triandafyllidou, "Regions, minorities and European Integration: A case study on Muslims in Western Thrace, Greece", (2007) *ELIAMEP/Romanian Journal of Political Sciences*, 100–125, accessed 11 February 2021, http://www.eliamep.gr/wp-content/uploads/en/2006/05/Case_study_report_Thrace.pdf. K. Tsitselikis, "The application of the Treaty of Lausanne in Greek Law. The Chapter on minorities" («Η εφαρμογή της Συνθήκης της Λωζάννης στο ελληνικό δίκαιο. Το κεφάλαιο περί των μειονοτήτων») in P. Pazartzis and K. Antonopoulos (ed.) *The 1923 Lausanne Peace Treaty at 90* (Hellenic Branch of the International Law Association, Nomiki Vivliothiki, 2014). Y. Ktistakis, *Charia, tribunaux religieux et droit grec, supra*, at 27–28 regarding the exception of Muslims of Dodecanese or at 71 and at 134–136 on conclusions.

15 Law No 4511/2018, Amendment of Article 5 of Legislative Act of December 24, 1990 "On Muslim Clerics" (A' 182) ratified by the Sole Article of Law 1920/1991 (A'11), Official Gazette of the Hellenic Republic, January 15, 2018 Issue A' (non-official translation) available at: https://www.minedu.gov.gr/publications/docs2018/Law_4511_2018_Reform_on_Mufti_jurisdiction_Sharia_law.pdf.

16 N. Kitsantonis, "Greece Scraps Compulsory Shariah for Muslim Minority", *The New York Times*, January 10, 2018, accessed 11 February 2021, https://www.nytimes.com/2018/01/10/world/europe/greece-shariah-law.html.

Article 1 of the 2018 Law inserted a paragraph as follows:

> 1. The following paragraph shall be inserted at the end of Article 5 of the Legislative Act of 24 December 1990, "On Muslim Clerics" (A' 182) ratified by the Sole Article of Law 1920/1991 (A' 11): "4.a. The cases of paragraph 2 are regulated by ordinary provisions (Civil Code), and only in exceptional cases are they subjected to the jurisdiction of the Mufti, provided that the parties file a request before him applying for their dispute to be resolved under Sharia law. Once the dispute is subject to the jurisdiction of the Mufti, this is irrevocable, and it precludes the jurisdiction of the Court on this particular dispute. If either party does not wish for the case to be subject to the jurisdiction of the Mufti, he or she may apply to the courts of civil law pursuant to ordinary substantive and procedural provisions, which in any case have the presumption of jurisdiction."[17]

All necessary procedural rules on the discussion of the case before the Mufti and on the issuing of his decisions, the procedure of application by the parties, the explicit, irrevocable statement of each party on the choice of this jurisdiction, the representation by authorized lawyers, the procedure of discussion and adoption of the decision, and any matter related to the implementation of this law shall be set out by Presidential Decree. It is worth mentioning that the law provides that succession relations of members of the Muslim minority in Thrace are regulated for under the provisions of the Civil Code, except if the testator draws up before a notary a declaration of property upon death, containing the expressive will of the testator exclusively to subject his succession under Sharia law. Concurrent application of the Civil Code and Sharia law on succession either in a percentage or on specific parts of it is prohibited.

As it has been referred to in the Law's explanatory report and reiterated by the ECtHR (paragraph 58), it seems that case law and the legal theory had dealt with various aspects of Sharia law's application, its provisions' hierarchy in the domestic legal order, and their conformity with the Constitution and

17 In the second subparagraph of Article 5(3), after the phrase "are contrary to the Constitution", the following phrase is added: "in particular to Article 4(2) and the European Convention on Human Rights". See article 4(2) of the Constitution: "Greek men and women have equal rights and equal obligations". See also para 4 of the Law: "Article 5(4)(a) of the Legislative Act of 24 December 1990 "On Muslim Clerics" (A' 182) ratified by the Sole Article of Law 1920/1991 (A' 11) shall enter into force as from the publication of the Presidential Decree referred to in 4(b)". In paragraph 5, an Expert Committee is to be formed to draw up a report on the procedural rules referred to in subparagraph 4b.

European human rights standards.[18] This kind of treatment of Sharia law is an indication of state law integrating Islamic law along with the application of the Greek Constitution and the European Convention on Human Rights. The not-so-similar *Sahyouni* case[19] of the ECJ, regarding divorce, legal separation and the recognition of a divorce decision delivered by a religious court in a third country, could also be recalled here to show the parallel directions that the two European Courts and European societies follow in such issues of integration of the religious law. It is interesting to underline the common dilemmas and legal questions before the two European Courts as the harmonization of judicial answers on religious issues in Europe becomes a challenge.

The presidential decree 52/2019[20] on the procedural rules on cases under the jurisdiction of the Muftis of Thrace and the establishment, organization, and operation of the Directorate for cases under the Mufti's jurisdiction at the Muftiates in Thrace is the next step of the aforementioned legal framework. The details on the local jurisdiction, the applicants and their age, the fundamental principles of the procedures, on the hearings and the decisions, and the *res judicata* and enforceability are to be taken into consideration in the discussion of the practical aspects of the role of Islamic law in the national legal framework. The judgment 1822/2020 of the Greek Supreme Administrative Court (plenary session),[21] referring to the *Molla Sali* case, decided that the provisions of the aforementioned presidential decree are constitutional and not contravening Article 9 in conjunction with Article 11 ECHR and Article 10 of the EU Charter of Fundamental Rights. We need to have in mind these developments for the third part of our contribution.

18 ECtHR, *Molla Sali v. Greece*, Appl. No. 20452/14, judgment (Grand Chamber), 19 December 2018, para 58.

19 ECJ, Case C-372/16, *Soha Sahyouni v. Raja Mamisch*, 20 December 2017. The request for the preliminary ruling concerned the EU Regulation No 1259/2010 on the law applicable to divorce and legal separation and the recognition of a divorce decision delivered by a religious court in a third country. The Court ruled that Article 1 of the Regulation must be interpreted as meaning that a divorce resulting from a unilateral declaration made by one of the spouses before a religious court, such as that at issue in the main proceedings, does not come within the substantive scope of that regulation.

20 Presidential decree 52/2019, Procedural rules on cases under the jurisdiction of the Muftis of Thrace – Establishment, organization and operation of the Directorate for cases under the Mufti's jurisdiction at the Muftiates in Thrace, Official Government Gazette of the Hellenic Republic, A' 90 11 June 2019, available at: https://www.minedu.gov.gr/publications/docs2020/Presidential_Decree_52_2019_Procedural_rules_on_cases_under_the_Muftis_jurisdiction.pdf.

21 Supreme Administrative Court (plenary session), No. 1822/2020 – Procedural rules for Muftis, 6 October 2020.

2.2 *The Revision of the Constitution and Challenges of Religious Neutrality*

During 2019, there was an ongoing procedure of a revision of the Constitution. Even though the respective provisions have not been revised, the legal discussion is not over yet, as it might not be over within the society. State neutrality is one point of this revision, while Greece has been traditionally following the engagement with the Greek Orthodox Church. It goes without doubt that the Greek Orthodox Church is a central aspect of the history of the Greek State, as is the case in other States with the respective Church or religion. We could say that it is part of the constitutional identity of the State given the Constitution's references in the preamble ("*In the name of the Holy and Consubstantial and Indivisible Trinity*") and in Articles 3, 13, and 16 (2).[22] Nevertheless, this does not prevent the legal dialogue and possible future proposals from transforming the constitutional identity. The political party of the Government in 2018, with its proposal of the Constitution's revision, sought to enshrine the religious neutrality of the Greek State in the country's Constitution. According to the relative procedure Article 3 of the Greek Constitution, regarding relations between Church and State, was subject to revision by the next Parliament but has not finally been amended. The initiative proposed to 'modernize' Article 3 and enshrine the State's religious neutrality in law while maintaining "recognition of the Orthodox Church as the dominant religion for historical and practical reasons". The changes might seem progressive, but, of course, they can be the object of criticism.

At the end of 2018, before the deliberation in the *Molla Sali* case, there was a dialogue between the Government and Archbishop Hieronymos II and members of the Holy Synod of the Church of Greece. This discussion included religious neutrality reforms and the payroll of 10.000 Church employees, who would have no longer had the status of civil servants but would have been paid

22 Article 3 reads as follows: "*Relations of Church and State. 1. The prevailing religion in Greece is that of the Eastern Orthodox Church of Christ. The Orthodox Church of Greece, acknowledging our Lord Jesus Christ as its head, is inseparably united in doctrine with the Great Church of Christ in Constantinople and with every other Church of Christ of the same doctrine, observing unwaveringly, as they do, the holy apostolic and synodal canons and sacred traditions* (...)". Article 13 refers to freedom of religious conscience, the freedom of known religions and the State supervision of the ministers of all known religions "*to the same obligations towards it as those of the prevailing religion*". Article 16 (2) reads as follows: "*Education constitutes a basic mission for the State and shall aim at the moral, intellectual, professional and physical training of Greeks, the development of national and religious consciousness and at their formation as free and responsible citizens*".

through an annual subsidy.[23] The meeting of the entire hierarchy of the Church of Greece rejected the agreement, but the Holy Synod decided to continue the State-Church dialogue. In contrast, the final agreement's accomplishment remained an open question[24] until now.

The principle of religious neutrality separates the roles of the State and religion, and it can lead to multifaceted cooperation of public policy such as cooperation in humanitarian action with different faith-based institutions while facing mixed migration. The neutral State does not contradict a State with historical links to a specific religion if it is neutral to all religious communities in its territory. The principles of neutrality, tradition, and, at the same time, society's evolving nature transform the state into a modern one, for it risks otherwise forgetting its past or neglecting its present.

An aspect that we deem equally crucial during such a procedure is whether those changes of the Constitution change the constitutional identity of the State. The theory on constitutional identity is not the subject of this contribution. However, we shall briefly refer to it given the constitutional dialogue raised on the change of this article. In this reference, we should not neglect the *Lautsi* case[25] dilemma between the Grand Chamber judgment of the ECtHR and the Court's Chamber of the Second Section. The respect of national and constitutional traditions and principles has been a point of reference and justification in the judgment, illustrating the constitutional dialogue's relevance and importance. However, we shall adhere to the opinion below:

> "Constitutional identity can be constructed on the basis of sameness or of selfhood, or more precisely, based on dynamic interaction between projections of sameness and images of selfhood" [...] and "plays an important and multifaceted role in constitutional interpretation [...] Viewed systematically and dialectically, constitutional interpretation produces

23 K. Kallergis, "Greece Church agreement to take 10,000 priests off payroll" and "Will anything change in Greece" BBC *News*, 7 November 2018, accessed 11 February 2021, https://www.bbc.com/news/world-europe-46122997.

24 E. Chalkiadakis and K. Papashathis, "February 2019: Tsipras-Hieronymus Agreement on the payroll of the Orthodox priests" (3 June 2019) *EUREL*, accessed 11 February 2021, https://eurel.info/spip.php?article3649&lang=fr.

25 ECtHR, *Lautsi and others v. Italy*, Appl. No. 30814/06, judgment (Grand Chamber), 18 March 2011, paras 3–4. The Grand Chamber held that crucifixes in Italian State schools do not violate article 2 of Protocol No. 1 ECHR, changing the Chamber's decision that has found that the crucifix was incompatible with the principle of secularism.

> constitutional identity and is at the same time shaped, filled, and molded by the latter."[26]

This interpretation in Greece is traced through the Greek Supreme Administrative Court judgments no. 660/2018 concerning the primary and middle school religious education programs and no. 926/2018 concerning the high school religious education program. The dialogue in the Greek legal context contains the different legal viewpoints as to what extent religious education, as structured by the State according to a specific curriculum, follows the Constitution and Article 16 (2) to the aim of the development of national and religious consciousness and is compatible with the international standards if it focuses on the prevailing religion or not. The arguments within the Court are based on Articles 16(2), 13(1) of the Greek Constitution, Article 2 of Protocol No. 1 to the ECHR, Article 4(1) of the Constitution, and Articles 14 and 9 ECHR given the designing of religious education. These two judgments of the Supreme Court annulled the respective religious education programs based on a ministerial decision which, according to the dissenting opinion, was published in light of the offer by the State of a polyphonic and neutral religious education adequately presenting the teaching of Orthodoxy. The dissenting opinion has referred to this pluralistic approach of the act in question and the religious neutrality that needs to be preserved with an extensive argumentation in paragraph 15 of the judgment, referring, among others, to the ECtHR's case law. This balancing of the Greek legal order between the constitutional identity and the European human rights standards has not finished yet.

The ECtHR has also treated the case *Papageorgiou and others v. Greece,*[27] as indicative of the same ongoing dialogue on these matters in the national legal order. The application was related to the participation of students in religious education without a chance of exemption which, according to the applicants, violated Article 2 Protocol 1 to the ECHR regarding their religious and philosophical convictions. It seems that religious education is a rather controversial subject in Greece.

---

26 M. Rosenfeld, "Chapter 35 – Constitutional Identity" in M. Rosenfeld and A. Sajó (ed.), *The Oxford Handbook of Comparative Constitutional Law* (Oxford, OUP, 2012), at 757, 771.

27 ECtHR, *Papageorgiou and others v. Greece*, Appl. Nos. 4762/18 and 6140/18, judgment, 31 October 2019. See also E. Fokas, "Stuck in the middle with Papageorgiou: Missed or new opportunities" (27 November 2019) *StrasbourgObservers*, accessed 11 February 2021, https://strasbourgobservers.com/2019/11/27/stuck-in-the-middle-with-papageorgiou-missed-or-new-opportunities/ and M. Markoviti, "In-between the Constitution and the European Court of Human Rights: Mobilizations Around Religion and Education in Greece" (2019) 12 *Politics and Religion* 31–54.

Given the different constitutional models and the kaleidoscope of constitutional and religious diversity in Europe, we can understand why these issues are under an ongoing dialogue and far from being solved and harmonized in a way that does not violate freedom of religion or State neutrality. A tradition, either a constitutional or a minority, can take multiple forms that may not change its nature and essence. This flexibility is a modern look at traditional instruments and does not prevent the State from following the principle of neutrality in a more effective and declaratory manner, also based on the ECtHR's approach. The answers are to be searched and found within the parallel need of the State for neutrality and religious pluralism.[28]

The Law 4301/2014 on the Organization of the Legal Form of Religious Communities and their organizations in Greece[29] can be considered a further development of the last decade in Greece, which might affect the future legal arguments given the challenges mentioned in parts II and III. The law contains, among other provisions, the concept of the religious community, the religious legal person, the registration for acquiring a legal personality, the establishment of worship places and monastic institutions, the "ecclesiastical" legal person, and the recognition of legal personality of the Catholic Church in Greece, the Anglican church, the Ethiopian Orthodox Church, the Coptic Orthodox Church, the Church of Orthodox Armenians, the German-speaking Evangelical Church, the Greek Evangelical Church, and the Assyrian Orthodox Church. All the provisions above could be considered the first step to create a platform of interreligious dialogue and interaction among the religious communities and the Greek State in order to face modern challenges of religious diversity by taking into account the actual identity of the society.

3 Legal Pluralism and the *Molla Sali* Effect

3.1 *The Minority within the Minority*

Coming to the content of the *Molla Sali* case, we need to briefly refer to the principal facts and complaints based on the judgment of the Grand Chamber.

28 P. Cumper and T. Lewis, "Introduction: freedom of religion and belief – the contemporary context" in P. Cumper and T. Lewis (eds.), *Religion, Rights and Secular Society – European Perspectives* (Cheltenham, Edward Elgar, 2012).

29 Law 4301/2014, Organization of the Legal Form of Religious Communities and their organizations in Greece (non-official translation), available at: https://www.minedu.gov.gr/publications/docs2014/publications/Law_4301_-2014_Organization_of_the_legal_form_of_religious_communities_and_their_organizations_in_Greece.pdf.

Upon the death of her husband, the applicant, Chatitze Molla Sali, a Greek national born in 1950 and resident in Komotini, inherited her husband's whole estate under a will drawn up by her husband before a notary. Subsequently, the deceased's two sisters challenged the will's validity, arguing that their brother had belonged to the Thrace Muslim community, that any question relating to inheritance in that community was subject to Islamic law, the jurisdiction of the "mufti", and not to the Greek Civil Code.[30] The two sisters' claims were dismissed by the Court of first instance and the Appellate Courts: in September 2011, the Thrace Court of Appeal ruled that the decision of the deceased person, a Greek citizen of Muslim faith and a member of the Thrace religious minority, to call on the services of a notary to draw up an official will, was in line with his legal right to dispose of his property after his death under the same conditions as all other Greek citizens. The Court of Cassation set that judgment aside, stating that matters of inheritance within the Muslim minority had to be dealt with by the mufti in accordance with the rules of Sharia law. The case was then referred to the Court of appeal, which on 15 December 2015 ruled that the law applicable to the deceased's estate was Muslim religious law and that the impugned will was devoid of legal effect. Ms. Molla Sali's appeal on points of law was dismissed on 6 April 2017.

Before the ECtHR, relying on Article 6 (1) read separately and in conjunction with Article 14, Ms. Molla Sali complained about the application of Sharia law to her inheritance dispute rather than the ordinary law applicable to all Greek citizens. She also submitted that she suffered discriminatory treatment on the grounds of religion. Relying on Article 1 of Protocol No. 1, Ms. Molla Sali complained that the Court of Cassation deprived her of three-quarters of her inheritance by applying Muslim religious law instead of Greek civil law. The Grand Chamber of the Court held unanimously that there had been a violation of Article 14 of the ECHR, read in conjunction with Article 1 of Protocol No. 1 to the Convention.

There is no need to focus on the legislative instruments, case law, and the applicable law in the national legal order as they are included in the judgment. In the latter, there is a section on "Provisions governing the application of Sharia law in Greek law and domestic practice", which describes the state of interaction between Islamic law and the national legal framework. However, we would like to point out the disagreement of the highest Greek Courts on whether the Treaty of Athens concerning the protection of the rights of minorities is still in

30 The sisters relied, in particular, on the 1920 Treaty of Sèvres and the 1923 Treaty of Lausanne, which provided for the application of Muslim customs and Islamic religious law to Greek nationals of Muslim faith.

force. At the same time, its scope is based on a dispute on the principle of equal treatment of members of minorities and other citizens in exercising their civil and political rights (para. 44). References are made in the National Commission for Human Rights on the application of Sharia law, in the explanatory report of the Law No. 4511/2018 and in the interaction between the case law of the Greek courts and that of the international courts (para. 58). The report acknowledged that the State had not acted on this matter for ninety-seven years, during which time conceptions, practices, and traditions had evolved at both international and national levels. Further, it noted that the State should not be a mere onlooker during a legal debate and should no longer leave it to the judiciary to resolve critical issues that affected Greek citizens.

The international law and practice part of the judgment is significant. There are references to the international treaties regulating the protection of the religious distinctiveness of Greek Muslims, the Vienna Convention on the Law of Treaties, and the Council of Europe Framework Convention for the Protection of National Minorities (hereinafter "Framework Convention" or FCNM). The Convention was adopted in 1995, came into force on 1 February 1998, and it has been signed but not ratified by Greece. Article 3(1) of this Convention provides:

> Every person belonging to a national minority shall have the right freely to choose to be treated or not to be treated as such and no disadvantage shall result from this choice or from the exercise of the rights which are connected to that choice.

The explanatory report on the Framework Convention constitutes a guide to the guarantees of the right and the criterion of free choice.

The findings of international bodies (e.g., the UN Committee on the Elimination of Discrimination against Women, the UN Human Rights Committee, the Commissioner for Human Rights of the Council of Europe, the Committee on Legal Affairs and Human Rights of the Parliamentary Assembly) and instruments of EU law (e.g., the Charter of Fundamental Rights of the European Union and Article 21 on non-discrimination, along with the Directive 2000/78/EC of 27 November 2000 establishing a general framework for equal treatment in employment and occupation) are some of the criteria set by the international legal framework.

Based on a comparative law perspective (para. 82),[31] the Court underlines that the documents available concerning the legislation of Council of Europe

31 For example, in the United Kingdom, in May 2016, the government commissioned an independent review into the application of Sharia law (in England and Wales) in order to

member states indicate that Sharia law may apply to them as a source of foreign law in the event of a conflict of laws in the framework of private international law. The third parties' interventions by Christian Concern, Hellenic League for Human Rights, and Greek Helsinki Monitor are helpful as they make an overview of different perspectives. We shall also focus on the applicant's statement that if Sharia law was to retain its place within the Greek legal order as a body of law protecting the Muslim minority, it should not be imposed against the person's wishes (para. 105).

3.2 *The "Modern Identity" of the Inhabitants of Europe*

The Government proposed an interesting approach (para. 111), inviting the Court to distinguish between the present case from *Refah Partisi (the Welfare Party) and Others v. Turkey*,[32] in its attempt to convince the ECtHR not to follow the same principles. They submitted that in the *Molla Sali* case, the Court was not called upon to consider *in abstracto* the application of a plurality of legal systems based on Sharia law or its compatibility with fundamental rights. The Government underlines very distinctively that

> "The present case had to be examined in concreto, having regard to such criteria as respect for multiculturalism in today's Europe and the difficulty of formulating policies applicable to religious communities. In view of the complexity of the "modern identity" of the inhabitants of Europe, the Court should conduct a case-by-case examination of each rule of Sharia law applying to actual cases concerning Muslims residing in non-Muslim

---

consider "whether Sharia law is being misused or applied in a way that is incompatible with the domestic law in England and Wales, and in particular whether there were discriminatory practices against women who use sharia councils". In its report of February 2018, that independent review explained that "Sharia councils have no legal status and no legal binding authority under civil law. Whilst sharia is a source of guidance for many Muslims, sharia councils have no legal jurisdiction in England and Wales. Thus, if any decisions or recommendations are made by a sharia council that are inconsistent with domestic law (including equality policies such as the Equality Act 2010) domestic law will prevail. Sharia councils will be acting illegally should they seek to exclude domestic law. Although they claim no binding legal authority, they do in fact act in a decision-making capacity when dealing with Islamic divorce". See Secretary of State for the Home Department, *The independent review into the application of sharia law in England and Wales,* February 2018, available at: https://assets.publishing.service.gov.uk/government/uploads/system/uploads/attachment_data/file/678478/6.4152_HO_CPFG_Report_into_Sharia_Law_in_the_UK_WEB.pdf.

32 ECtHR, *Refah Partisi (the Welfare Party) and Others v. Turkey*, Appl. Nos. 41340/98, 41342/98, 41343/98 *et al.*, judgment (Grand Chamber), 13 February 2003.

> States. The complexity criterion should be especially decisive in a case such as the present one, since the domestic courts had referred to international treaties as being the basis of Sharia law."[33]

The terms of "the modern identity" of the inhabitants of Europe, the proposal for a "case-by-case examination of each rule of Sharia law" and the "complexity criterion" are, to our viewpoint, central aspects of this case and an explicit statement of a State party to the Convention before the ECtHR. It is the acknowledgment of the factual religious pluralism of European states like Greece. This statement is considered necessary, given the distinction of Sharia law rules based on the criterion of their compatibility with national law and ECHR. This examination *in concreto* is very firmly proposed by the Government considering also the complexity of the present conditions of the mixed migration and the current state of the Greek and European society. This seems to be a great moment of the State's acknowledgment of the religious kaleidoscope in Greece and Europe and, at the same time, of Islamic law's role in respective societies along with the proposal for the *in concreto* examination, either the latter is considered a solution or not.

3.3 *The Nexus of Difference of Treatment and Sharia Law*

It is essential to underline the fundamental conclusion of the Court for the outcome of the case. Firstly, it considers that the main focus of the present case is the Court of Cassation's refusal to apply the Greek Civil law of inheritance. Secondly and most importantly, the primary issue arising is whether there was a difference in treatment potentially amounting to discrimination as compared with the application of the law of succession, as laid down in the Civil Code, to those seeking to benefit from a will as drawn up by a testator who was not of Muslim faith. Therefore, the case will be considered solely under Article 14 of the Convention read in conjunction with Article 1 of Protocol No. 1.

The Court's assessment focused its reasoning on the fact that the applicant's right to inherit can raise a claim based on the concept of 'possession' and the denial of all or part of a particular asset as a complaint under Article 14 in conjunction with Article 1 of Protocol No. 1. Thus, the ECtHR concluded that the applicant would have inherited her husband's whole estate had the testator not been of the Muslim faith and that the difference of treatment for a beneficiary of a will drawn up in accordance with the Civil Code by a testator of Muslim faith as compared to a non-Muslim testator had no objective and reasonable

33 ECtHR, *Molla Sali v. Greece*, *supra*, para. 111.

justification.[34] As a result, the application of Sharia law to the estate in issue had severe consequences for the applicant, depriving her of three-quarters of the inheritance.[35]

The Court noted that, while in signing and ratifying the Treaties of Sèvres and Lausanne, Greece undertook to respect the customs of the Muslim minority, those treaties do not require Greece to apply Sharia law.[36] At this point, we need to consider the references of Dominic McGoldrick regarding the historical, legal, and social contexts of Muslims in Greece and the interpretation of treaty obligations.[37] In this context, the reference of the Court in the divergences of the Greek courts' case law is particularly illustrative.[38] It mainly raises the question of whether the application of Sharia law is compatible with the principle of equal treatment and with international human rights standards. Such divergences exist among courts of the same judicial branch, between the Court of Cassation and the civil courts, between the Court of Cassation and the Supreme Administrative Court, and within the Court of Cassation itself. Such divergences create legal uncertainty, which is incompatible with the requirements of the rule of law.

By referring to the significant case *İzzettin Doğan and Others v. Turkey,*[39] the ruling stated

> The Court reiterates that according to its case law, freedom of religion does not require the Contracting States to create a particular legal framework in order to grant religious communities a special status entailing specific privileges. Nevertheless, a State which has created such a status must ensure that the criteria established for a group's entitlement to it are applied in a non-discriminatory manner.[40]

---

34 ECtHR, *Molla Sali v. Greece, supra*, paras 130 and 162.

35 We should take into account the reference of para 148: "*The main consequence of the approach adopted by the Court of Cassation in inheritance cases since 1960 and followed by certain lower courts, to the effect that inheritance matters involving members of the Muslim minority should be governed by Sharia law, is that notarised wills drawn up by Greek nationals of Muslim faith are devoid of legal effect because Sharia law only recognises intestate succession, except in the case of Islamic wills*".

36 ECtHR, *Molla Sali v. Greece, supra*, para 151.

37 D. Mc Goldrick, "Sharia Law in Europe? Legacies of the Ottoman Empire and the European Convention on Human Rights" (2019) 8 *Oxford Journal of Law and Religion* 517–566, at 524, 547.

38 ECtHR, *Molla Sali v. Greece, supra*, para 153.

39 ECtHR, *İzzettin Doğan and Others v. Turkey,* Appl. No. 62649/10, judgment (Grand Chamber), 26 April 2016, para 164.

40 ECtHR, *Molla Sali v. Greece, supra*, para 155.

The Court also stated that "Nor can the State take on the role of guarantor of the minority identity of a specific population group to the detriment of the right of that group's members to choose not to belong to it or not to follow its practices and rules".[41]

Further, the Court noted that Greece was the only country in Europe that had applied Sharia law to a section of its citizens against their wishes until the material time. That was particularly problematic in the present case because the application of Sharia law had led to a situation that was detrimental to the individual rights of a widow who had inherited her husband's estate in accordance with the rules of civil law but who had then found herself in a legal situation which neither she nor her husband had intended.[42]

Regarding the new law mentioned above and the relevant changes brought before the Parliament following the applicant's complaint, while the Court "noted with satisfaction" the change in legislation, the new law "had no impact on the situation of the applicant" as the final rulings in her case had been made under the old system.

4 Lessons Learned for Islamic Law in Greece and Europe

4.1 *Mixed Migration Presenting New Challenges of Religious Diversity*

Considering the surrounding debate, it is clear that the *Molla Sali* case impacts not only the Greek judicial system but the overall role of Islam and Sharia law in Europe. This shall allow us to understand which lessons we can learn from the debate on the *Molla Sali* case that can be relevant for the many new Muslim communities of migrant origin spread out in Europe. This European perspective vis-à-vis new communities of migrant origin is a necessary aspect of the new context being created. However, unlike the historical Muslim minority of Thrace these communities do not have the special collective right to derogate from the Civil Code in favor of Islamic law.[43]

Given the different religious communities of refugees, we shall consider the intersection among different fields of law such as private or public international law, Islamic law, and national law based on religious marriage, inheritance, or

41 ECtHR, *Molla Sali v. Greece, supra*, para 156.

42 Molla Sali's husband had drawn up his will according to Greek law, and both a first instance and an appeals court initially ruled in her favor in the dispute with her sisters-in-law. However, other court decisions ruled that inheritance issues within the Muslim minority had to be dealt with under Islamic religious law, and the will was deemed invalid.

43 Y. Ktistakis, *Charia, tribunaux religieux et droit grec* (Istanbul, istos, 2013), at 139.

other issues that may arise in such contexts. This aspect is essential considering the needs to manage and regulate any family or other relations between refugees in the destination countries. Thus, this legal side of refugees' relations is included in integration or inclusion contexts and is necessary to fulfil their rights, such as family unity, the right to respect for family life, and the right to marriage.

The mixed migration context indicates the considerable change in the religious landscape of Greece and Europe during the last decades. Despite the reasons for forced migration which seem to be the same over the years, the phenomenon in Greece and part of Europe was unprecedented and relatively new given the increased numbers and humanitarian situation formed in 2015. This humanitarian crisis and the emergency can also be proved by the responses of the respective EU institutions, such as EASO. This can show that this religious diversity resulting from the mixed migration is one of the main forces that explain the context under construction in Greece and Europe, including the EU Member States and institutions.

The commonalities of an abundance of judgments from the two European courts, dealing with significant asylum cases,[44] can prove that European law on asylum and migration, European human rights law, and international refugee law can be interconnected more closely than ever before in the judicial reasoning. The latter can be explained if we consider that freedom of religion, religious grounds of persecution, and refugee law are closely related to the reasoning of asylum judgments and treatment on asylum grounds. The cases *Y (C-71/11) and Z* (*C-99/11*) before the Grand Chamber of European Court of Justice (hereinafter ECJ)[45] show exactly this interconnection, especially as far as it concerns freedom of religion and membership to the religious community of Ahmadiyya. These cases demonstrate that the refugees and migrants' rights

44 ECJ, Case C-411/10 *NS c/ SSHD*, 21 December 2011. ECtHR, *M.S.S. v Belgium and Greece*, Appl. No. 30696/09, judgment (Grand Chamber), 21 January 2011.

45 ECJ, Case *Y (C-71/11) and Z (C-99/11)*, 5 September 2012. For the Muslim Ahmadiyya community, which the applicants claimed to be an Islamic reformist movement in Pakistan, see paragraphs 30, 31, 39 etc. With this judgment the ECJ interprets articles 9 (1)(a) and 2(c) of Directive 2004/83 on minimum standards for the qualification and status of third country nationals or Stateless persons as refugees or as persons who otherwise need international protection. The articles focus on the interpretation of the act of persecution as a result of the interference with the external manifestation of the freedom of religion and the well-founded fear of engaging in religious practices upon return to the applicant's country of origin, which will expose him to a real risk of persecution. In assessing an application for refugee status on an individual bases, the national authorities cannot reasonably expect the applicant to abstain from those religious practices.

have come to the forefront of the dialogue in Greece and Europe. This must persist to preserve those refugee and religious communities and ensure the protection of their rights.

Further, the legal framework of such judgments or mechanisms such as relocating eligible applicants for international protection from Greece to another European country and the EU-Turkey agreement[46] finally impacts religious diversity and integration measures in terms of policies, given the secondary movements inside the EU and to a third country such as Turkey. Besides, there is proof of religious diversity through the dynamic presence of faith-based humanitarian agencies/organizations, such as the International Catholic Migration Commission, Islamic Relief Worldwide, HIAS (Hebrew Immigrant Aid Society), Jesuit Refugee Service. These humanitarian agencies and even their cooperation can play a great role in promoting religious coexistence. This presence can indicate that religious diversity derives from different sources and not only from refugees and migrants but also through a humanitarian agency or institution, Churches, or various religious communities.

In general, refugee and migrant communities reveal the religious diversity of Greece and Europe, which need to be addressed through constitutional, legislative and state practice's protection. For this reason, *Molla Sali* is incredibly significant for understanding how European states can approach legal pluralism and the potential presence of Islamic law to accommodate their rising diversity.

4.2 *The Interrelation between the Constitution and Minority Protection*

The first conclusion that we can draw from the elements mentioned above for Greece and Europe is related to the constitutional identity's focus and content. According to Michel Rosenfeld:

> The place and function of constitutional identity is determined by the need for dialectical mediation of existing, evolving, and projected conflicts and tensions between identity and difference [...] [and]constitutional identity should be channeled into a cogent narrative that will guide the determination under a particular set of circumstances of whether a multi-ethnic or mono-ethnic or a national or multinational constitution would best bind together the diverse groups and/or ideologies or

46 The EU-Turkey statement, which was agreed on 18 March 2016, determines that all migrants and asylum seekers arriving from Turkey to Greek islands and whose applications have been declared inadmissible will be returned to Turkey.

> interests within a polity into a sufficiently unified and cohesive constitutional shelf.[47]

Combining such an approach with the current issues deriving from the *Molla Sali* case, we shall highlight the interaction between Islamic law and State law and the evolving role of Islamic law in the respective societies for members of minorities. This role may change through interaction with the State law, the ECHR, and other human rights instruments. Its application may change in favor of the minorities inside the broader minorities, as was the case for Molla Sali. This interaction and evolution need to be observed and relevant conclusions for Greece and other European legal contexts need to be drawn.

A second conclusion comes from a more practical aspect of the case. In the case of *Molla Sali,* the deficiencies in legislative and administrative regulation and judicial response were apparent. This needs to be identified in other European countries as well. A comparative law approach to such cases and a legal framework of the existence and use of Islamic law could be of particular importance for the regulation to be achieved in a European context given the needs, challenges and opportunities mentioned above for an equivalent regulation for all refugee and migrant communities. This kind of harmonization appears as a need from taken cases before the CJEU as well.

Further, Stephanos Stavros noted a significant impact of the Molla Sali case and the public dialogue on the protection of minority rights:

> Greece's efforts to modernize its minority-protection legislation (which include reconciling the preservation of distinct religious identities with non-discrimination) deserve attention. However, Greece has always approached national-minority issues as aspects of its relations with neighbouring countries. Matters have to be placed in a multilateral context, that of the Council of Europe and its specialized conventions. In *Molla Sali,* the Court reminded Greece that lots have been changed since the pre-WWII treaties; standards had evolved, for example, on minority members' right to free self-identification.[48]

47 M. Rosenfeld, "Chapter 35 – Constitutional Identity" in M. Rosenfeld and A. Sajó (eds.), *The Oxford Handbook of Comparative Constitutional Law* (Oxford, OUP, 2012), at 761.

48 S. Stavros, "The European Court of Human Rights' judgment in Molla Sali: A call for Greece to modernize its system for national-minority protection?" (17 January 2019) *Oxford Human Rights Hub*, available at: https://ohrh.law.ox.ac.uk/the-european-court-of-human-rights-judgment-in-molla-sali-a-call-for-greece-to-modernise-its-system-for-national-minority-protection/.

This approach needs to consider that Greece is one of the member states of the Council of Europe that still have not ratified the Framework Convention. The Court included in its reasoning this approach by referring to the right of members of religious minority to voluntarily opt for and benefit from ordinary law and the right to free self-identification.[49] This part of the Court's analysis is one of the most interesting aspects of the case and a promise for the future regarding the use of the FCNM. The right to free self-identification is not a right specific to the FCNM. As referred by the Court, it is the "cornerstone" of international law on the protection of minorities in general and this applies especially to the negative aspect of the right: no bilateral or multilateral treaty or other instrument requires anyone to submit against his or her wishes to a special regime in terms of protection of minorities.

Thus, considering the interplay between religious rules and State law from the angle of legal pluralism, we need to identify existing instruments that could enhance the pluralism of norms in the society.[50] To evaluate this suggestion, we need to dive deeper into the meaning and practice of State neutrality. The European Courts of Strasbourg and Luxembourg and their case law are crucial actors for exploring the variables of State neutrality, legal pluralism, and religious diversity. The trend in the Courts' jurisprudence for example on freedom of religion is significant. As changes happen within societies, it is interesting to wonder whether this trend will change and develop to a new understanding of relevant issues which might be more effective, inclusive, and holistic. The content of this contribution supports the idea that issues of religion, issues that derive from the very essence of freedom of religion or belief, could be considered without focusing on the system of the relation between States and Churches but by taking into account local sensibilities. Neutrality is an instrument that can lead to such results.

In a more theoretical approach, the overlapping consensus of John Rawls[51] that could be implemented in such cases should be considered, given the consensus between religions and human rights and among different legal orders. Additionally, concepts of national or constitutional identity, religion,

---

49 ECtHR, *Molla Sali v. Greece, supra*, Para 157: "*The negative aspect of this right, namely the right to choose not to be treated as a member of a minority, is not limited in the same way as the positive aspect of that right. The choice in question is completely free, provided it is informed. It must be respected both by the other members of the minority and by the State itself*".

50 S. Ferrari, "Religious Rules and Legal Pluralism: An Introduction" in B. Rossella *et al.* (eds.), *Religious Rules, State Law, and Normative Pluralism – A Comparative Overview* (Switzerland, Ius Comparatum – Global Studies in Comparative Law, Springer, 2016).

51 V. Nurock, *Rawls : Pour une démocratie juste* (Paris, Ed. Michalon, 2008), at 85, 112.

and citizenship overlap and will continue to overlap more and more in the future. On the other hand, we shall reflect on how Dworkin's approach on interpretation of constitutional concepts can positively impact such cases.[52] Thus, religion and freedom of religion or belief, defined according to various approaches, can include claims related to specific rights. This matter, irrespective of definitions, is crucial in the interaction of Islamic law and human rights in the legal framework of a European State.

Neutrality seems to be the solution to many of our questions in Europe. As the notion of secularism may be stricter in practice, modern times need modern solutions. The term "modern" is used as a living instrument, of an evolving procedure, provided that traditional instruments need to be living instruments. The new challenges are already present in modern societies. Traditional instruments, as defined before, can positively impact new challenges when societies and States use them with a different and more holistic perspective. Thus, there is an urgent need to rethink the foundations of freedom of religion and the protection of religious minorities, taking into consideration the changing role of religion, human rights, and human dignity in the legal discourse.

4.3 *Judicial Answers between Traditional and Modern Instruments*

The pluralism that this contribution supports is a type of pluralism that does not only contain tolerance but respect as well. It is pluralism that includes an aspect of evolution while protecting human rights and not one that simply accommodates them. This could be characterized as a reasonable accommodation. The European debate on religious legal pluralism has mainly revolved around possible formulas for soft accommodation of religious norms such as "interactive pluralism," an accommodation not *per se* inconsistent with the ECHR.[53] Besides, according to J. Martínez-Torrón:

> the examination of the "Islamic cases" decided by the ECtHR leads to the conclusion that, in some areas, the Court has applied to Islam the same

52 R. Dworkin, *Religion without God* (London, HUP, 2013), at 108–109: "[…] the interpretation of basic constitutional concepts does not depend on common understanding or dictionary definitions. They are interpretative concepts whose use demands a very different kind of test. Such interpretative concepts – liberty, equality, dignity, religion, and the rest – form the nerve of political ideals. We use them to decide what to protect as human and constitutional rights, and we must define them so as to make sense of that crucial role […]".

53 A. Cebada-Romero, "Religion-Based Legal Pluralism and Human Rights in Europe" in L. J. Cohen and C. Laborde (eds.), *Religion, Secularism & Constitutional Democracy* (New York, Columbia University Press, 2016), at 402, 406, 409 and footnote 63, 412.

> principles that it has applied to other religions which does not mean that those principles are not objectionable or are expressed with sufficient precision.[54]

Conversely, Muslim communities (in common with other societies) must ensure consistent alignment of constitutional norms with evolving norms on human rights and minority rights.[55]

National, European, and international courts certainly have a role to play in that direction. The role of the European Court of Human Rights and the Greek Council of State have been important for cases of freedom of religion or belief. The latter can play a more inclusive and evolving role in the future, as the dissenting opinion has done in the cases referred above. The cases before them have a direct impact on Greek national society and on the European public sphere, which strives to confront new challenges. The religious diversity, which sometimes includes the aspect of discrimination, as cases before the courts show, needs to slowly turn to pluralism in order for the religious difference, the religious minority, the religious "other" to become a vital part of the society and the State. The fact of a religious "other" does not neglect the fact of citizenship. An individual or a group can have different roles and shall coordinate these roles according to the law. This assumes that constitutional or human rights law can interact or coordinate with Islamic law and the opposite. This can be done as it seems from the Greek experience or the examples of other European countries.

Although European judges have missed the unique chance to set concrete standards for the exercise to choose a religious legal order in civil law matters, the aspect of the right to a voice[56] needs to be further elaborated. The basis of the *Molla Sali* case is the first step for this development.

---

54 J. Martínez-Torrón, "Islam in Strasbourg: Can Politics Substitute for Law?" in C. W. Jr Durham *et al.* (eds.), *Islam, Europe and Emerging Legal Issues* (Famham/Burlington, Ashgate, 2012), at 21, 59.

55 J. Rehman, "Islam vs the Shari'a: Minority Protection within Islamic and International Legal Traditions" in A. Emon *et al.* (eds.) *Islamic Law and International Human Rights Law, Searching for Common Ground?* (Oxford, OUP, 2012), at 378.

56 E. Kalampakou, "Is There a Right to Choose a Religious Jurisdiction over the Civil Courts? The Application of Sharia Law in the Minority in Western Thrace, Greece", (2019) 10 (4), 260 *Religions* (*Special Issue: Religions, Religious Freedom, and Human Rights: A Social Scientific Approach*). See also M. Berger, "The Last Shari 'a Court in Europe. On Molla Sali v. Greece (ECHR 2018)", (2020) 1 (1) *Harvard Law School Journal of Islamic Law* 115–134.

5 Conclusion

As a final remark, even if there is no common approach or practice for Islamic law, religion is a factor of integration of refugees who were subject to forced displacement and thus it must be promoted in such policies or soft law instruments. Its identification as an important dimension in Greece and Europe, in general, could support religious intolerance and persecution towards survivors harming their ability to live as a group or individually together with the rest of the society. Faith-based and other organizations and institutions need to support such efforts given the general approach of the Council of Europe on the intercultural cities programme and the linkage with refugee communities.[57] Faith communities and faith leaders are part of this dialogue. Such approaches are necessary in order to engage different actors towards issues of religious diversity. Different beliefs are welcomed and have a role to play in the public sphere. This process will benefit all the actors, such as the refugees, the host communities, and their common community.

Questions raised, such as those coming from the *Molla Sali* case, will be arising in the future. It is of utmost importance to prepare or correct the legal framework and practice to avoid future rights violations, different legal responses in national and European legal orders, and an unbearable workload for the national and European courts. This can be done with case studies and issues arising from different religious backgrounds. Interdisciplinary research and comparative law approaches in issues of Islamic law or other religious rules and traditions need to be the focus during the next years in order to explore unconsidered dimensions of such fields and their interaction with the State law. Academic discussions and policies need to promote this concept in order for the notions of religion and culture to be preserved in the context they flourish, either in a minority that is part of a broader community or an individual within a minority.

The paradigm needs to change to a more interactive approach of different normative systems in specific platforms of national, European, or international human rights law. This will help to observe the convergences and divergences and reach conclusions regarding human rights protection given their universality; even this might be considered practically relative.[58] The same interaction somehow exists with indigenous rights and other religious rules or other

57 CoE, Intercultural cities programme – Intercultural Cities and Refugees, available at: https://www.coe.int/en/web/interculturalcities/intercultural-cities-and-refugees.

58 J. Donnelly, "The Relative Universality of Human Rights", (2007) 29 (2) *Human Rights Quarterly* 281–306.

religious communities' rules aside from the Muslim communities in Europe. The "translation" of religious rules to rights of a Constitution, the ECHR, or the EU Charter of Fundamental Rights may be part of this process. The ongoing academic or judicial dialogue on legal pluralism can only bring positive impact to present challenges. This is the feedback that could be drawn from or further discussed based on the *Molla Sali* judgment in terms of refugee context and religious communities in Greece and Europe but also given developments towards neutrality. Both traditional and modern instruments can be part of this procedure and be directed to an effort not to square the circle but to interconnect them with an intention to reach a positive normative consensus.

Bibliography

Anagnostou, D. and Triandafyllidou, A., "Regions, Minorities and European integration: a Case Study on Muslims in Western Thrace, Greece", (2007) *ELIAMEP/ Romanian Journal of Political Sciences* 100–125, accessed 11 February 2021, available at: http://www.eliamep.gr/wp-content/uploads/en/2006/05/Case_study_report _Thrace.pdf.

Berger, M., "The Last Shari 'a Court in Europe. On Molla Sali v. Greece (ECHR 2018)", (2020) 1 (1) *Harvard Law School Journal of Islamic Law* 115–134.

Cebada-Romero, A., "Religion-Based Legal Pluralism and Human Rights in Europe" in L.J. Cohen and C. Laborde (eds.), *Religion, Secularism and Constitutional Democracy* (New York, Columbia University Press, 2016).

Chalkiadakis, E. and Papashathis, K., "February 2019: Tsipras-Hieronymus Agreement on the payroll of the Orthodox priests" (3 June 2019) *EUREL*, accessed 11 February 2021, available at: https://eurel.info/spip.php?article3649&lang=fr.

Council of Europe/ECtHR/Research Division, Article 9 – Application of Islamic law in the domestic legal order, (2017), available at: https://www.echr.coe.int/Docume nts/Research_report_application_islamic_law_ENG.PDF.

Council of Europe, Intercultural Cities Programme – Intercultural Cities and Refugees, available at: https://www.coe.int/en/web/interculturalcities/intercultural-cit ies-and-refugees.

Cumper, P. and Lewis, T., "Introduction: Freedom of Religion and Belief – the Contemporary Context" in Cumper, P. and Lewis, T. (eds.), *Religion, Rights and Secular Society – European Perspectives* (Cheltenham, Edward Elgar, 2012).

Donnelly, J., "The Relative Universality of Human Rights", (2007) 29 (2) *Human Rights Quarterly* 281–306.

Dworkin, R., *Religion without God* (London, HUP, 2013).

European Court of Human Rights, *Molla Sali v. Greece*, Appl. No. 20452/14, judgment (Grand Chamber), 19 December 2018.

European Court of Human Rights, *M.S.S. v Belgium and Greece,* Appl. No. 30696/09, judgment (Grand Chamber), 21 January 2011.

European Court of Human Rights, *Papageorgiou and others v. Greece*, Appl. Nos. 4762/18 and 6140/18, judgment, 31 October 2019.

European Court of Human Rights, *Lautsi and others v. Italy*, Appl. No. 30814/06, judgment (Grand Chamber), 18 March 2011.

European Court of Human Rights, *İzzettin Doğan and Others v. Turkey,* Appl. No. 62649/10, judgment (Grand Chamber), 26 April 2016.

European Court of Human Rights, *Refah Partisi (the Welfare Party) and Others v. Turkey*, Appl. Nos. 41340/98, 41342/98, 41343/98 et al., judgment (Grand Chamber), 13 February 2003.

European Court of Justice, Case C-411/10 *NS c/ SSHD*, 21 December 2011.

European Court of Justice, Case *Y (C-71/11) and Z (C-99/11)*, 5 September 2012.

European Court of Justice, Case C-372/16, *Soha Sahyouni v. Raja Mamisch*, 20 December 2017.

Ferrari, S., "Religious Rules and Legal Pluralism: an Introduction" in B. Rossella *et al.* (eds.) *Religious Rules, State Law, and Normative Pluralism – a Comparative Overview*, (Switzerland, Ius Comparatum – Global Studies in Comparative Law, Springer, 2016).

Fokas, E., "Stuck in the Middle with Papageorgiou: Missed or New Opportunities", (27 November 2019) *StrasbourgObservers*, accessed 11 February 2021, available at: https://strasbourgobservers.com/2019/11/27/stuck-in-the-middle-with-papageorgiou-missed-or-new-opportunities/

IRC, *Refugees in limbo, Greece crisis briefing*, available at: https://www.rescue.org/country/greece.

Kalampakou, E., "Is There a Right to Choose a Religious Jurisdiction over the Civil Courts? the Application of Sharia Law in the Minority in Western Thrace, Greece", (2019) 10 (4), 260 *Religions* (*Special Issue: Religions, Religious Freedom, and Human Rights: a Social Scientific Approach*).

Kallergis, K., "Greece Church Agreement to Take 10,000 Priests Off Payroll" and "Will anything Change in Greece" *BBC News*, November 7, 2018, accessed 11 February 2021, https://www.bbc.com/news/world-europe-46122997

Kitsantonis, N., "Greece Scraps Compulsory Shariah for Muslim Minority", *The New York Times*, January 10, 2018, accessed 11 February 2021, https://www.nytimes.com/2018/01/10/world/europe/greece-shariah-law.html.

Ktistakis, Y., *Charia, tribunaux religieux et droit grec* (Istanbul, istos, 2013).

Markoviti, M., "In-between the Constitution and the European Court of Human Rights: Mobilizations Around Religion and Education in Greece", (2019) 12 *Politics and Religion* 31–54.

Martínez-Torrón, J., "Islam in Strasbourg: Can Politics Substitute for Law?" in Durham, C. W. Jr et al. (eds.), *Islam, Europe and Emerging Legal Issues* (Famham/Burlington, Ashgate, 2012).

McGoldrick, D., "Sharia Law in Europe? Legacies of the Ottoman Empire and the European Convention on Human Rights", (2019) 8 *Oxford Journal of Law and Religion* 517–566.

Molokotos, L., "Greece – Religious belonging and Religious Demography – Homogeneousness and Evolution", (19 September 2012) *EUREL*, available at: https://eurel.info/spip.php?rubrique274.

Molokotos, L. and Akgönül, S., "Greece – Other Religious and Non-religious Groups – Religious Minorities" (19 September 2012) *EUREL*, available at: https://eurel.info/spip.php?rubrique683&lang=en.

Nurock, V., *Rawls : Pour une démocratie juste* (Paris, Ed. Michalon, 2008).

Nussbaum, M., *The New Religious Intolerance – Overcoming the Politics of Fear in an Anxious Age* (Cambridge – London, The Belknap Press of HUP, 2012).

Rehman, J., "Islam vs the Shari'a: Minority Protection within Islamic and International Legal Traditions" in A. Emon *et al.* (eds.), *Islamic Law and International Human Rights Law, Searching for Common Ground?* (Oxford, OUP, 2012).

Rosenfeld, M., "Chapter 35 – Constitutional Identity" in M. Rosenfeld and A. Sajó (eds.), *The Oxford Handbook of Comparative Constitutional Law* (Oxford, OUP, 2012).

Stavros, S., "The European Court of Human Rights' judgment in Molla Sali: a call for Greece to modernize its system for national-minority protection?" (17 January 2019) *Oxford Human Rights Hub*, accessed 11 February 2021, https://ohrh.law.ox.ac.uk/the-european-court-of-human-rights-judgment-in-molla-sali-a-call-for-greece-to-modernise-its-system-for-national-minority-protection/.

Tsitselikis, K., "The application of the Treaty of Lausanne in Greek Law. the Chapter on minorities" («Η εφαρμογή της Συνθήκης της Λωζάννης στο ελληνικό δίκαιο. Το κεφάλαιο περί των μειονοτήτων») in Pazartzis, P. and Antonopoulos, K. (eds.) *The 1923 Lausanne Peace Treaty at 90* (Hellenic Branch of the International Law Association, Nomiki Vivliothiki, 2014).

UNHCR, Operational Portal – Refugee Situations (07 February 2021), available at: https://data2.unhcr.org/en/situations/mediterranean/location/5179.

UNHCR, Greece, updated September 2020, available at: https://www.unhcr.org/greece.html.

UNHCR, *Routes towards and Western and Central Mediterranean Sea, UNCHR's Updated Risk Mitigation Strategy and Appeal* (January 2021), available at: https://reporting.unhcr.org/sites/default/files/UNHCR%20Western%20and%20Central%20Mediterranean%20Appeal%202021.pdf.

UNHCR, *UNHCR calls for EU to ensure a new chapter for refugee protection* (12 January 2021), accessed 11 February 2021, https://www.unhcr.org/news/press/2021/1/5ffc80f74/unhcr-calls-eu-ensure-new-chapter-refugee-protection.html

UNHCR, Global Focus – UNHCR Operations Worldwide, Operation: Greece, 2016 Year-End report, available at: https://reporting.unhcr.org/sites/default/files/pdfsummaries/GR2016-Greece-eng.pdf.

CHAPTER 6

Rabbinical Court Decisions and Their Impact on Jewish Society

Elimelech Westreich and Avishalom Westreich

1 Introduction*

In this paper, we focus on the legal influence of rabbinical courts on Jewish society in Israel. Rabbinical courts in Israel are a religious institution officially recognized by the law of the state, with jurisdiction over the Jewish population in some matters of personal status and family law. Intuitively, we expect rabbinical courts to apply Jewish law, and civil courts to apply secular civil law. But this is not always the case; the complex structure of Israeli family law leads to various situations, as for example, when religious law is applied by a secular civil court, and secular law is applied by a religious court. This intricate situation is part of the complexity of the societal place of rabbinical courts within Jewish society, as discussed below. We review various areas in which decisions of rabbinical courts affect Jewish Israeli society, and evaluate the role of this influence in the life of the citizens.[1] We show how the effect of the decisions of rabbinical courts depends on various elements: the extent of their jurisdiction, the extent of the involvement of civil law in their decisions, and the extent of the integration of religious law in the decisions of the civil legal system, and presumably also the influence of civil courts on religious law itself.

Rabbinical courts can have several types of jurisdictions: exclusive, parallel, and attached (or bound) jurisdiction. Exclusive jurisdiction is imposed by law and cannot be changed at the will of the parties. This is the case in matters of marriage and divorce, in which Jewish religious law applies. Parallel jurisdiction

* This research was supported by the Israel Science Foundation (grant No. 922/16). We wish to thank also the David Berg Institute for Law and History, at the Buchmann Faculty of Law, Tel Aviv University for its support. Special thanks to the editors of this book, Kerstin Wonisch and Roberta Medda-Windischer, for their valuable insights, and to Gabriel Lanyi for excellent English editing.

1 This pattern is not unique to the rabbinical courts and the Jewish community; it applies to other Israeli religious communities as well – those of the Moslems, Christians, and Druze, who are subject to the jurisdiction of their religious courts in similar matters. In this paper, however, we focus exclusively on rabbinical courts.

 | DOI:10.1163/9789004446816_008

is granted to civil court unless all parties to the case agree to transfer it to the rabbinical court, so that both civil and rabbinical courts might have jurisdiction. We found this type of jurisdiction in suits of spousal maintenance or in suits of children's maintenance. Attached or bound jurisdiction exists when one of the parties filed a suit for divorce and attached an additional matter to the suit, usually spousal maintenance (not by agreement) or property division. The attachment brings the issue under the exclusive jurisdiction of the rabbinical court, together with the exclusive jurisdiction over the divorce suit.

The question of jurisdiction is of great importance in discussing the presence of rabbinical courts in the life of Jewish citizens, because it frames the boundaries of influence of the religious courts in society, including on the non-religious majority and other groups, such as a few modern-liberal religious groups that are not interested in being tied to (the more conservative) religious courts. But the scope of jurisdiction is not the only factor affecting society. Religious law may be applied in certain circumstances even by civil courts, as for example, in spousal and children's maintenance. In these cases, civil courts usually adopt religious law as interpreted by rabbinical law, but occasionally they propose innovative interpretations that incorporate liberal values into religious law, which may cause conflict with the religious system. Religious law applied by civil courts is thus another significant component of the influence of religious law on Jewish society.

It is clear, therefore, that both from the point of view of the choice of law and of religious jurisdiction, religious law and religious courts have a marked presence in legal family matters. Their influence is not absolute, however, and it is subject to significant limitations and supervision, including intervention in Jewish religious law itself by civil courts, mainly the Israeli Supreme Court, either in its role as a high court of appeals or as the High Court of Justice. Often the objective of these interventions is the secularization of family law and the expansion of civil jurisdiction at the expense of religious jurisdiction, which, again, could lead to power conflicts within Israeli Jewish society. Yet, despite these tensions and the conflicts that arise from time to time, the basic character of rabbinical courts and the influence of religious law on the Jewish society are significant and have not changed dramatically in the last several decades.

2 Historical Background

The phenomenon of a religious court that has jurisdiction in family matters in the Land of Israel began in the 19th century with the decline of the Ottoman Empire, which occupied the Middle East, including the territories that later became the State of Israel. All three monotheistic religions practiced in the Ottoman empire, Judaism, Islam, and Christianity, enjoyed jurisdiction in family matters.[2] Every religion had its own court system, applying its religious law to members of this religion.

In 1917, the British Empire captured the Land of Israel from the Ottoman Empire. In 1922, the British Empire accepted from the League of Nations the charter of the Mandate on Palestine and soon enacted The King's Order in Council, 1922, according to the guidelines of Chapter 8 of the Charter. The King's Order in Council adopted the basic idea of sharing jurisdiction in family matters between civil and religious courts and between religious and civil law. (As we have already mentioned, the courts and the law are not always equivalent, as for example, when cases are decided according to religious law but under civil jurisdiction.) All religious courts were granted exclusive jurisdiction in matters of marriage, divorce, alimony, maintenance, and wills, although many of these were later dropped or substantially changed by legislation of the Israeli Parliament or by case law. Rabbinical courts for Jews and the courts of the Christian communities were provided with parallel jurisdiction in other matters of personal status, as defined in Chapter 51 of The King's Order in Council, 1922–1947, upon mutual agreement between both parties to their jurisdiction. Muslim Courts, by contrast, enjoyed exclusive jurisdiction in all matters of personal status.[3]

The British Mandate, accordingly, adopted the Ottoman basic structure regarding the special legal status of family matters. It included in certain aspects even sole jurisdiction granted to religious courts, although modified and crystalized according to the more modern visions of the British Mandate. In addition to defining the complex relationship between civil and religious tribunals, the British Mandate made some internal changes within the religious legal system, for example, establishing a religious court of appeal, an important procedural act that had significant substantive effect as well.[4]

2 See Chapter 51 of The King's Order in Council, 1922–1947. Later, after the establishment of the State of Israel, Druze religion became recognized as well by the Knesset that enacted the Law of the Druze Religious Court, 1962. Regarding Christian denominations, the second addition to The King's Order in Council, 1922–1947, recognized nine denominations, including the Eastern Orthodox Church, the Catholic Church, and more.

3 Here also Israeli law changed the situation. Section 3 of the Family Court law, 5755–1995 (5th amendment, 2001), provided civil courts with parallel jurisdiction over Muslims as well, so that jurisdiction of Muslim Courts was made equal to that of the Rabbinical and Christian Courts.

4 It was not easily accepted by the religious legal system and within the religious law discourse. See A. Radzyner, "Rabbi Ouziel, the Tel-Aviv-Jaffa Rabbinate and the Rabbinical Court of Appeal: A Play in Four Acts", (2004) 21 *Bar-Ilan Law Studies* 129–243.

The most recent historical development in the jurisdiction of religious courts and the applicability of religious law occurred after the establishment of the State of Israel. Israel in general continued the Mandatory arrangements that provided religious courts with jurisdiction over family matters and recognized religious law in some aspects of family matters, but with substantial changes. Some of these arrangements reaffirmed the authority of religious courts, for example, with regard to marriage and divorce, but many others limited the scope of this authority, for example, in the areas of inheritance, and later, in matters of financial matrimonial relations. These somewhat contradictory trends have led to ongoing tension around the relations between religious law and civil law, and consequently, between religious and civil courts. These arrangements are one of the identifying characteristics of the Israeli legal system, and they have significantly affected Israeli society to this day,[5] as discussed below.

3 Change of Course since the Establishment of the State of Israel

The status of rabbinical courts has not remained static since the establishment of the State of Israel. The Knesset (Israeli Parliament) and the Supreme Court have been intervening in many ways in areas that fall under the jurisdiction of the religious courts. Below we describe the main changes that took place over the years and discuss their influence on crystallizing the Israeli legal system in family matters. The discussion will help clarify the position of rabbinical courts in Israel and their legal influence on Israeli society.

Immediately after the establishment of the State of Israel, in 1948, to prevent a legal vacuum, Israel incorporated the laws of the British Mandate into its laws, including the structure of these laws in family matters.[6] Accordingly, both civil and religious courts were given jurisdiction and could apply both civil law and religious law, depending on the issue and the circumstances. Later, Israel legislated new laws, amended the old ones, and multiple court rulings were handed down, which dramatically affected the law. One of the important new laws that

5 On the dynamics in the relations between the legal authorities, including recent trends to reduce the tension, see, e.g., A. Westreich, "Accommodating Religious Law with a Civil Legal System: Lessons from the Jewish Law Experience in Financial Family Matters," (2018) 33 *Journal of Law and Religion* 481–503.

6 See section 11 of the Law and Administration Ordinance, 1948, enacted by the Provisional Council of the State a few days after the Declaration of the Establishment of the State of Israel.

had a significant influence on the relations between civil and religious law was the Women's Equal Rights Law 1951. Section 1 decrees as follows:

> A man and a woman shall have equal status with regard to any legal proceeding; any provision of law which discriminates, with regard to any legal proceeding, against women as women, shall be of no effect.

This law affected immediately the status of women within the family and family matters in general. For example, Section 8 banned bigamy and coerced divorce of the wife for all religious groups. But the overall effect of the law went beyond that of its individual provisions, and it directly affected the religious courts, which were instructed to follow it in their decisions: "All courts shall act in accordance with this Law" (Section 7). Marriage and divorce, however, were explicitly excluded from this provision, as stated in Section 5: "This Law shall not affect any legal prohibition or permission relating to marriage or divorce." Thus, the legislation did not change the religious aspects of marriage and divorce, despite the fact that they contained some discriminatory elements. It did change, however, other aspects of the institution of. For example, an important section of this law affected matrimonial financial relations:

> A married woman shall be fully competent to own and deal with property as if she were unmarried; her rights in property acquired before her marriage shall not be affected by her marriage.[7]

This important declaration regarding the financial autonomy of the wife had many practical implications. With regard to Jewish family law, it cancelled the right of the husband to enjoy the fruits of his wife's property during the marriage and to administer her estate. A few decades later, the Supreme Court used this rule to implement radical changes in the laws of economic relations between husband and wife, as discussed below.

In the first decades after the establishment of the State of Israel, the Knesset began to restructure family law, directly changing the boundaries of jurisdiction of religious courts and the extent to which religious law was present within the Israeli ~~the~~ legal system. Active involvement of the Supreme Court extended the reach of these changes, and often increased the tension between the religious and civil systems. Three significant issues within family law were affected by this process, influencing Israeli society (Jewish and non-Jewish) to

7 Women's Equal Rights Law, 5711–1951, Section 2.

this day: marriage and divorce, maintenance, and matrimonial property relations. We discuss these in the following sections.

4 Marriage and Divorce: Exclusive Jurisdiction and Jewish Law

Marriage and divorce are regulated by the Rabbinical Courts Jurisdiction (Marriage and Divorce) Law, 1953, which decreed:

1. Matters of marriage and divorce of Jews in Israel, being nationals or residents of the State, shall be under the exclusive jurisdiction of rabbinical courts.
2. Marriages and divorces of Jews shall be performed in Israel in accordance with Jewish religious law.

On the basis of this law, these essential topics remained under the exclusive jurisdiction of rabbinical courts, as under the British Mandate, with some modifications that expanded their jurisdiction. They are governed by the Jewish religious laws (similarly to the other recognized religions), and the presence of civil law with respect to them is marginal. This arrangement is an extension of the status quo that was in effect in British Mandate Palestine, but in fact, since early years of the State of Israel, it has been understood by many as a significant aspect of the Jewish identity of the young state (while others dispute it).[8] Yet, this situation has a significant effect on Israeli society, forcing residents and citizens to conduct their marriage and divorce according to religious law (according to its Orthodox interpretation), even if it contradicts their believes. This is not merely a question of faith or of freedom of (and from) religion.[9] This legal situation has practical consequences for both marriage and divorce. With regard to marriage, religious law imposes significant limitations on the right to marry based on religious considerations, for example, in cases of interfaith marriage or when certain religious restrictions are in force, like the prohibition against Jewish *kohanim* (priests) marrying divorced women. Jewish religious law allows divorce, but generally adopts a regime of fault-based divorce or divorce by agreement.[10] To this day, there are circumstances in which one spouse refuses to divorce, and because of religious demands, the

8 A. Westreich and P. Shifman, *A Civil Legal Framework for Marriage and Divorce in Israel* position paper, Ruth Gavison (ed.), trans. Kfir Levy((Jerusalem, Mezila Center, 2013).

9 G. Sapir and D. Statman, "Religious Marriage in a Liberal State," (2009) 30 *Cardozo Law Review* 2855–2880; Westreich and Shifman, "A Civil Legal Framework" *supra*, at 48–71.

10 A. Westreich, "The Right to Divorce in Jewish Law: Between Politics and Ideology", (2010) 1 *International Journal of the Jurisprudence of the Family* 177–196.

divorce cannot be carried out, although this situation has been changing in recent years.[11]

Despite the sole jurisdiction of rabbinical courts in matters of both marriage and divorce, and despite the clear legal requirement to follow religious law in these matters, civil courts have found ways to bypass religious law, mostly, but not exclusively, in marginal cases. According to the Rabbinical Courts Jurisdiction (Marriage and Divorce) Law 1953, marriage and divorce must be performed in accordance with Jewish law. Nevertheless, in an ongoing progress, civil courts granted nearly full recognition to *de facto* marital relationships. Thus, cohabitants are given all the marital rights provided to married couples.[12] Moreover, in a compromise with the High Rabbinical Court, the High Court of Justice (2006) recognized almost completely civil marriages of Jewish couples performed abroad, so that on one hand, civil marriages performed abroad are recognized, but their dissolution is under the jurisdiction of the rabbinical court.[13]

The situation regarding divorce is similar, but because divorce is considered a critical issue from a religious perspective, and *a priori* rabbinical courts approach it with greater stringency, the relations between the religious and the civil systems are more complex and tense. An issue that reflects these tensions is that of tort compensation for men or women whose spouse refuses to divorce, as discussed below.

The basic requirement in Jewish law of a mutual agreement for divorce has created a social problem and elicited much criticism from liberal circles, because of the option of husbands to refuse granting their wives a writ of divorce (*get*), resulting in a "chained woman" (*agunah*). Often rabbinical courts do not coerce a divorce when one party refuses, even in cases of marital breakdown.[14] Since the early 2000s, a new legal practice has emerged to

11 See A. Westreich and A. Radzyner, "Revolutionism and Conservatism in the Rulings of the Israeli Rabbinical Courts: Divorce Enforcement on the Grounds of '*Ma'is 'Alai*' (He Is Repulsive to Me)", (2020) 42 *Tel Aviv University Law Review* 639–686 (Heb.).

12 See S. Lifshitz's *Cohabitation Law in Israel in Light of a Civil Theory of the Family* (Heb.) (Haifa, Haifa University Press 2005).

13 P. Shifman, "Civil Family Laws Gone Public: On President Barak's Contribution to Family Lawat " in E. Zamir *et al* (eds.), *Barak's Festschrift* (Jerusalem, The Faculty of Law, Hebrew University Press 2009) (Heb.); A. Westreich, "Rhetoric and Substance 'Came Down Wrapped Together'? On Civil Marriage in Israel Following the Noahide Decision", (2013–2014) 6–7 *Family in Law Review* 543–578 (Heb.).

14 This is not always the case, and as noted, there are significant efforts to resolve this situation. See A. Westreich, "The Right to Divorce in Jewish Law: Between Politics and Ideology" *supra*; A. Westreich and A. Radzyner, "Revolutionism and Conservatism in the Rulings of the Israeli Rabbinical Courts: Divorce Enforcement on the Grounds of '*Ma'is 'Alai*' (He Is Repulsive to Me)" *supra*.

confront the problem of *get* refusal: men or women whose spouses refused to divorce and who could not obtain a divorce through the rabbinical courts have sued for tort compensation in civil family courts.[15] Rabbinical courts objected to this practice, arguing that it is an intervention in matters of marriage and divorce which are under their sole jurisdiction, but civil courts argued that tort compensation is an independent civil remedy. According to civil family courts, preventing one's divorce (and preventing remarriage) violates one's autonomy, and can therefore be considered a civil wrong, usually on the basis of negligence.[16] This practice is still pursued over the objection of rabbinical courts, but at times with a silent agreement of the rabbinical court system.[17]

Thus, rabbinical courts play a significant role in marriage and divorce, and Jewish Israeli society is subject to their legal jurisdiction. There are, as discussed, recognized civil alternatives to marriage, like cohabitation (which has civil recognition) or civil marriage abroad (which enjoys civil and partial religious recognition), and ongoing efforts to bypass the difficulties caused by the religious divorce regime. Nevertheless, the core of marriage and divorce in Israel is religious and under religious control.[18]

5 Spousal Maintenance: Parallel and Bound Jurisdiction and Jewish Law

In 1959, the Family Amendment (Maintenance) Law was legislated. The law lists various maintenance obligations and states:

15 See, for example, two of the first such cases: Family Court File 19270/03 *K.S. v. K.F.* (21 December 2004); Family Court File 024782/98 *N.S. v. N.Y* (14 December 2008).

16 Section 35 of the Tort Ordinance (New Version). On this practice see, e.g., B. Shmueli, "Commodifying Personal Rights and Trading the Right to Divorce: Damages for Refusal to Divorce and Equalizing the Women's Power to Bargain", (2015) 22 *UCLA Women's L.J.* 39–105.

17 A. Radzyner, "'The Essential Thing is not studying, but Deed': *Get* Procedures after Tort Claims and the Publications Policy of Rabbinical Courts Judgments", (2015) 45 *Mishpatim – Hebrew University Law Journal* 5–84.

18 There are ongoing calls to change this situation. See, e.g., Westreich and Shifman, "A Civil Legal Framework," *supra*. As for today, however, as mentioned, marriage and divorce are under sole jurisdiction of religious courts, so that couples who get divorce do not have any option other than handling their case in a religious court. Other issues related to family matters, on the other hand, are sometimes under parallel jurisdiction, and are many times characterized by "forum shopping"; see below.

> 2(a) A person is liable for the maintenance of his[19] spouse in accordance with the provisions of the personal law applicable to him, and the provisions of this law shall not apply to him.

During the British Mandate, the Supreme Court understood personal law to refer to religious law. As a result, Israeli citizens were obligated to maintain their spouses according to their religious law, which in the case of Jews is Jewish law. Israeli law has not changed this situation, although some workarounds were developed in certain cases. Thus, Israeli Supreme Court offered several civil options for spousal maintenance, such as restorative maintenance, in cases when religious law does not provide sufficient financial resources for the needs of the spouse, usually the wife.[20] There are also some gaps between rabbinical and civil courts in some areas of the practical application of religious maintenance law, for example, whether a wife is required to work and whether her maintenance is to be reduced as a result. Rabbinical courts were generally flexible on this matter and ruled in favor of the wife.[21] In most cases, therefore, the law being applied is the religious one, whether in religious or in civil court.

Rabbinical courts have parallel jurisdiction if both parties agree to it.[22] Yet, Israeli law added another option for providing rabbinical courts with sole jurisdiction – bound jurisdiction. Section 3 of the Rabbinical Courts Jurisdiction (Marriage and Divorce) Law, 1953 decrees:

> Where a suit for divorce between Jews has been filed in a rabbinical court, whether by the wife or by the husband, a rabbinical court shall have exclusive jurisdiction in any matter bound to such suit, including maintenance for the wife and for the children of the couple.[23]

This section has sparked intensive wrangling over jurisdiction between rabbinical and civil courts and between the parties themselves (sometimes defined as race for jurisdiction, or, more gently: forum shopping).[24] Although the

19 Third person in Hebrew distinguishes between feminine and masculine forms. It is not gender neutral, and usually the masculine form is preferred, both in spoken and in formal Hebrew. Although in recent years there is a gradual process of change in this matter, the law still uses masculine forms. Our translation, accordingly, follows this structure.

20 See, e.g., Family Appeal Request 3151/14 *Plonit v. Ploni* (5 November 2015), Justice Barak-Erez's opinion.

21 See file 4553/53 R.L.R. v. 1, at 90–94.

22 Section 9 of the Rabbinical Courts Jurisdiction (Marriage and Divorce) Law, 5713–1953.

23 Rabbinical Courts Jurisdiction (Marriage and Divorce) Law, Israel Gazette, 1953, at 165.

24 This characterization of Israeli family law is not new and quite common. See, e.g., A. Rosen-Zvi, "Forum Shopping between Religious and Secular Courts (and Its Impact on the Legal System)", (1989) 9 *Tel Aviv U. Stud. L.* 347–396. Yet, there are indications that

straightforward reading of this section appears to provide rabbinical courts with automatic jurisdiction in matters related to the divorce suit, Israeli Supreme Court rejected this position by interpreting the section as requiring an explicit act of binding various issues related to divorce, including spousal maintenance, to the divorce suit. Therefore, rabbinical courts have jurisdiction in these matters only when they are explicitly attached to the divorce suit. Several conditions were also added to providing jurisdiction to rabbinical courts based on this section, mainly that the divorce suit be *bona fide*.

6 Children's Maintenance: Unsolved Tensions over Jurisdiction

In recent years, child support has been one of the fascinating areas for examining the relationships between rabbinical courts and the civil legal system, and it has become a litmus test for the place of rabbinical courts and religious law in the changed Israeli society. The issue produced a revolutionary interpretation of substantive Jewish law by the Supreme Court and imposed a significant limitation of rabbinical court jurisdiction in this matter, in order to bring it closer to the modern liberal view of the family, and in particular – of gender equality within it. The complexity of this case makes it a good example of the intricate situation of religious law in Israel.

The Family Amendment (Maintenance) Law, 5719–1959, states that:

> 3(a) A person is obligated for the maintenance of minor children and the minor children of his spouse in accordance with the provisions of the personal law applying to him.[25]

Similarly to spousal support, Israeli citizens are obligated to maintain their children according to their religious law, which in the case of Jews is Jewish law. The question of jurisdiction, however, is different, and may be granted to either a civil or a religious court (parallel jurisdiction), with preference for the civil court. Following High Court of Justice decisions, rabbinical courts have jurisdiction only when all parties to the suit agree. But there is another alternative for providing rabbinical courts with jurisdiction: the "bound" provision

---

in recent years this situation has been improved, and more cooperation between these legal authorities can be seen. See A. Westreich, "Three Crossroads in the Relationships between Rabbinical Court and Civil Court: Child Support, Property Distribution and the Litigations Arrangement Law" (2022) 52 *Mishpatim – Hebrew University Law Journal* 217–274.

25 Family Amendment (Maintenance) Law, Israel Gazette, 1959, at 72.

in Section 3 of the Rabbinical Courts Jurisdiction (Marriage and Divorce) Law 1953, which we have already met, that states:

> Where a suit for divorce between Jews has been filed in a rabbinical court, whether by the wife or by the husband, a rabbinical court shall have exclusive jurisdiction in any matter connected with such suit, including maintenance ... for the children of the couple.[26]

About 50 years ago, in the famous *Shragai* case, the High Court of Justice interpreted this paragraph in a narrow manner as relating only to a suit that the wife filed against her husband to recover her expenses for child maintenance.[27] The children themselves, however, have the right to sue their father for maintenance separately in the civil court, even if their mother attached her maintenance suit to a divorce suit submitted in rabbinical court. In practice, the children's suit against their father is submitted by their guardian – usually, in these kinds of cases, their mother, so in practice this option may nullify any decision made by rabbinical court.

In the last two decades, this issue kept swinging like a pendulum between two extremes. Based on the above position, rabbinical courts have expanded their jurisdiction to even more cases of child support. Child support cases were formally described as reimbursement of expenses, but which in reality were substantive debates on maintenance, while the civil system gradually limited the option of submitting separate suits in the name of the children in civil courts. An ambiguous decision of the High Court of Justice, from 2014, has been understood as reversing the *Shragai* ruling not only *de facto* but also *de jure*, and providing rabbinical courts with jurisdiction over children's maintenance.[28] Despite a clarification by Chief Justice Grunis, according to whom this was not the intention of the decision, rabbinical courts continued, on this basis, to adjudicate cases of child maintenance. This process was blocked in 2019 by another Supreme Court ruling, which drove back the pendulum to limit the jurisdiction of the rabbinical courts.[29] At present, rabbinical courts have limited jurisdiction over child maintenance, either by attaching a reimbursement suit according to Section 3 of the Rabbinical Courts Jurisdiction

26 Rabbinical Courts Jurisdiction (Marriage and Divorce) Law *supra*.

27 Civil Appeal Request 120/69 *Shragai v. Shragai*, LR. v. 23(2), at 161.

28 HCJ 5933/14 *Plonit v. Ploni* (11 September 2014).

29 Family Appeal Request 7628/17 *Plonit v. Ploni* (22 September 2019). There are first signs that rabbinical courts do not completely adhere to this decision, see High Rabbinical Court File 1250217/3 *Ploni v. Plonit* (10 October 2021).

Law or by agreement, under supervision of a civil court, to make sure that the best interest of the child is served.

As noted, religious law applies in this domain. This, however, did not prevent the Supreme Court from instigating dramatic changes in this area as well, which affected Jewish couples and led to extensive debates in rabbinical courts. In July 2017, a revolutionary verdict was issued by the Supreme Court regarding child support.[30] Traditionally, according to Jewish law, the maintenance obligation was imposed exclusively on the father, consistent with the paternalistic family structure of the past. The Supreme Court challenged this approach and ruled that in cases of shared custody, when the financial resources of the parents are relatively equal, the maintenance obligation should be mutual. Because children's maintenance is adjudicated according to Jewish religious law, as noted above, the court based its ruling on an analysis of Jewish legal sources. Jewish law distinguishes between children below the age of 6, toward whom the father has a strong and stable maintenance obligation, and children above the age of 6. For the latter, the obligation is based on the Talmudic laws of charity, which were applied specifically to children above 6,[31] and on an enactment of the Chief Rabbinate from 1944.[32] The Supreme Court argued, based on the opinion of quite a few Jewish law scholars, that the enactment of 1944 did not make a substantive change in the source of the obligation for maintenance, which is still based on the laws of charity. Therefore, it was possible to take the next and highly significant step of imposing the obligation on the mother as well, if she had sufficient financial resources to meet such an obligation.[33]

The Supreme Court did not seek to conceal its modern liberal considerations in reaching this decision:

> We must choose [the interpretation] that is consistent with the basic conceptions and basic values of Israeli law ... I believe that the interpretation that best suits the basic values of our legal doctrine is that between

30 Family Appeal Request 919/15 *Plonit v. Ploni* (19 July 2017).

31 See Babylonian Talmud, 49a – 50a.

32 See Rabbi I. Halevi Herzog, *A Constitution for Israel According to the Torah,* Vol. 3, (I. Warhaftig ed. Jerusalem, Mossad Harav Kook 1989), at 118–121 (Heb.). Chief Rabbi Herzog, together with Chief Rabbi Ben Zion M. H. Uzi'el, were the driving force behind this and few other enactments. On the 1944 enactments see E. Westreich and A. Westreich, "Chief Rabbinate Regulations on Economic Issues at the End of the Mandate Period", (2022) 5 *Law, Society & Culture: Law, Economy, and Institutions in Israel* 437–487. (Heb.).

33 See Family Appeal Request 919/15 *Plonit v. Ploni* (19 July 2017), *supra*, paragraphs 24–27 of Justice Fogelman opinion.

the ages of 6 and 15 the maintenance obligation is based on the laws of charity, which apply equally to both parents.

Many rabbinical courts rejected this interpretation and continued to hold that as far as the child's basic needs are concerned, the maintenance obligation is imposed on the father, whereas additional expenses are in principle imposed equally on both spouses.[34] Some courts, however, did accept the basic approach of the Supreme Court.[35] Does it really make a difference, however? Since the jurisdiction of rabbinical courts was significantly limited, the effect of their objections would be minor. It may be relevant when both parties agree to provide jurisdiction to the rabbinical court, but it is difficult to see why a woman would agree to grant jurisdiction to the rabbinical court knowing that the result would be imposing a financial obligation on him. Only if the jurisdiction pendulum were to move again to expand the jurisdiction of the rabbinical courts, it really would make a difference. Meanwhile, the complexity of this case illustrates how the legal control of rabbinical courts over Jewish couples (as regards jurisdiction) is reduced, while the basic status of religious law is preserved, albeit with a revolutionary liberal interpretation by the secular Supreme Court.

7 Matrimonial Property and Financial Relations: Bound Jurisdiction and Civil Law

During the British Mandate, economic matrimonial relations were included in matters of marriage, and therefore under the exclusive jurisdiction of the rabbinical courts, which applied Jewish law.[36] In the 1960s, the Supreme Court began to develop an alternative civil arrangement – equal property sharing – arguing that it arose from Section 2 of the Women's Equal Rights Law, 1951.[37] As a result, civil courts gained jurisdiction over the spouses' economic relations

34 See, e.g., a few days after the publication of the Supreme Court decision: Rabbinical Court File (Be'er Sheva) 147728/12 *Ploni v. Plonit* (24 July 2017). The objections did not fade away over time. See, e.g., Rabbinical Court File (Ashkelon) 969794/12 *Ploni v. Plonit* (23 March 2019).

35 See, e.g., Haifa Regional Court File 1169832/6 *Ploni v. Plonit* (28 October 2019), expressing some reservations about the Supreme Court decision, but nevertheless adopting its general approach.

36 See, e.g., Justice Zilberg's opinion in Civil Appeal 8/59 *Goldman v. Goldman*, PD 13 1085 (1959).

37 See, e.g., Chief Justice Agranat, Civil Appeal 253/65 *Briker v. Briker*, PD 20(1) 589 (1966).

(excluding matters of maintenance), and ruled in such matters according to civil law, specifically, according to the legal presumption of shared property. Rabbinical courts continued to have jurisdiction in economic matters only when the economic suit was bound to a divorce suit based on Section 3 of the Rabbinical Courts Jurisdiction Law, discussed above. Rabbinical courts, however, were not committed to the civil doctrine of shared property presumption until the 1990s. The Bavli v. Bavli case changed this situation entirely. In this case, the High Court of Justice ruled that property matters are not considered part of personal law and should not be adjudicated according to religious law. Rabbinical courts could still have jurisdiction if monetary matters were bound to the divorce suit according to Section 3. Nevertheless, because these matters were no longer considered as belonging to the area of personal law, they were forced to rule according to civil law, specifically, according to the shared property presumption doctrine. Not surprisingly, the ruling elicited criticism both from the rabbinical establishment and from public religious groups, but despite these objections, rabbinical courts today usually follow the civil approach.[38]

A significant legal development regarding matrimonial property preceded the Bavli ruling, although without significant resistance. In the early 1970s, the legislator introduced a new law: the Property Relations between Spouses Law 1973, which replaced the doctrine of the shared property presumption by one of equitable distribution – different in its legal construction, but similar in its objective to achieve equal distribution of property:

> 5.a) Upon termination of the marriage in consequence of divorce or of the death of one spouse ... each of the spouses is entitled to half the value of the aggregate property of the spouses, except property they had owned immediately before the marriage or received by way of gift or inheritance during the marriage.

This new arrangement applied to couples that married on or after January 1, 1974. The previous shared property presumption continued to be applied for couples that married until that date, for cohabitants who were not formally married, and with regard to certain assets that did not fall under the legal arrangement of the new law, as for example, gifts and inheritance.

The doctrine of equitable distribution was imposed immediately on rabbinical courts (although without limiting their jurisdiction) without resistance:

38 See Westreich, "Accommodating Religious Law" *supra* 5.

> 13(a) This Law is not designed to affect the jurisdiction of the religious courts; (b) In a matter involving this Law a religious court shall act in accordance with the provisions of this Law.

Why was it easier for rabbinical courts to adopt this law than the shared property presumption? Possibly, because of the difference between formal legislation and Supreme Court rulings, which traditionally provoked tension. The result is that today, in most cases, rabbinical courts follow the civil approach in monetary matters. Nevertheless, there are still gaps and differences, including some tendencies of rabbinical courts to take into account traditional considerations, including unequal property distribution when one of the spouses is at fault.[39]

A possible solution to the complex situation of adopting civil law while trying to retain some conservative ideas is the use of the *ketubah* payment, which is part of the husband's obligations in the traditional Jewish marriage contract, in cases of spousal fault. The Property Relations between Spouses Law did not entirely replace the old Jewish structure in economic matters. One component of economic rights in Jewish law – the *ketubah* payment – survived and continued to be applied by rabbinical courts according to the ruling of section 17 of the Property Relations between Spouses Law 1973: "This Law shall not derogate from … the rights of a woman under her *ketubah* (marriage contract settlement)." The *ketubah* is an old Jewish instrument originating from the era of the Hasmoneans (2nd – 1st centuries BCE).[40] According to Jewish law, the *ketubah* includes a sum of money that the wife is entitled to receive after the dissolution of her marriage. The sum usually includes three components: the essence of the *ketubah*, which is obligatory by law; the additional part, which is a gift of the husband; and the dowry brought by the wife into marriage. It also contains important economic elements of the spouses' relations, which is based on the doctrine of separate ownership. The value of each element in the *ketubah* is not completely clear, which provides rabbinical courts a range of interpretative options. Courts are highly flexible in using these options, so that *ketubah* payment can be imposed on the husband or denied, depending on various considerations, including spousal fault.[41]

This issue complicates the picture of the influence rabbinical courts exert in family matters. We witness here a significant limitation of their power, together with substantial assimilation of the rabbinical courts themselves within civil monetary legal arrangements. Notwithstanding this, rabbinical courts still

39 *Ibid.*

40 See, e.g., Babylonian Talmud, Shabbat 14b.

41 See Westreich, "Accommodating Religious Law" *supra*.

have jurisdiction when monetary issues are bound to the divorce suit,[42] and as noted above, they are still able to modify secular law based on traditional fault considerations. Thus, despite the erosion in the jurisdiction of rabbinical courts and in the applicability of religious law, in important aspects, both from a social perspective and in the public consciousness, rabbinical courts and Jewish law still have significant presence in matters of family law.

8 Additional Aspects of Rabbinical Court Presence in Family Matters

We discussed above the central family law issues, in which rabbinical courts intensively interact with Jewish Israeli society. To complete the picture, below we review several issues related to family law in which rabbinical courts have limited or no jurisdiction. The first group involves inheritance, adoption, and guardianship – topics in which rabbinical courts accept the restrictions imposed on their jurisdiction. The second group relates to surrogacy and egg donation, where, by contrast, some rabbinical courts claim jurisdiction although the legislature has explicitly denied it to them.

8.1 *Inheritance, Adoption, and Guardianship*

During the British Mandate, rabbinical courts enjoyed exclusive jurisdiction in matters of confirmation of wills, and parallel jurisdiction in matters of successions, legacies, adoption, and guardianship of minors. At the same time, the civil court applied religious law in matters of successions, legacies, adoption, and guardianship of minors in cases in which it had jurisdiction. In the 1960s, the Knesset made significant changes in all these topics. It enacted the Law of Adoption, 5720–1960 (later replaced by Children Adoption Law, 5741–1981), the Law of Guardianship and Legal Capacity, 5722–1962, and the Law of Inheritance, 5725–1965. All three laws substituted civil law for religious law and denied jurisdiction of rabbinical courts. According to this legislation (which is binding today as well) Rabbinical courts retain jurisdiction only if all parties agree to it and have to apply the civil law. Religious law can be applied in rabbinical courts only in cases of inheritance and only if the parties agree to it explicitly.

---

42 According to the Supreme Court ruling, rabbinical courts cannot have jurisdiction by agreement in monetary matters because these are not matters of personal law. See HCJ 8638/03 *Sima Amir v. The Rabbinical Court of Appeal*, LR. v. 61(1) 269–300. Therefore, the only possible way to obtain jurisdiction is by binding monetary matters to the divorce suit according to Section 3 of the Rabbinical Courts Jurisdiction Law.

Yet, despite the option of applying religious law (upon explicit agreement) in almost all cases in which the parties agree to grant jurisdiction to rabbinical courts, these courts apply civil principles in their adjudication, as for example, providing inheritance rights to the wife and practicing gender equality in inheritance rulings, despite the different approach of Jewish law with regard to these issues.[43] Therefore, lack of jurisdiction in these three topics does not lead to a conflict of jurisdictions or to tension between the religious and civil systems, or to feelings of religious coercion. A different picture emerges in cases of surrogacy and egg donation, as discussed below.

8.2 *Affecting Life: Bypassing Lack of Jurisdiction (Surrogacy and Egg Donation)*

The influence of religious law in Israel goes far beyond the formal jurisdiction of rabbinical courts. First, in legislation, religious law is taken into consideration by the legislators in many sensitive issues, even if they are not formally required to do so, because of the nature of the State as Jewish and democratic, and because of pragmatic considerations, to make the law more easily acceptable. Issues such as the legal definition of brain death, organ transplantation, and artificial procreation are good illustrations.[44] Discussing the influence of religious law on legislators is, however, beyond the scope of this chapter.

Second, the influence of religious law is felt in rabbinical court decisions. Rabbinical courts address some issues that are under civil jurisdiction but are nevertheless influenced by religious law. The question of religious affiliation in surrogacy and egg donation is a good test case.

Israeli law considers surrogacy and egg donation to be a civil matter. Although religious considerations are taken into account, for example, by limiting interfaith donations,[45] in general, the process is under the jurisdiction

43 D. Hacker, "Religious Tribunals in Democratic States: Lesson from the Israeli Rabbinical Courts", (2012) 27 *Journal of Law and Religion* 59–82.

44 See A. Westreich, *Assisted Reproduction in Israel: Law, Religion, and Culture* (Leiden, Brill Publication, 2018), at 16–19; 39–43. In surrogacy and egg donation, for example, it is reflected in limiting interfaith donations. See below.

45 Section 2(5) of the Embryo Carrying Agreements Law, 5756–1996, requires that the surrogate mother will belong to the same religion as the intended mother. Similarly, section 13(e)(3)(a) of the Egg Donation Law, 5770–2010, requires that both donor and recipient will belong to the same religion, although in the case of egg donation, if the ova were already taken, the process would be approved under condition that the physician in charge would inform the intended parents of the difference in religious affiliation and receive their written agreement for the process (*ibid*, 13(e)(4)). For discussing these restrictions and their legal and cultural reasons. See Westreich, *Assisted Reproduction*, at 16–19.

of civil family court, except in cases of marriage and divorce resulting from surrogacy or egg donation.[46] Religious affiliation determines religious jurisdiction. Thus, children who were involved in a process of artificial procreation and would like to be declared Jewish, need to approach the rabbinical court for determining their religious status.

In October 2019, the district rabbinical court of Be'er Sheva made a dramatic decision in a case of a woman who received an anonymous egg donation:[47] her request to declare her child Jewish was rejected by the rabbinical court. According to Jewish law, one is considered Jewish if one's mother is Jewish. In case of surrogacy and egg donation, Jewish law decision-makers are divided on who is considered to be the mother: the gestational mother who gives birth to the child or the genetic mother (the owner of the egg). As a result, a dispute arises whether a child is considered Jewish when one of the "mothers" is not Jewish. In the Be'er Sheva case, the gestational mother was Jewish and the egg donor was anonymous, although the donor was registered in the population registry as Jewish,[48] which justified the gestational mother's claim that the child should be considered Jewish. The Be'er Sheva rabbinical court rejected her request, however, arguing that the population registry is not even a *prima facie* evidence of religious affiliation. Because many argue that motherhood and religious affiliation should be determined according to the genetic mother, and because the possibility exists that the genetic mother is not Jewish, the child, according to the Be'er Sheva court, cannot be declared Jewish.

This problematic decision is currently under consideration in the High Rabbinical Court. The main problem is that based on the Jewish legal construction of a "doubtful situation," there is sufficient basis to consider the child Jewish.[49] But the Be'er Sheva court ignored this and other arguments, and refused to even discuss them, including a formal opinion submitted by the Jewish Law Unit of the Israeli Ministry of Justice. The court did discuss its proposal that could be construed as a demand that the rabbinical system should be exposed to the details of egg donors, so that it would be possible to confirm her religious affiliation. The court suggested the following:

46 *Ibid.*

47 Rabbinical Court File (Be'er Sheva) 1216693/1 *Request of Plonit (mother) and Ploni (child)* (28 October 2019).

48 This was known based on the testimony of the physician involved in the process, as required by Israeli law.

49 A. Westreich and A. Stav, "Conversion of Children Born through Non-Jewish Egg Donation or Surrogacy", (2021) 41 *Techumin* 167–178 (Heb.).

> The Ministry of Health shall direct the egg donor to a religious court in her living area. The donor shall undergo a simple and accepted process of clarification of Jewishness, without stating the goal of this process, and without anyone, including the rabbinical court, knowing that she is an egg donor. A Ministry of Health representative, accepted by the Chief Rabbinate, shall confirm having seen the Jewish affiliation of the egg owner, based on which the newborn child shall be certified as Jewish.
>
> Without an announcement by the Ministry of Health that this was done, unfortunately we have no option other than to close this file in the absence of any data regarding the Jewish affiliation of the egg donor, despite the fact that it is clear that a great injustice was done to the son and his mother.[50]

This ruling is striking. The rabbinical court deliberately chose to ignore substantial considerations based on Jewish law and preferred to demand to be involved in a process that is not under its jurisdiction. In our opinion, this is an extreme example of a case in which rabbinical courts actively demand an expansion of their jurisdiction. If this demand is accepted, it will extend the influence of rabbinical courts on Jewish society significantly beyond where it currently stands.

From the perspective of the court, the decision was not merely political, but rather a necessary act aimed at preserving religious values, in this case regarding religious affiliation. Legal decisions, and religious-legal decisions among them, involve multiple tiers of considerations, including standards and various types of values that affect the final decision.[51] Yet, when the courts take extreme positions, against the straightforward meaning of the law contrary to other types of considerations,[52] it is difficult to accept their arguments. Thus, we consider this ruling as a misguided step aimed at expanding the jurisdiction of the court. We assume and hope that the High Rabbinical Court would adopt a different approach in this case.

---

50 File 1216693/1, at 11.

51 R. Dworkin, *Taking Rights Seriously* (Cambridge, Harvard University Press, 1978), at 14–45.

52 For example: privacy considerations of the egg donor or social interest in egg donations (which might be hurt if the rabbinical court's proposal would be accepted). See Westreich and Stav, "Conversion of Children" *supra*.

9 Conclusion

The unique legal system in family law in Israel provides an opportunity for examining the influence of religious courts and religious law on a given society through its legal system. In this paper, we discussed the dynamic relationships within this system, both diachronically, along a timeline, and synchronically, regarding various issues within the legal framework.

A well-known starting point is that Jewish courts[53] have significant influence in family matters (involving most, if not all, Jewish residents and citizens). Yet, an ongoing process has attempted and succeeded over the years to reduce this influence in certain areas. This includes limiting the jurisdiction of rabbinical courts, limiting the scope of Jewish law as applied in certain family matters, and integrating liberal aspects to the interpretation of Jewish religious law by secular civil courts. But the pendulum does not stay in one place, and these and other aspects are changing all the time – at times in one direction, at other times in the opposite one. In any event, the place of rabbinical courts and Jewish law within Israeli law, their relevance to Israeli individuals and couples, and their influence over them remain significant. This situation, static at its foundations and dynamic on its surface, is still debated within Israeli society.

Bibliography

Babylonian Talmud, Shabbat 14b.
Civil Appeal 253/65 Briker v. Briker, PD 20(1) 589 (1966).
Civil Appeal 8/59 Goldman v. Goldman, PD 13 1085 (1959).
Civil Appeal Request 120/69 Shragai v. Shragai, LR. V. 23(2) 161.
Dworkin, R., *Taking Rights Seriously* (Cambridge, Harvard University Press, 1978).
Egg Donation Law, 5770–2010.
Embryo Carrying Agreements Law, 5756–1996.
Family Amendment (Maintenance) Law, 5719–1959.
Family Appeal Request 3151/14 *Plonit v. Ploni* (5 November 2015).
Family Appeal Request 7628/17 *Plonit v. Ploni* (22 September 2019).
Family Appeal Request 919/15 *Plonit v. Ploni* (19 July 2017).
Family Court law, 5755–1995.
Family Court File 19270/03 *K.S. v. K.F.* (21 December 2004).

53 For Jewish citizens. Similar phenomena can be identified for other religious denominations.

Family Court File 024782/98 *N.S. v. N.Y* (14 December 2008).

Hacker, D., "Religious Tribunals in Democratic States: Lesson from the Israeli Rabbinical Courts", (2012) 27 *Journal of Law and Religion* 59–82.

HCJ (High Court of Justice) 5933/14 *Plonit v. Ploni* (11 September 2014).

HCJ 8638/03 *Sima Amir v. The Rabbinical Court of Appeal*, LR. v. 61(1) (2006).

High Rabbinical Court File 1250217/3 *Ploni v. Plonit* (10 October 2021).

King's Order in Council, 1922–1947.

Lifshitz, D., *Cohabitation Law in Israel in Light of a Civil Theory of the Family* (Haifa, Haifa University Press 2005).

Rabbi Itzhak Halevi Herzog, *A Constitution for Israel According to the Torah*, Vol. 3, (I. Warhaftig ed. Jerusalem, Mossad Harav Kook 1989) at 118–121.

Rabbinical Court File (Ashkelon) 969794/12 *Ploni v. Plonit* (23 March 2019).

Rabbinical Court File (Be'er Sheva) 1216693/1 *Request of Plonit (mother) and Ploni (child)* (28 October 2019).

Rabbinical Court File (Be'er Sheva) 147728/12 *Ploni v. Plonit* (24 July 2017).

Rabbinical Courts Jurisdiction (Marriage and Divorce) Law, 5713–1953.

Radzyner, A., "Rabbi Ouziel, the Tel-Aviv-Jaffa Rabbinate and the Rabbinical Court of Appeal: a Play in Four Acts" (2004) 21 *Bar-Ilan Law Studies* 129–243.

Radzyner, A., "'The Essential Thing is not Studying, but Deed': *Get* Procedures after Tort Claims and the Publications Policy of Rabbinical Courts Judgments", (2015) 45 *Mishpatim – Hebrew University Law Journal* 5–84.

Rosen-Zvi, A., "Forum Shopping between Religious and Secular Courts (and Its Impact on the Legal System)", (1989) 9 *Tel Aviv U. Stud. L.* 347–396.

Sapir, G. and D. Statman, "Religious Marriage in a Liberal State", (2009) 30 *Cardozo Law Review*, 2855–2880.

Shifman, P., "Civil Family Laws Gone Public: On President Barak's Contribution to Family Law" in E. Zamir et al (eds.), *Barak's Festschrift* (Jerusalem, 6The Faculty of Law, Hebrew University Press, 2009)(Heb.).

Shmueli, B., "Commodifying Personal Rights and Trading the Right to Divorce: Damages for Refusal to Divorce and Equalizing the Women's Power to Bargain", (2015) 22 *UCLA Women's L.J.*, 39–105.

Westreich, A., "Accommodating Religious Law with a Civil Legal System: Lessons from the Jewish Law Experience in Financial Family Matters", (2018) 33 *Journal of Law and Religion* 481–503.

Westreich, A., *Assisted Reproduction in Israel: Law, Religion, and Culture* (Leiden, Brill Publication 2018), at 16–19; 39–43.

Westreich, A., "Rhetoric and Substance 'Came Down Wrapped Together'? On Civil Marriage in Israel Following the Noahide Decision", (2013–2014) 6–7 *Family in Law Review* 543–578 (Heb.).

Westreich, A., “The Right to Divorce in Jewish Law: Between Politics and Ideology”, (2010) 1 *International Journal of the Jurisprudence of the Family* 177–196.
Westreich, A., “Three Crossroads in the Relationships between Rabbinical Court and Civil Court: Child Support, Property Distribution and the Litigations Arrangement Law”, (2022) 52 *Mishpatim – Hebrew University Law Journal* 217–274.
Westreich, A. and A. Radzyner, “Revolutionism and Conservatism in the Rulings of the Israeli Rabbinical Courts: Divorce Enforcement on the Grounds of ‘*Ma’is ‘Alai*’ (He Is Repulsive to Me)”, (2020) 42 *Tel Aviv University Law Review* 639–686 (Heb.).
Westreich, A. and P. Shifman, *A Civil Legal Framework for Marriage and Divorce in Israel* position paper, R. Gavison (ed.), trans. Kfir Levy (Jerusalem, Mezila Center 2013).
Westreich, A. and A. Stav, “Conversion of Children Born through Non-Jewish Egg Donation or Surrogacy”, (2021) 41 *Techumin* 167–178 (Heb.).
Westreich, E. and A. Westreich, “Chief Rabbinate Regulations on Economic Issues at the End of the Mandate Period”, (2022) 5 *Law, Society & Culture: Law, Economy, and Institutions in Israel* 437–487 (Heb.).
Women’s Equal Rights Law, 5711–1951.

CHAPTER 7

Legal Pluralism, Religious Identity and Citizenship in the State of Israel: The Case of Non-Orthodox Jews

Anna Parrilli

1 Introduction

It is well-known that Israel's stances on religion and religious communities have been shaped by two features, namely the foundation of the State as the *national home* of Jewish people[1] and the adoption of the *millet* system of personal laws.[2]

As far as the attitude of the State towards religion is concerned, Israel exhibits no separation between the State and religion. Religious institutions and religious courts are integrated in the State system. Furthermore, the Declaration of Independence (1948) defines Israel as a "Jewish and Democratic" State, meaning that both democracy and the Jewish values are considered as fundamental characters of the State and part of its normative vision. The Jewishness of the State creates a strong connection between Israel and the Jewish cultural and legal tradition.[3]

This close link has both symbolic and practical implications. Firstly, Jewish culture and symbols dominate the public sphere. Secondly and most importantly, religious affiliation acquires legal significance in the determination of rights and obligations of Israeli citizens. The latter implication encompasses both personal status matters, and several public-law issues, such as immigration law, citizenship rights, access to public services and facilities, participation in State religious institutions.

1 The Balfour Declaration, dated 2 November 1947, is a letter sent by the former UK's Interior Minister Balfour to the leader of the British Jews, Lord Rothschild, to support the foundation of a Jewish State in Palestine. The Declaration was then incorporated into the British Mandate in Palestine. See S. Navot, *The Constitution of Israel. A Contextual Analysis* (Oxford and Portland, Hart Publishing, 2014), at 2.

2 Y. Sezgin, "The Israeli Millet System: Examining Legal Pluralism through Lenses of Nation-Building and Human Rights", (2010) 43(3) *Israel Law Review* 631–654.

3 I. Englard, *Religious Law in the Israel Legal System* (Jerusalem, Hebrew University of Jerusalem, 1975).

 | DOI:10.1163/9789004446816_009

When it comes to the relationship between the State and religious confessions, in the aftermath of Israel's foundation (1948), the government kept in place the Ottoman *millet* structure of personal laws. Under this system, fourteen religious communities (Jews, Muslims, ten Christian denominations, Druze and Bahai) are currently granted exclusive jurisdiction on marriage and divorce, and parallel jurisdiction over other matters of personal status.[4]

At the same time, a prominent position among State institutions is granted to the Chief Rabbinate of Israel (hereinafter, the Rabbinate), which is the supreme religious authority for Judaism in Israel and a public law institution with both religious and administrative tasks.[5] For historical and political reasons, the Orthodox stream of Judaism holds the control of the Rabbinate, Jewish religious courts, and local religious councils.

This contribution investigates the implications of both the partial establishment of Orthodox Judaism within State religious institutions and the adoption of the *millet* structure on the individual and collective rights of religious minorities. The topic has been extensively debated by legal scholars with regard to the legal status of non-Jews, especially Palestinian-Arabs.[6] The focus of this contribution lies instead on the legal status of non-Orthodox Jews within the Jewish majoritarian community.

The difficulties encountered by non-Orthodox Jews in exercising some constitutionally protected rights, such as freedom of religion (and *from* religion), equality before the law, the right to marry and have a family life, as well as identity rights are indeed paradigmatic of the structural shortcomings of the Israeli model of management of religious diversity.

The chapter proceeds as follows: its first section examines the attitude of the State towards religion and the State's relationship with religious denominations. Section two portrays the interplay of different legal sources and the implementation of the law, including the plurality of civil and religious courts dealing with personal status. Against this background, the third section addresses the legal position of non-Orthodox Jews in Israel, discussing three significant and interrelated matters: immigration and the right to immediate citizenship under the Law of Return; family law (marriage and divorce); and conversion to Judaism. The last section outlines the phenomenon of deep legal

---

4 Y. Sezgin, "The Israeli Millet System" *supra*.

5 D. Sinclair, "Jewish Law in the State of Israel" in N. S. Hecht *et al.* (eds.), *An Introduction to the History and the Sources of Jewish Law* (Oxford, Oxford University Press, 1996), at 399.

6 See, among others, the recent work by M. Karayanni, *A Multicultural Entrapment. Religion and State Among the Palestinian-Arabs in Israel* (Cambridge, Cambridge University Press, 2020).

pluralism as an example of the reaction of religious groups against the Israeli system for governing religious diversity.

This chapter maintains that Israel's attitude towards the majority religion (Judaism) and the *millet* system are based on a communitarian paradigm which constructs citizenship along ethno-religious lines. In doing so, it differentiates among ethno-religious communities, which are regarded as homogenous entities. However, this "oversimplified archetype of homogeneous groups"[7] hardly mirrors reality. Most importantly, it poses serious challenges to both non-Jewish minorities living in the country, as well as to non-Orthodox Jewish people in their daily life.

2 Law and Religion in the State of Israel

Since its foundation in 1948, the "Jewish and Democratic" nature of Israel has deeply been embedded in the constitutional and legislative structure of the State. The dual character of the State is explicitly mentioned in the Declaration of the Establishment of the State of Israel (1948) (hereinafter: The Declaration). The Declaration does not enjoy constitutional status, whereas the principles contained in it were included into the two Basic Laws on human rights;[8] therefore, they are given preferred constitutional value.[9] Furthermore, the Basic Law: the Knesset (1992) prohibits participation in elections for lists and candidates which negate the existence of Israel as "Jewish and Democratic".[10] Recently, the Jewish character of the State has been further strengthened by the provisions contained in the Basic Law: Israel as the Nation State of the Jewish People (hereinafter: 2018 Basic Law), approved by the Knesset on July, 2018. Most notably, the 2018 Basic Law affirms the exclusive right to self-determination of Jewish people; thus, widening the divide between the Jewish nation and other ethno-religious communities in Israel. The Supreme Court jurisprudence complements this constitutional framework in as much as it

7 F. Palermo, "Current and Future Challenges for International Minority Protection" in *European Yearbook of Minority Issues, vol. 10, 2011* (Leiden-Boston, Brill, 2013), at 31–32.

8 Art. 1, Basic Law: Human Dignity and Liberty, passed by the Knesset on 17 March 1992; art. 2, Basic Law: Freedom of Occupation (1994) passed by the Knesset on the 9 March 1994, which repeals and replaces the Basic Law: Freedom of Occupation enacted in 1992.

9 See, among others, A. Maoz, "The Application of Religious Law in a Multi-religion Nation State: The Israeli Model" in R. Bottoni *et al.* (eds.), *Religious Rules, State Law, and Normative Pluralism. A comparative Overview* (New York, Springer, 2016), at 213.

10 Section 7, *Basic Law: The Knesset* passed by the *Knesset* on 12 February 1958.

recognizes the Jewish character of the State to be a "fundamental constitutional fact" alongside the democratic one.[11]

The concept of "Jewish State" has been construed in two ways: national and religious. Dating back to the secular Zionists ideology,[12] the first view, interprets the term "Jewish" as referring to the common cultural and historical heritage of the Jewish people. Contrariwise, the religious view maintains that the national and religious component of Judaism cannot be separated; being a Jewish State, Israel must pursue Jewish religious objectives.[13] The chapter does not intend to enter this considerable debate. Suffice it to remember that, when discussing Israel's approach to religious pluralism, the "unique connection between nation and religion in Judaism"[14] must be taken into consideration. The reason is twofold: firstly, the connection stems from the incorporation of Jewish law in the Israeli legal system;[15] secondly, the State communitarian approach towards religious diversity has led, as already noted, to the partial establishment of Orthodox Judaism in State law and institutions.

When it comes to considering the place of Jewish tradition within the constitutional context, Israel is not a "*medinat halakha* (a State based on Jewish law)".[16] Nevertheless, Jewish law occupies a prominent role in the Israeli legal system at the level of general principle and in specific legislations. Religious laws are not enforced in Israeli civilian courts, except for some personal status matters.[17] The Foundations of Law Act (1980) grants Jewish tradition official

---

11 See *Electoral Appeal, 1/65 Yeredor v. Chairman of the Central Election Committee for the Sixth Knesset*, PD, 19(3), at 20 (J. Agranat).

12 See, among others, C. Gans, "Jewish and Democratic: Three Zionism and post-Zionism" in G. Sapir *et al* (eds.), *Israeli Constitutional Law in the Making* (Oxford and Portland, Hart Publishing, 2013), 473–486.

13 See, for instance, Rabbi YI Herzog's unfinished work, *A Constitution for Israel According to Tora* (Jerusalem, Mosad HaRav Kook, 1989) (in Hebrew). On Herzog's constitutional project see A. Kaye, *The Invention of Jewish Theocracy. The Struggle for legal authority in modern Israel* (New York, Oxford University Press, 2020), at72–98.

14 G. Sapir, *The Israeli Constitution: From evolution to revolution* (New York, Oxford University Press, 2018), at 173.

15 S. Baldin, "La rilevanza del diritto ebraico nello Stato d'Israele" in S. Baldin (ed.), *Diritti tradizionali e religiosi in alcuni ordinamenti contemporanei* (Trieste, EUT, 2005), at 66.

16 R. Hirschl, *Constitutional Theocracy*, (MA – London, England, Harvard University Press, 2010), at 140–141.

17 Such as the role of religious law in Israeli legal system has been addressed in several Supreme Court's decisions. In *Mitral*, Justice Orr clarifies that "It is a basic principle in Israel that civilian and citizens enjoy freedom of religion and freedom from religion. Religious edicts and principles that draw on religion are not laws in Israel" (HCJ 3872/93 *Mitral v. The Prime Minister and the Religious Affairs Minister*, ver. 47(5), 54 [1997], para. 485 and para. 506). However, one can argue, religious principles are not laws in Israel

status as a source of interpretation.[18] Talmudic and rabbinical principles and norms are indeed part of this tradition, and they are frequently quoted in the Supreme Court's rulings. Furthermore, Jewish norms and practices are incorporated into primary legislation.[19] Some telling examples are the law pertaining public transport; the closing of commercial activities during *shabbat*; the issuance of *kashrut* certificate;[20] the legal arrangements allowing Jewish farmers and businesses to bypass *schmita* rule (the prohibition to cultivate the soil every seventh year).[21]

With regard to the attitude of the State towards religion, there is no established religion in Israel.[22] Institutions and courts of the recognized religious communities are integrated into the State legal system, and they enjoy a

---

as long as they are not incorporated into the Israeli legal system, whether by means of primary legislation or jurisprudence.

18 Art. 1 of the Act affirms that, when a court facing with a legal question "finds no answer to it in statute law or case-law or by analogy, it shall decide it in the light of the principles of freedom, justice, equity and peace of *Israel's heritage*". See Foundations of Law, 5740, 1980 passed by the *Knesset* on 23 July 1980, at 163. English translation in *Laws of the State of Israel: Authorized translation from the Hebrew* (Israel, Government Printer, (1948–1989)), at 181.

19 See R. Hirschl, *Comparative Matters: The renaissance of Comparative Constitutional Law*, (Oxford, Oxford University Press, 2014), at 42–67.

20 Other religiously oriented acts regulating dietary matters are the 1964 Ban on Growing Pig Law, applying to Jews and Muslim; and the Kosher meet Import Law 1994.

21 Art. 3 of the Israel Lands Law (5720–1960) passed by the *Knesset* on the 25 July 1960.

22 In the Established Church States, the constitutional and legal frameworks recognize a particular religion and Church the status of official or national religion of the State. In these Countries, the Church is institutionalized, and it is an organ of the State. In this respect, the Anglican Church constitutes a paradigmatic example. In Sweden, the Evangelical Lutheran Church under public law is ensured by art. 76 of the Constitution, while the Orthodox Church is regulated by the Orthodox Church Act (521/1969) and the supplementary Statute (179/1970) Similarly, art. 4 of the Danish Constitution grants the Evangelical Lutheran Church the status of established church. Art. 3 of the Greek Constitution accords the Eastern Orthodox Church of Christ the status of "prevailing religion". State religion model applies in the absence of churches and churches hierarchy. In Muslim majority countries, Islam is recognized as the official religions of the State by art. 2 of the Constitutions of Egypt, Afghanistan, Iran, Maldives, Pakistan, Somalia. When it comes to Israel, there is no constitutional or legal provision which grants Judaism the status of State established religion. Nevertheless, Jewish tradition and institutions are *de facto* given a prominent role among State institutions by virtue of the "Jewish and Democratic" character of the State. On different model of State-religion relationship, see M. Mancini and M. Rosenfeld, "Unveiling the limits of Tolerance: Comparing the Treatment of Majority and Minority Symbols in the Public Sphere", (2010) 309 *Benjamin N. Cardozo School of Law Working Paper* 3–4; B. Neuberger, "Religion and State in Europe and Israel", (1999) 6(2) *Israel Affairs* 65–84.

"semi-national status".[23] They are financed by the State treasury and their employees are public servants.[24]

With respect to the Jewish community, the Rabbinate acts as a statutory State body which is comprised of a rabbinical council and two Chief Rabbis belonging to the Ashkenazi and Sephardi Jews respectively.[25] The Rabbinate has a say over the authorization of *dayanim* (Jewish religious judges). Moreover, it enjoys the monopoly over the supply of public religious services, such as the issuing of *kashrut* and conversion certificates, and licensing marriages and divorces among Jews.[26]

As abovementioned, Jewish religious institutions are mostly controlled by Orthodox Judaism, which has long been the sole branch of Judaism recognized by the State.[27] This privileged status displays several consequences in terms of citizenship rights and duties. For instance, in Israel, military service is mandatory for Jewish (men and women), as well as Druze and Circassian (only men) over the age 18. However, students enrolled in full-time Orthodox *yeshivot* (Jewish schools of Talmudic learning) are granted deferral to mandatory defense service until the termination of their studies.[28]

---

23 S. Navot, *The Constitution of Israel a contextual analysis* (Oxford-Portland, Hart Publishing, 2014), at 74.

24 See G. Sapir and D. Statman, *State and Religion in Israel. A philosophical-Legal Inquiry* (New York, Cambridge University Press, 2019), at 59. See, further, H. Lifhshitz and G. Sapir, "Jewish Religious Services Law – A proposed Framework for Privatization Reform", (2006) 23 *Bar-Ilan Law Studies* 117–194 (in Hebrew).

25 The Chief Rabbinate of Israel Law, 35, L.S.I, 97, 1980 rules the functions, composition and the election process of the Rabbinical council and the Chief Rabbis. The Law on Religious Public Service (consolidated version) (5731–1971) establishes the terms of work of city rabbis under the supervision of the Rabbinate.

26 See Kashrut (Prohibition of Deceit) Law, 37 L.S.I. 147, 1982–83; Rabbinical Courts' Jurisdiction Law (Marriage and Divorce) (5713–1953).

27 R. Hirschl, "Constitutional theocracy" *supra*, at 141.

28 In 1992, the Supreme Court held the deferral from defense service lacked legislative grounds (HCJ, *Rubinstein v. Minister of Defense*, 525 PD HC 3267/97 [1998]. In 2002, The Deferment of Military Draft for Yeshiva Students Whose Occupation Is the Study of Torah Law (5762–2002) (Tal Law) was passed by the *Knesset*. In 2006, the Court was called to review the constitutionality of the law at hand. Since the Tal Law included the provision that it would expire within five years of the publication, the Court decided to postpone the judgment to evaluate its effects on military service participation. Eventually, in 2012, the Court found the Tal Law unconstitutional on the ground that it infringes Israeli citizens' right to equal treatment before the law (HCJ *6427/02 Movement for Quality of Government v. Knesset*, 54; HCJ *6298/07 Ressler v. Knesset*, 63).

The partial establishment of Orthodox Judaism has served, since the foundation of the State, as a tool of identity and nation-building.[29] The primary objective was to create the "Israeli Jew" out of the newcomers of the Diaspora.[30] To this end, Israeli immigration law and the Supreme Court jurisprudence adopted a secular, inclusive, definition of "Jew" to favor Jewish immigration. As explained later on in this chapter, the said definition only partially fits the religious criteria (matrilineal descent and conversion to Judaism) followed by Rabbinical institutions and courts to determine Jewish status for the purposes of marriage and divorce law, as well as for granting access to public religious services provided by the Rabbinate and the Ministry of Religious Services.[31]

3 State Control and Community Identity: the Israeli *Millet* System

Israel's *millet* grants recognized religious communities a large degree of autonomy in matters of personal status, which fall under the exclusive or concurring jurisdiction of religious courts.[32]

This system of personal laws dates back to the Ottoman ruling period. Established in 1452 by Mehmet II, the *millet* was based on the Islamic legal tradition of *dhimma*, sanctioned by the *qur'an* (9: 1–3), and the *hadith* tradition.[33]

29 See, among others, Y. Sezgin, "Human Rights under State-enforced Religious Family Laws" in Y. Sezgin, *Human Rights under State – enforced Religious Family Laws in Israel, Egypt and India* (New York, Cambridge University Press, 2013), at 93.

30 M. Masri, *The Dynamics of Exclusionary constitutionalism. Israel as a Jewish and Democratic State* (Oxford-Portland, Hart Publishing, 2017), at 76–125. The term "Diaspora" derives from a Greek word meaning 'dispersion'. The word has been used to describe different periods in the Jewish history. It characterized the status of Jews during the Babylonian captivity in the sixth century B.C, as well as the Jewish community that lived in Alexandria before the rise of Christianity. More recently, the word "Diaspora" has been referred to Jewish communities which flourished outside Palestine after the destruction of the Jerusalem temple in 70 A.D. The mass exodus of Jews from Palestine led to the creation of several "dispersed" Jewish communities all over the globe. See, A. Ages, *The Diaspora Dimension* (Dordrecht, Springer, 1973).

31 Religious services provided by State to the Jewish population of Israel include, for instance, the supervision of *kosher* certificate and regulation, burial and cemeterial services, marriage ceremonies and registration, the development of the relationships with Jewish communities all over the world.

32 S. Navot, *The Constitution of Israel a contextual analysis* (Oxford-Portland, Hart Publishing, 2014).

33 The *hadith* tradition records the sayings and deeds of Prophet Muhammad, and it constitutes one of the primary sourcers of Islamic law. These religious legal sources regulated the personal and public affairs of those religious minorities living under the Ottoman rulers. See A. Osman, "The Qur'an and the Hadith as sources of Islamic law" in. K. Abou

The system was preserved under the British mandatory regime in Palestine.[34] Until its abolitions in the nineteenth century, the *millet* granted space for self-government and a certain degree of legal autonomy to Greeks (*rum milleti*), Jews (*yahudi milleti*) and the Armenians (*ermeni milleti*), while Muslims were considered as part of a single tradition and nation (*umma islamiyya*).[35]

When the State of Israel was founded in 1948, the first government decided to maintain a *millet*-like structure with some minor modifications, owing to the fact that Jews became the majoritarian religious community.[36]

The reasons behind the government's decision have been broadly discussed by the literature.[37] The majority of authors suggests that, initially, Israeli authorities preferred to avoid harsh confrontations on religious matters.[38] Hence, religious courts were left jurisdiction over issues of personal status (marriage, divorce, and some ancillary issues) and they were incorporated into the State institutional structure. In doing so, potentially conflicting legal systems were kept in force but partially reconducted under State control.

However, the implementation of the *millet* system was also aimed at "the preservation and homogenization of Israeli-Jewish identity; and the differentiation of non-Jewish identities".[39] In other words, the *millet* manages diversity in society by drawing the communities along ethno-religious lines, while, at the same time, favoring the creation of a common national identity among Israeli Jews.

In this respect, it is important to remember that Israel was primarily conceived as a country of Jewish immigration. As declared in section five of the

---

El Fadl *et al.* (eds.), *Routledge Handbook of Islamic Law* (Abingdon, Routledge Handbooks Online, 2019); M. Ayoub, "Dhimmah in Qur'an and Hadith [with Commentary]", (1983) 5(2) *Arab Studies Quarterly* 172–191.

34 Law and Administration Ordinance 5708–1948, May 19, 1948.

35 See K. Hashemi, *Religious Legal Traditions, International Human Rights Law and Muslim States* (Leiden – Boston, Martinus Nijhoff Publishers, 2008), at 133.

36 Law and Administration Ordinance, 1948, 1 LSI 9 (1948). See E. Don-Yehiya, "The resolution of religious conflicts in Israel" in Stuart A. Cohen and E. Don-Yehiya (eds.), *Conflict and Consensus in Jewish Political Life* (Ramat Gan, Bar-Ilan University Press, 1986), at 203–218; I. Englard, "Religious Law in the Israel Legal System" *supra*, at 13; A. Rubinstein, "Law and Religion in Israel", (1967) 380 *Israel Law Review* 384–99.

37 See, among others, R. Harris, *Historical opportunities and absent-minded Omissions: on the incorporation of Jewish Law*, in *Nascent Israeli Law* in M. Bar-On and Z. Zameret (eds.), *Both sides of the Bridge: Church and State in Early Israel* (in Hebrew) cited in Y. Sezgin, "The Israeli Millet System" *supra*, at 638.

38 See D.M. Sassoon, "The Israel Legal System", (1968) 16(6) *The American Journal of Comparative Law* 405–415.

39 Y. Sezgin, "How to integrate Universal Human Rights into Customary and Religious Legal Systems", (2010) 60 *Journal of Legal Pluralism*, at 5.

Basic Law: Israel as the Nation State of the Jewish People (2018): "the State shall be open for Jewish immigration, and for the Ingathering of the Exiles". Similarly, the 1948 Declaration calls the Jewish Diaspora "to rally round the Jews of Eretz-Israel in the tasks of immigration and upbuilding" of the State.

Jews coming to Israel from all over the world constitute a highly differentiated group, as they have been born and educated in different countries of origins.[40] Hence, State authorities aim at building a common Israeli Jewish identity out of the plurality of identities of Jewish immigrants.

To this aim, inter-religious marriages cannot be celebrated (and other forms of inter-denominational unions are discouraged), and Jewish symbols and rituals dominate the public sphere. Moreover, the sole Orthodox interpretation of Jewish law is recognized, incorporated into the general legal system, and applied by religious courts to *all* Jews, regardless of the streams of Judaism they belong to.[41]

At the same time, the Palestinian Order in Council 1022–194 gave non-Jewish religious communities recognized by the State a large degree of jurisdictional autonomy over personal status issues, drawing clear ethno-religious boundaries between Jews and non-Jews.[42]

Not only Jewish tribunals (*batei din*), but also *shari'a* courts maintain exclusive jurisdiction over Muslim marriages and divorces, while on matters of inheritance both Islamic and Israeli laws apply. All other personal status issues fall under the exclusive competence of the *Knesset*.[43] Similarly, the Druze,

40 A walk through the city of Jerusalem can be quite revealing of the persisting connection between Israeli Jews and their countries of origins (or those of their ancestors). For instance, two of the most prominent neighborhoods get their name from the communities who came from Europe: the German Colony and the French Hill. Latin American, Italian, Eastern-European and Northern American Jews also tend to live close to one another. Moreover, Jews coming from different countries understands the meaning and practice of "being Jews" according to their cultural specificities.

41 I. Englard, "Religious Law in the Israel Legal System" *supra*, at 13 and 49–56; S. Baldin, "La rilevanza del diritto ebraico nello Stato di Israele" *supra*.

42 In addition to the Jewish and Sunni Muslim communities, the second schedule of the Palestine Order in Council (1922) recognizes the following Christian religious groups: the Latin Catholic Community, the Eastern Orthodox Community, the Gregorian Armenian Community, the Catholic Armenian Community, the Catholic Syrian Community, the Chaldean Community, the Maronite Community, the Orthodox Syrian Community, and the Greek Catholic Mellcite Community. Moreover, the Druze (1957) and the Bahai (1971) communities are recognized.

43 Originally, Muslim tribunals were granted exclusive jurisdiction on all personal status issues under art. 52 of the Palestine Order in Council 1022–1947. Artt. 53–54 of the said Order granted Rabbinical and Christian courts' exclusive jurisdiction over marriage, divorce, alimony, and confirmation of wills only. Following the enactment of the

Bahai and Christians tribunals are assigned exclusive jurisdiction on marriages and divorces between members of their respective communities, while ancillary issues – such as child's custody, adoption, and inheritance – may be conducted under religious law upon the litigating parties' consent.[44]

In 1995, the picture showing the plurality of courts and sources of law applicable to the personal status has been further complicated by the establishment of the Family Courts. These are civil tribunals with parallel jurisdiction to the religious courts on family law and related issues (with the sole exception of marriage and divorce).[45]

Therefore, in Israel, matters over which religious tribunals have exclusive competence are decided under the communities' religious law, while others are subject to both secular and religious law. However, since religious laws and institutions are incorporated into the Israeli legal and institutional system, religious and secular law frequently overlap.

This is especially true with regard to Family Courts. The civil judges sitting in these courts follow a civil code of procedure and a civil code of evidence, mainly oriented to ensure non-discrimination between men and women during the proceedings. At the same time, however, they are supposed to apply the religious law of the applicants on family, inheritance, and personal status matters.[46] For instance, if litigants are Jews, the judge will decide the case according to Jewish law; if they are Muslims, the judge will apply Islamic law.

Although Family Courts' judges and lawyers are highly educated and trained in family law, several difficulties arise during the proceedings. Firstly,

---

Succession Law 5725–1965, Muslim courts' jurisdiction on matters of inheritance was downgraded from exclusive to concurrent. The same law grants secular courts priority over Muslim religious courts in matters of inheritance: the transfer of jurisdiction from the family court to Muslim tribunals is subjected to a written agreement within all the parties involved (art. 151(a)). Moreover, the Family Court Law of 2001, further reduced Muslim, and Christian courts' powers by limiting their exclusive jurisdiction to marriage, divorce and *waqf*. As a result of the legislative interventions by the *Knesset*, at present, Muslim and Christian courts' jurisdiction equals that of Jewish courts. See I. Shahar, *Legal Pluralism in the Holy City: Competing Courts, Forum Shopping and Institutional Dynamics in Jerusalem* (London – New York, Routledge, 2016), at 29–40.

44 The Rabbinate controls Jewish courts, while Muslim and Druze Court are placed under the supervision of the Ministry of Justice. Christian tribunals' organization differs from that of other religious courts as they are autonomous institutions, which are granted extra-territorial personal jurisdictions. See, among others, Y. Sezgin, "The Israeli Millet System" *supra*.

45 Family Court Law 5751–1995.

46 People not-belonging to recognized religious communities and same-sex couples may also litigate before a family court.

as noted by Justice Silberg, "Jewish law applied by a civil court is different from a Jewish law applied by religious court"[47] because the same norms and principles are likely to be subject to different interpretations by religious and secular judges.[48] The same applies to the laws of the other religious communities. Secondly, family judges are mainly Jews who are called to interpret and implement unfamiliar normative system, such as Canon Law and Muslim law. To this aim, they heavily rely on external experts and translators.[49] Finally, when deciding a controversy according to religious law, the judges' "philosophy of life, [and] faith"[50] shall not be overlooked as their ruling may be nuanced by their personal ideology and background. This is particularly true with regard to sensitive matters, such as child custody, adoption, paternity/maternity.

The system of personal laws also raises other complex issues. With regard to Jewish citizens and permanent residents, the *Rabbinical Courts' Jurisdiction Law (Marriage and Divorce)*, 1953, grants Jewish religious tribunal exclusive and unique jurisdiction over marriages and dissolution of marriages; concurrent jurisdiction on other ancillary issues, such as alimony.[51]

On matters of concurring jurisdiction, the principle of "one judge for one family applies";[52] therefore, the plaintiff who chooses the courthouse

47 I. Englard, "Religious Law in the Israel Legal System" *supra*, at 104.

48 *Ibid.*, at 103–135.

49 It is worth notice that the proceedings before the Family Courts are in Hebrew. Simultaneous translation is provided.

50 C.A *238/55 Cohen, Buslik v.* A.G., PD 4, 19 (English translation in 2 SJSC 239, 254).

51 See *HCJ 8638/03, Amir v. Great Rabbinical Court* [2006]. Jewish tribunal act in their capacity of State courts. There are twelve Regional Rabbinical courts placed under the supervision of the Ministry of Religious Services. The President of the Great Rabbinical Court is at the head of the rabbinical court system, and he serves as chief rabbi of Israel. The Great Court in Jerusalem acts as an appellate court. The institution of the appellate court is alien to the Talmudic legal culture, which according to the majority of the literature does not recognize the doctrine of *res judicata*. See for instance the J. Aganat and J. Cohen concurring opinion in CA *54/65 Mekitan v. Mekitan*, 19, PD 2 at 666 and at 657; CA 395/60 *Amrani v. Attorney General*, 15 PD 594, 602, (J. Berenson); *Haham v. Haham*, 20 PD 2 199, 207–208.

52 Family Court Law 5157–1995. The "one family-one judge" model, which is likely to be inspired by the US experience of Family Courts, is designed to allow family issues to be litigated entirely before a highly specialized and trained judge, assisted by a team of qualified experts. Family Courts are aimed at producing tailored solution for families matters in a more efficient and compassionate way. However, compared to the US, Israeli family judges exercise broader discretion in term of both rules of evidence and substantive law, which leads to a degree of legal uncertainty. For the United States see, among others, B.A. Babb, "Reevaluating where we stand: A Comprehensive survey of America Family Justice System", (2008) 46(2) *Family Court Review* 230–257. In Israel, the family judge's task is

determines: 1) whether the civil or religious jurisdiction solves the controversy; 2) and which law is to be applied.[53]

A particularly negative consequence of this mechanism is the "jurisdiction race" between the spouses to file the case in the civil or a religious court. In brief, the court (civil or religious) in which the first claim is made is the court which will decide the case. Usually, women prefer to resort to Family Courts, which are perceived as less patriarchal, whereas the men defendants tend to litigate before religious courts. In addition, since State official response to reduce discrimination against women – particularly in matters of divorce – rarely finds application in religious courts,[54] Israeli women developed several "unofficial" mechanisms to turn religious norms at their favor.[55]

In this respect, another widespread phenomenon in Israeli legal system is "forum shopping", namely "[t]he practice of choosing the most favorable jurisdiction or court in which a claim may be heard".[56] This practice is commonplace among Jews, Muslims (since 2011)[57] and, to a lesser extent, Christians.[58] Women tend to go forum shopping between religious courts and Family Courts with regard to matters of concurring jurisdiction. The main reason lies behind the will to bypass the patriarchal religious codes applied by religious tribunals, which often lead to unsatisfactory decisions for women, by implicating their rights protected under both Israeli and international law.[59]

---

made more complicated by the millet system and the application of different religious laws in a civil court.

53 See K.C. Yefet, "Israeli family law as civil-religious hybrid: a cautionary tale of fatal attraction", (2016) 1505 *University of Illinois Law Review* 1528–1533.

54 Both Israeli law and Rabbinical law provide for sanctions against the husband who refuses to give a get and it grants disciplinary power to rabbinical courts that decide on divorce. See Y. Kaplan, "Enforcement of Divorce Judgments in Jewish Courts in Israel: The Interaction between Religious and Constitutional Law", (2012) 4 *Middle East Law and Governance* 1–68.

55 On the topic see P. Fournier, "Halacha, The Jewish State and the Canadian Agunah: Comparative Law at the intersection of Religious and Secular Orders", (2013) 44(65) *The Journal of Legal Pluralism and Unofficial Law* 165–204.

56 B.A. Garner (ed.), *Black's Law Dictionary* (Chicago, St. Paul, MN – Thompson Reuters, 2001).

57 Until 2001, forum shopping was an option for Jews and Christians only. Muslims, instead, were obliged to appeal to shari'a courts for personal status issues falling under religious courts' domain. Following a long public campaign promoted by several women's rights organizations, the Knesset eventually amended the Family Courts Law 5755–1995, allowing Muslims to resort to Family Courts in all personal status matters, except for marriage and divorce. See. I. Shahar, "Legal Pluralism in the Holy City" *supra*, at 151.

58 See, for instance, the description of the West Jerusalem Court's functioning and case law provided by the legal anthropologist I. Shahar, "Legal Pluralism in the Holy City", *supra.*

59 In this respect, three brief observations are worth making. As mentioned above, Family Courts follow a civil code of procedure and a civil code of evidence to avoid gender-based

In this respect, it must be remembered that religious courts are part of the State court system; thus, their activities are supervised by the Israeli Supreme Court, in its capacity of High Court of Justice, and they shall comply with Israel legislative and constitutional provisions, in particular the Basic Law: Human Dignity and Liberty.[60] The Supreme Court further intercedes when religious tribunals have acted *ultra vires* – i.e. beyond their legal authority – or in case of failure of natural justice. Finally, religious courts must adhere to the legal principles governing every public institution, in particular the legality principles.[61]

As already mentioned, while establishing legal pluralism among the fourteen recognized religious communities, the *millet*-like system also serves the purpose of the preservation of the Jewish identity.[62] To this aim, only Orthodox *dayanim* (judges) sit into Rabbinical Courts.[63] These judges adhere to the Orthodox interpretation of Judaism, replacing "the inherent plurality of Jewish

---

discrimination during the proceedings. However, where permitted by Israeli law, substantive law applied by Family Courts is religious law. Therefore, the possible discriminatory outcomes for women, originating from the application of patriarchal religious rules, are only partially mitigated by courts' obligation to comply with constitutional and statutory law on human rights, or Israel's obligations under international law (for instance, the Basic Law on Human Dignity and Liberty (1992), the Equal Rights for Women Law (1951) and the Convention on the Elimination of all forms of Discrimination against women (1979)). Indeed, Family Courts are more likely to comply Israeli law then religious courts, which often does not fell bound by State law. On the other hand, in recent times, it was not uncommon for religious courts to interpret religious laws in a more 'gender-neutral' way. This is especially true with regard to Muslim courts. On this topic, see A. Natour, *Promoting Women's Rights in Islamic Law in a Non Muslim State – Israel* (Lanham – Maryland, Lexington Books, 2021). Finally, State's official response to reduce discrimination against women, particularly in matters of divorce, does not always find application in religious courts. Consequently, as noted above, Israeli women – especially Jewish women – developed "unofficial" mechanisms to turn religious norms at their favor. See further P. Fournier, "Halacha" *supra*.

60 See, for instance, HC *3914/92, Lev v. Tel Aviv Regional Rabbinical Court* [1994] PD (2) 502–505; HC *6751/04, Sabag v. The High Rabbinical Court of Appeal* [2004] PD 59 (2) 834.

61 As repeatedly pointed out by the Supreme Court, the *Knesset* established religious tribunals by law. "[T]heir orders become the voice of the State and it is the State that enforce them" (Justice Amir in HCJ *3269/95 Yosef Katz v. The Jerusalem Regional Rabbinical Court*, PD 50(4) 590, 602). Therefore, at least in principles, their decisions must not contravene Israeli (secular) law, nor State's obligations under international law.

62 Y. Sezgin, 'How to integrate Universal Human Rights" *supra*, at 5.

63 *Dayanim* are appointed by the President of the State upon the recommendation of a committee composed by both religious and government representatives (the Sephardi and Ashkenazi chief rabbis, two judges from the Rabbinical Court of Appeals, the Minister of Justice and another government minister, two representatives of the Knesset and two members of the Israel Bar association). See Religious judges (Dayanim) Law (Ordination and its arrangements) 1955, KT 537, 1273.

law with a uniform legal structure".[64] Limiting the scope of interpretation to Orthodox Jewish law contributes to the creation of a single Jewish-Israeli community, sharing the same characteristics, values and rules.[65]

Since, in Israel, religious affiliation – for the purpose of personal status – is not the result of a voluntary choice but it is primarily determined by the State, once the Rabbinical Courts Jurisdiction Law (1953) subjected *all* Jews to State-run religious courts, including non-conformist groups (Reformist, Conservative, Karaites, Samaritans etc.),[66] the State shall also take the responsibility to ascertain "who are Jews?".

The extensive case law of the Supreme Court addressing, mostly indirectly, this fundamental question, and the parliamentary debate around the definition of "Jew" reveals the contradictions underling Israeli forms of State as "Jewish and Democratic", as well as the shortcomings of the *millet* system.

As highlighted in the next section, it occurred that the criteria adopted by the State to ascertain a persons' belonging to the Jewish community partially diverge from the religious criteria followed by Rabbinical Courts. This discrepancy raises serious questions regarding the legal status and rights of non-Orthodox Jewish minorities, as well as non-religious people in Israel.

4 Non-Orthodox Jewish Minorities in the Jewish and Democratic State

4.1 *The Law of Return and the Definition of "Jew"*

The Law of Return (hereinafter: LR) (1950)[67] constitutes "one of the clearest reflections of the State of Israel as a Jewish State".[68] As is known, according to the present law and the Nationality Law (1952),[69] Jewish immigrants in Israel are immediately entitled to right to full citizenship, as well as other benefits which are not granted to non-Jews, such as financial assistance, educational programs, income tax benefits, reductions on property purchase tax and long term mortgage assistance.

64 N.L. Zucker, *The Coming Crisis in Israel: Private Faith e Public Policy* (Cambridge, Mass., The MIT Press, 1973), at 76–86.

65 Y. Sezgin, 'How to integrate Universal Human Rights" *supra*, at 5.

66 *H.C. 47/82 Fund for the Reform Judaism v. Minister of Religions,* 43(2) PD, 661. See further, S. Navot, "The Constitution of Israel" *supra,* at 76.

67 Law of Return, 5710–1950.

68 S. Navot, "The Constitution of Israel" supra, at 76.

69 Nationality Law 5712–1952.

Such a piece of legislation finds its justification in the Jewish nature of the State and, recently, the 2018 Basic Law. The latter, as highlighted above, recognizes the right to self-determination to Jews only; thus, strengthening the Jewish character of Israel. Consequently, under the 2018 Basic Law, Jewish citizens fully enjoy both collective and individual rights, whereas citizens belonging to ethno-religious minorities are only granted individual rights.[70] As regards non-Jewish collective rights, they are recognized as far as they are "not perceived to threaten the exclusivity of the Jewish right to self-determination".[71]

From this constitutional and legal framework derives the prevalence of the ethnic concept of nationality over the civic concept of citizenship.[72] Furthermore, since the status of Jews qualifies as a prioritizing factor for citizenship, religious affiliation becomes a core political and legal issue in Israel.

Following the entering into force of the LR, the Orthodox establishment has been trying to maintain the monopoly over the definition of Jewish status and conversion. However, these attempts have been partially balanced by the Supreme Court, acting as a "standard-bearer of secularism".[73]

Under Jewish law, a Jew is a person who was born to a Jewish mother or who converted (*ghiur*) to Judaism.

Under Israel secular law, the definition of the term "Jew" has been subject to harsh political and legal debate. Originally, the LR did not provide for a

70 Section 1.3 of the Basic Law: Israel as the Nation State of the Jewish People. See A. Harel, "Basic Law: Israel as the Nation State of the Jewish People", (2021) 49(2) *Nationalities Papers* 262–269.

71 For instance, with regard to cultural and linguistic rights, in 1999 the Supreme Court censored the decision of the Municipality of Tel Aviv to use only English and Hebrew on street signs. However, while ruling the use of Arabic as well, the judges emphasized that Arabic and Hebrew languages do not enjoy equal status. As explained by A. Harel in "Basic Law" *supra*, at 266: "The use of Arabic, especially its presence in the public sphere, is not considered to be a merely technical matter; it is perceived to touch upon the collective right to the culture of the Palestinian minority in Israel".

72 In CA 630/70, *Georges Raphael Tamarin v. the State of Israel* [1972], known as "The Tamarin Decision", Justice Agranat held that in order to grant a declaratory order about one's membership of a certain nationality, there must be objective evidence about the existence of that nationality. A subjective belief is insufficient for determining the existence of a certain nationality for purposes of registering in the Population Registry. In addition, J. Agranat affirmed that there was no evidence that an "Israeli" nationality was formed in the State of Israel that is separate and distinct from the Jewish nationality. The "Tamarin decision" was confirmed in the subsequent ruling *CA 8573/08 Ornan v. Ministry of the Interior*. See S. Baldin, "Lo Stato nazione del popolo ebraico. Considerazioni sulla forma di Stato israeliano alla luce della legge fondamentale del 2018", (2018) 24 *Revista general de derecho publico comparado*, at 10.

73 *Ibid.*, at 10.

definition of "Jew" for the purposes of *aliyah* (Jewish return to Israel). In 1958, the Ministry of Interior adopted a subjective criterium prescribing that it is considered "Jew" a person who declares himself a Jew "in good faith", provided that he/she does not belong to other religions. The Orthodox religious parties refused the government's definition, calling for the application of Jewish law in determining religious affiliation.

In 1962, in *Rufeisen* (*Brother Daniel*), the Supreme Court held that, being the LR a secular law, the Court shall decide the meaning of "Jew" for the purpose of this law by applying the ordinary rules of interpretation instead of the religious criteria.[74]

The precedent-setting decision is well-known. Mr. Rufeisen was a Polish Jew who converted to Christianity, becoming a Carmelitan monk by the name Brother Daniel. In 1953, he moved to Israel and sought to be recognized as Jew under the LR. Israeli authorities refused his request since, according to the said law, the term "Jew" does not apply to a person who converted to another religion. The judges reasoned that "in the absence of a definition either in the statute itself or in the decided cases", the term "Jew" must be interpreted according to its "ordinary meaning", i.e., taking into consideration the perception of the community on "who is a Jew". Since a Jew who converted to Christianity is considered to be no longer a Jew by his or her community, Mr. Rufeisen/Brother Daniel was not regarded as Jew for the purpose of the LR[75] (albeit he might still have been considered Jew under Jewish law).[76]

In 1968, in *Shalit*, the Supreme Court, applying the secular-national test developed in *Rufeisen*, ordered the registration as Jew in the Population Registry of a child born to a Jewish father and a non-Jewish mother.[77] Therefore, a child who was not Jew under religious law, was still considered Jew in Israeli jurisprudence.[78]

---

74 See *HCJ 72/62 Rufeisen v Minister of the Interior*, P.D.16, 2428 [1962].

75 In the dissenting opinion, J. Cohn diverged from the "communal understanding" test by favoring a subjective approach which took into consideration Mr. Rufeisen's declaration of being Jew because of his subjective feeling. See, J. Cohn dissenting opinion, *HCJ 72/62 Rufeisen v Minister of the Interior*, P.D.16, 2428 [1962].

76 According to Jewish law a person who is born Jew is part of the Jewish people, even though he/she decides to convert to another faith or does not fulfill his/her religious obligations.

77 *HCJ 58/68 Shalit v. Minister of the Interior* P.D. 23(2). Similarly, in *Beresfords*, Justice Barak held that the applicant, who declared to be Messianic Jews, did not qualify as Jews under the Law of Return because the Jew "from the marketplace" would not have recognized them as part of the Jewish people. *HCJ 265/87 Beresford v. Minister of the Interior* 43(4) PD 793 [1987].

78 It must be underlined that the child was registered as a Jew under the Registration of Inhabitants Ordinance 1949, which preceded the Population Registry Law of 1965, by

Following *Rufeisen* and *Shalit*, the *Knesset* repeatedly amended the LR. Under the current formulation of the law, a "Jew" is "a person who was born of a Jewish mother or has become converted to Judaism, and who is not a member of another religion". Parliament does not entirely depart from Jewish tradition, as the LR accepts the matriarchal rule. However, contrary to Jewish law – according to which a Jew converted to another religion is still a Jew –[79] as shown in application of the *Rufeisen* case, a Jew converted to another religion is not considered part of the Jewish community by the State.

Most important, section 4a of the LR further departs from the religious tradition by broadening the scope of the law to include other family members of a Jew: the spouse, children (and their spouses), and even grandchildren (and their spouses). In sum, even family members who are not considered Jews under Jewish law qualify as Jews under Israeli LR.

As part of an effort to build the Jewish State, the current formulation of the LR allows a great number of people to come to Israel as Jews and to obtain immediate citizenship. However, those immigrants under the secular LR, whose Jewishness is contested by the Rabbinate under Orthodox religious law, are left in a "limping legal status".

This occurs because, in Israel, religious affiliation is legally relevant on matters of personal status, which is partially regulated by religious laws. Uncertainties with regard to the religious status of the person may jeopardize her/his constitutionally protected rights, in particular the rights to freedom of religion (and *from* religion), to marry and family life, to non-discrimination in the access to public religious services, to be equal before the law, as well as children and women's rights.

---

filling the entry *le'um*, a term generally referred to the (very different) concepts of "peoplehood", "ethnicity", "nationality" but whose translation is almost impossible, and not under the entry "dat", which indicates religious affiliation for the purpose of personal laws. On the *Shalit* case, see further A.R. Petty, "The Concept of 'Religion' in the Supreme Court of Israel", (2014) 26 *Yale Journal of Law and the Humanities* 211–268.

79 From the point of view of Jewish law there is no way to leave Judaism. Having said that, there is a great deal of variety in how the "always a Jew" rule is interpreted by those Jews who converted to other religions. Some converts no longer consider themselves as Jews, while other maintain a dual identity. For instance, a Jew converted to Christianity may consider himself/herself as ethnically Jew, even if he or she adheres to a different religion. See H.H. Ben-Sasson *et al.* "Apostasy" in M. Berenbaum and F. Skolnik (eds.), *Encyclopaedia Judaica*, Vol. 2, II (Detroit – USA, Macmillan Reference, 2007), at 269–277.

4.2 *Family Issues between Secular and Religious Law*

In Israel, no civil marriage and divorce exist. In the absence of a state civil law applicable to all citizens, marriage and divorce law depend on denominational affiliation. *All* Jews in Israel marry and divorce under Jewish law.

However, the system reveals evident shortcomings deriving from the partially divergent definition of the term "Jew" accepted by secular and religious authorities. Firstly, a person who acquires Israeli citizenship under the LR, but whose Jewishness is contested by the Rabbinate is unable to get married in Israel. In addition, since Orthodox *halakha* is the sole interpretation of Jewish law officially recognized by the Rabbinate, only Orthodox rabbis and judges are authorized to conduct marriage ceremonies and to preside over affairs of divorce. Consequently, those couples where the Jewishness of one of the spouses is contested on Orthodox *halakhic* grounds have the following options: to marry abroad and have their marriage registered in Israel under private international law;[80] or cohabitation as persons "known to the public" and common law marriages.[81] With regard to non-denominational couples, they may sign a Spousal Agreement and be registered in a special register. Family Courts are given exclusive jurisdiction over matter arising in connection to non-denominational families.

In sum, different options exist for Jews who wish to marry outside the Rabbinate, as well as non-denominational or inter-faith couples. Nevertheless, religious authorities may still object against the recognition of these unions, if it is believed that one of the spouses belongs to one of the recognized religious communities and, thus, he or she must follow the religious law of that specific community.[82]

Moreover, even Jewish couples who marry outside the Rabbinate, such as those who married abroad, are often unable to bypass religious tribunals' jurisdictions. This occurs because the Supreme Court held that divorces among *all* Jewish people fall under the exclusive domain of Jewish law;[83] consequently

80 The same holds true for mixed couples. *HCJ, 143/62 Funk-Schlesinger v. Minister of Interior* [1963], IsrSC 17(1) 225; *HCJ 2232/03 Anonymous v. Regional Rabbinical Court Tel-Aviv Yafo*, 23 [2006]. In both decisions, the Court held that registration of marriages celebrated abroad is due for statistical purposes only. The decisions further address the effect of same-sex marriages performed abroad.

81 Common law marriages are 'informal' marriages where the parties simply agree to consider themselves married. The cohabitation is recognized only in case of separation on the base of factual evidence. *CrimA 384/61 State of Israel v. Pesler*, 15 PD 102 (5722/23-1962).

82 Section 6 of the Law on Spousal Agreements for Persons without a Religion, 5760–2010.

83 According to the *Torah*, the husband issues a *get* (a divorce document) to the wife to divorce her. Wife's consent and acceptance of the *get* is not required by biblical law. Since divorce is a private act willingly performed by the husband; no religious tribunal

all Jewish couples are required to go through religious tribunals to dissolve their union in Israel. In other words, although Israeli law recognizes marriages conducted abroad, it does not allow the couples to divorce in a civil procedure. Consequently, Jewish couples are required to initiate a *get* process (Jewish divorce) or to obtain a divorce decree in the religious courts.[84]

Interestingly, even if the majority of these unions do not have internal validity under Jewish law, a religious divorce is considered necessary "so as to remove the remotest doubt of validity because of the seriousness with which Jewish law regards adultery".[85] Otherwise, the couple would still be considered married by religious authorities and would not be possible for them to legally re-marry in Israel.[86]

As far as divorce is concerned, if the Jewishness of one of the spouses is contested by the Rabbinate – for instance, because she/he belongs to a non-Orthodox stream of Judaism recognized by the State for the purposes of the LR, but not by religious authorities for the purpose of personal law – the couple may not be able to divorce in Israel.

Finally, the refusal to recognize non-*halakhic* marriages and marriages conducted under non-Orthodox ceremonies registered under Israeli secular law may also negatively affect the rights of the children. For instance, their

can pronounce a divorce judgment. When there are "grounds for divorce", the Rabbinical courts issue an order to "convince" the husband to initiate a *get* process. Sanctions exists under Israeli law to compel the husband to give the get. However, they are rarely applied by Rabbinical Courts. In case of get refusal by the husband, the wife asking for divorce remains married under Jewish law. She becomes an *agunah* (chained wife) and she cannot remarry according to Jewish law. Moreover, if she enters a new relationship, she commits adultery. On the get refusal, its consequence and frequency in Israeli and other countries, see further M. De Blois, "Religious law versus secular law. The example of the get refusal in Dutch, English and Israeli law", (2010) 6(2) June *Utrecht Law Review* 93–114.

84 *HCJ, 2232/03 A v. Tel-Aviv-Jaffa Regional Rabbinical Court*. However, the Supreme Court and the Great Rabbinical Court in a supplementary judgment, recognize the validity of divorce decrees (different from the *get*), issued when "the court finds that there is no possibility of a reconciliation between the couple". The Great Rabbinical court grounds the legitimacy of divorce decrees to the "universal custom of the Children of Noah" – according to which separation between husband and wife is sufficient to regard them as divorced – and on the "widespread practice" of rabbinical courts' to dissolve civil marriages between Jewish people by decree (para. 245).

85 I. Englard, "Religious Law in the Israeli Legal System" *supra*, at 106.

86 Under Section 176 of the Israeli Criminal Law bigamy is a criminal offence. Moreover, shall be stressed that considerable difference exists, under Orthodox religious law, between a woman and a man. While the latter may still ask religious authorities the permission to take another wife, no such possibility exist for the woman.

affiliation to the Jewish community may be contested, as parents bequeath their "limping status" to children.

Children born by a Jewish woman and a man who is not her husband under religious law are *memzerim* (sing. *mamzer*, bastard) in the eye of the religious authorities and the community. The status of *mamzer* is passed down through generations. The *memzerim* are "effectively excluded from Judaism",[87] they shall only marry other *memzerim* and they face social discrimination.[88]

4.3 *Conversion for the Purpose of the Law of Return*

Conversion to Judaism is the process whereby a person belonging to another religion becomes Jew.[89] In Israel, the validity of conversion is an essential factor for the purposes of Jewish immigration under the LR – as the law applies to Jews only – and, then, for the determination of the personal status law applying to the newcomers, in particular on matters of marriage and divorce.

Section 4b of the LR establishes that immediate citizenship rights are vested in people who converts to Judaism. Since "conversion in the context of this Law is a public-civil act",[90] it requires supervision by the State. In this respect, the Conversion Authority in the Prime Minister's Office and conversion courts assist Israeli citizens or permanent residents who wish to convert to Judaism in Israel. Despite the importance of this matter, a conversion law is still lacking,[91] and regulation of conversion has been mainly left to government decisions.[92]

---

87 J.A. Nichols, "Multi-Tiered Marriage: Ideas and Influences from New York and Louisiana to the International Community", (2007) 40(1) *Vanderbilt Journal of Transnational Law*, at 155.

88 In Israel, the phenomenon of *memzerim*, as well as that of the *agunot* – namely women whose husbands refuses the divorce – is claimed to be widespread by women's rights organizations, such as the Organization for the Resolution of Agunot (ORA). However, neither the Rabbinical courts, nor other Israeli institution provide periodic and accurate statistics on this issue.

89 It has been noted how the term "conversion", deriving from a Christian expression, is somewhat inaccurate to describe *giyyur* as it "does not succeed in capturing the ethnonational meaning that constitute an inseparable part of Jewish identity, all the more so for Jewish identity in the Jewish state". In brief, it is not accurate in describing public-community implication of conversion to Judaism, whose effects unfold outside the personal sphere. See M. Kravel-Tovi, "Jews by choice? Orthodox conversion, the problem of choice, and Jewish religion and politics in the Israeli state", 2019 (20)1 *Ethnography* 47–67.

90 HCJ 7625/06 *Rogachova v. Minister of Interior* [2016] (President Naor).

91 At the time of writing, a Conversion Bill proposed by the Interior Minister and leader of the Shas party, Aryeh Deri, is under discussion. The scope of the bill is limited to conversion performed within Israel and it would recognize legal validity to Orthodox conversion only.

92 Government decisions n. 3613 (4 July 1998) and n. 3155 (14 February 2008).

With regard to conversion performed abroad, the Ministry of Interior only accepts conversion certificates issued by rabbinical authorities belonging to recognized Jewish communities. The application is accompanied by a letter by the rabbi at the head of the community, describing in detail the process of conversion and the duration of the involvement of the converts in his/her community. In addition, a letter by the converts explaining the motivation behind the decision to become Jew is needed.[93] The controversies arising around conversion have been decided by courts on a case-by-case basis.

In particular, the courts have been confronted with the recognition of conversions performed under the auspices of both Orthodox and non-Orthodox private courts, i.e., non-State rabbinical fora, located in Israel or abroad, for the purposes of the LR. A new question therefore raises: "Who is Jew by choice?"

According to the Supreme Courts' established jurisprudence, the term "converted" in section 4b of the LR refers to a person who joins a "recognized Jewish community",[94] that is "an established, active community with a common, known Jewish identity, which has fixed frameworks of communal administration and which belongs to one of the streams recognized by the international Jewish community".[95] Under this inclusive criteria set by the Supreme Court, not only Orthodox conversion, but also Reformed and Conservative conversion performed both in Israel and abroad are recognized by the State for the purposes of the LR.[96]

Overall, the Supreme Court seems to pursue a secularizing agenda on matters of conversion, as several rulings ordered the registration of non-Orthodox conversions as citizens under the LR for the purpose of the Population

93 Overall, administrative authorities enjoy wide discretion on matters of recognition of the validity of conversions performed abroad. In deciding if the confession is "sincere" they adopt multiple criteria. For instance, they require documents that proves the active involvement of the converts in the activities of the community for at least nine months.

94 See the key-decisions HCJ 264/87 *Sepharadi Torah Guardians, Shas Movement v. Population Registrar*, IstrAr, 43(2); HCJ 2597/99 *Rodriguez-Tushbeim v. Minister of Interior*, IsrSC 59(6), 721; HCJ 1031/93 *Pessaro (Goldstein) v. Minister of the Interior*, 1995, IsrSC 49(4), *HCJ 5070/95 Naamat v. Minister of the Interior* [2002] *IsrSC 56(2) 721*, HCJ 7625/06 *Rogachova v. Minister of Interior* [2016]. Lower courts further contributed to the cause of non-Orthodox converts. For instance, in 1998, the Chief judge of the District Court in Jerusalem ruled the Ministry of the Interior to register as Jews 23 immigrants who converted under non-Orthodox procedures in Israel. *Gigi v. Minister of the Interior*, 5757(3) P.M. 454 [1998]. A list of Jewish communities recognized by the Rabbinate was published in 2018.

95 CJ 7625/06 *Rogachova v. Minister of Interior* [2016] (President Naor).

96 *Rodriguez-Tushbeim v. Minister of Interior*, IsrSC 59(6), 721; HCJ 1031/93 *Pessaro (Goldstein) v. Minister of the Interior*, 1995, IsrSC 49(4), HCJ 7625/06 *Rogachova v. Minister of Interior* [2016].

Registry.[97] Reacting to the Supreme Court relaxation of criteria and processes of conversion, numerous conversion bills have been proposed, mainly with the purpose of setting more rigid criteria for conversion. However, the drafts were never approved by the Parliament. Currently, backed by the *Knesset*, the Orthodox control over State conversion remains solid.[98]

In spite of different approaches displayed by State secular authorities on matters of conversion, what is certain is the Rabbinate refusal to recognize non-Orthodox conversions for the purposes of personal status falling under religious jurisdiction, as well as other conversions performed – whether in Israel or abroad – by private *halakhic* courts.

Alongside matrimonial and divorce matters, citizens whose conversion is contested by State religious authorities may face discrimination in accessing public religious services such as funeral and burial services; or religious facilities, such as public *mikvaot* for ritual bath and conversions.[99]

This contestation is of utmost importance, and it reveals the shortcomings of the Israeli system of religious diversity governance, which regards religious communities as homogeneous groups; thus, ignoring their inherent pluralism. Throughout the years, a growing number of Ethiopian, Russian, Indian and American Jews immigrated to Israel and automatically obtained Israeli citizenship under the LR. Most of them belong to non-Orthodox streams of Judaism. In Israel, they are *de facto* religious minorities within the Jewish majoritarian community.[100]

It is important to stress that non-Orthodox Jewish minorities portray themselves as an integral part of the Jewish community; therefore, they generally do not demand differentiated rights. Yet, imbrications and divergence between

97 *HCJ 5070/95 Naamat v. Minister of the Interior* [2002] IsrSC 56(2) 721; *HCJ 2597/99 Rodriguez-Tushbeim v. Minister of the Interior* [2005] IsrSC 58(5) 412 [2004].

98 N. C. Richmond, "Israel's Law of Return: Analysis of Its Evolution and Present Application", (1993) 12(1) *Penn State International Law Review* 95–133.

99 *AAA 587/10, Conservative Movement v. Be'er Sheva Religious Council* [2016].

100 According to the Jewish Agency for Israel, in 2020 nearly 20.000 people immigrated under the Law of Return, assisted by the Ministry of Aliyah and Integration and the Ministry of Interior. The Agency's data record that approximately 10.200 arrived from the countries of the former Soviet Union, around 3.120 from Western Europe, 2.850 from Northern America (2.550 from the United States), 1500 from Latin America, 280 from South Africa, about 90 from Australia and New Zealand, 1200 from Ethiopia. While they are all recognized as Jew under the Law of Return and, thus, entitled to immediate citizenship according to the (secular) Nationality law (1952), many of them are not regarded as Jews under Orthodox religious law applied by State religious institutions and courts.
See, "The Jewish Agency for Israel, More Than 20,000 Olim from 70 Countries Moved to Israel in 2020", survey accessed May 26, 202, available at: www.jewishagency.org.

Israeli citizenship legislation and Jewish law jeopardize non-Orthodox citizens' rights protected under State constitutional law, as well as Israeli obligations under international law (freedom of religion, freedom to marry and have a family life, equal access to public religious services, equality before the law, children and women's rights).

5 Deep Legal Pluralism and Private Jewish Courts

The previous sections dealt with "State-law pluralism"[101] in Israel, i.e., the incorporation of religious norms and religious adjudication on matters of personal status into the State legal system.[102] However, when trying to untangle the complexities of the Israeli legal experience, unofficial legal pluralism shall also be taken into consideration.[103]

Unofficial (deep) legal pluralism is commonplace in post-colonial countries, and it constitutes a growing phenomenon in Western countries as well. In South Africa, for instance, the 1996 Constitution affirms that the State may (but it is not obliged to) pass legislation recognizing personal status laws, provided that they are not inconsistent with any provision of the Constitution and the Bill of Rights.[104] That is to say that South African Muslim and Jews can resort to their own communal courts. The decisions are only binding *inter partes* and cannot be appealed against in State courts. Nevertheless, unofficial legal pluralism frequently comes to the surface in civil court proceedings, and it requires the judges to find suitable accommodation (when possible) between State law and religious legal systems in marriage, divorce or inheritance matters.[105] Similarly, in India, State-recognized Hindu-law interacts and frequently

101 In HCJ 7625/06 *Rogachova v. Minister of Interior* [2016] the Supreme Court defines a "recognized Jewish community" as an "established, active community with a common, known Jewish identity, which has fixed frameworks of communal administration, and which belongs to one of the streams recognized by the International Jewish community" (para. 30).

102 I. Englard, "Religious Law in the Israel Legal System" *supra*, at 33–48.

103 A. S. Hofri-Winogrdow, "A plurality of discontent: Legal pluralism, religious adjudication and the State", (2010–2011) 26 *Journal of Law and Religion* 101–133. See further K. Topidi, "Customary Law, Religion and Legal Pluralism in Israel: Islamic Law and Shari'a Courts in constant motion", (2019) 26 *Revista General de Derecho Pùblico Comparado* 1–19.

104 The Constitution of the Republic of South Africa, 1996, art. 15(3)(a)(b). However, the State is not compelled to give effect to religious laws, nor to recognize and enforce the decisions issued by the communities' informal courts.

105 In these respects, the *Hassam v. Jacobs*, NO 2009 11 BCLR 1148 (CC) SA case is of particular interest. In this landmark decision, the Constitutional court recognized the proprietary

clashes with unwritten traditional Hindu legal practices.[106] In Europe, Canada and the United States, Jewish *batei din* have a long, established history and Islamic shari'a councils started to emerge in Europe the 1980s.[107]

In Israel, deep legal pluralism dates back to the Ottoman era and it survived the British mandate. Private *halakhic* courts have been established alongside State-run religious and civil courts and they act as alternative and competing fora for the adjudication of disputes under a variety of communal laws, including non-Orthodox interpretation of Jewish law.

The member of the ultra-Orthodox *haredi* community, in particular, prefer to litigate before their private tribunals, since they have no confidence in State courts, not even in State religious adjudication. Interestingly, although official religious courts quite frequently employ *haredi* judges, *haredim* consider the State of Israel as an abomination and State courts as equal to non-Jewish courts.[108] Consequently, they prefer to resort to the *haredi batei din* and to appear in State courts only when forced by State's authorities.[109] Unofficial religious courts draw their authority from the community itself, whose internal cohesion ensures that the summoned parties appear in court and that they complied with the decisions. Otherwise, they will be subject to community sanctions.

Apart from the *haredi* courts, private tribunals developed alongside the State judicial system, allowing both Orthodox and non-Orthodox Jews to "forum shop" between State-run Rabbinical Courts and their communal courts. In particular, Reformist and Conservative Jews often resort to private courts as they apply different marriage and divorce ceremonies and agreements, which are perceived to be "more egalitarian" or because the official religious courts refuse to hear their case on account of uncertainties over their religious belonging.

The impact of halachic private courts on the State legal system would need further research as the phenomenon is slowly developing. Indeed, the major

---

consequences of a polygynous marriage under Islamic law within the context of the Intestate Succession Act 81 (1987).

106 See, among others, W. Menski, "The Uniform Civil Code Debate in Indian Law: New Development and Changing Agenda", (2008) 9(3) *German Law Journal* 211–250.

107 See, A. Rinella, *La Sharia in Occidente. Giurisdizioni e diritto islamico: Regno Unito, Canada e Stati Uniti d'America* (Bologna, Il Mulino, 2021); M.S. Berger, "Understanding Sharia in the West, Journal of Law", (2018) 6(2–3) *Religion and State* 236–273.

108 See E. Shochetman, *The Halachic Status of the Courts of the State of Israel*, (1991–1992) 12 Techumin 337, [in Hebrew].

109 Communal rules prescribe that, before filing a suit in a State court, Haredim need a permission from their private courts. See A.S. Hofri-Winogradow, "A plurality of discontent" *supra*, at 57–89.

consequences are currently visible with regard to conversion to Judaism performed by private courts.[110]

6 Conclusions. Jewish State, Personal Laws and Minority Rights: Trapped into the Communitarian Paradigm?

Founded to be the national homeland for Jewish people, Israel constantly faces the challenge to create a strong and stable political community, while addressing the demands of numerous ethno-religious minorities living in its territory.[111]

As explained in this chapter, the Israeli *millet* mainly serves two purposes. Firstly, it builds a new Israeli-Jewish identity out of the people "returning" to Israel which are different in terms of nationality, language, culture, ideologies. Secondly, it draws clear ethno-religious boundaries between Jews and non-Jews, discouraging inter-denominational marriages and favoring Jewish immigration under the LR. The system founds its legitimacy in the very nature of the State as "Jewish and Democratic". In addition, legal pluralism and the partial establishment of Orthodox Judaism in State institutions and religious courts coexist.

The main consequence of Israeli eclectic system of religious diversity governance and control is that citizens – and, to some extent, permanent residents – frequently find themselves "trapped" into their ethno-religious communities. Their rights and obligations *vis-à-vis* the State are determined by religious affiliation. However, as highlighted in this chapter, the criteria adopted by secular legislation to ascertain a persons' belonging to the Jewish community often diverge from the religious criteria applied by Rabbinical Courts. This discrepancy, it has been argued, raises serious questions regarding Jewish religious minorities, their legal status and rights.

In this respect, some considerations can be briefly drawn. Firstly, by combining legal pluralism and the establishment of Orthodox Judaism, Israel constructs well-defined, homogeneous communities. These are seen as monolithic blocks for the purposes of nation-building (Judaism) and the governance or religious minorities. In so doing, the system tends to neglect that religious

110 HCJ 7625/06 *Rogachova v. Minister of Interior* [2016].

111 J. Marko, "Ethnopolitics: The Challenge for Human and Minority Rights Protection" in C. Corradetti (ed.), *Philosophical Dimensions of Human Rights: Some Contemporary Views* (Dordrecht, Heidelberg, Springer, 2012), 265–291.

identity is usually nuanced, and it also stands at the intersection with other individual identities: ideology, nationality of origin, gender, age.[112]

With regard to communal courts' structure, the religious communities enjoy a degree of autonomy on sensitive matters of personal status. By contrast, neither the Jewish majority nor religious minorities seem to be fully satisfied with the personal law system. The application of the orthodox interpretation of Jewish law in religious courts to *all* Jews, regardless of their adherence to different streams of Judaism, favored the establishment of a growing number of private religious courts. Ultra-Orthodox and non-Orthodox Jews often prefer to litigate before their informal fora and be subject to their communal law. The consequences are significant for what concerns private conversions for the purpose of the LR. Moreover, the system creates the conditions for "jurisdiction races" and "forum shopping" between secular and religious courts. This further complicates the relationships between the different components of the Israeli judicial system, at the risk of jeopardizing citizens' rights and equality before the law.

Finally, the prevalence of an ethno-religious conception of citizenship over a civic one recently acquired constitutional legitimacy in the 2018 Basic Law creates issues. In affirming the right to self-determination to Jews only, the 2018 Basic law appears to exclude non-Jewish citizens from being constituent units of the State. At the same time, the Jewish character of Israel prevails over the democratic one. As it may be seen, this principle is not mentioned in the 2018 Basic Law. This may not come without consequences with regard to Jewish minorities, whose legal position in the State of Israel remains uncertain. Although Reformed and Conservatives streams of Judaism are usually recognized by the State for the purposes of the LR, government authorities still enjoy a high degree of arbitrariness in determining who is Jew.

Even more important, State religious courts firmly refuse to recognize non-Orthodox minorities for the purposes of marriage, divorce and ancillary issues; thus, leaving a growing number of people immigrating under Israeli immigration law in a "limping status".

The Supreme Court, which displays considerable cautiousness in deciding on sensitive religious issues, on several occasion ruled in favor of the non-Orthodox Jewish minority. In this respect, the judges stressed the multi-faced nature of Judaism and called for a well-defined approach by the government and the *Knesset* towards the determination of who is a Jew.

112 W. Kymlicka, *Multicultural odyssey. Navigating the new international politics of diversity* (New York, Oxford University Press, 2007).

Concretely, some attempts have been made to promote inclusion of non-Orthodox Jews in Israeli public life. In the last few years, steps forwards have been made with regard to State religious services. In 2016, the Supreme Court recognized to non-Orthodox Jews the right to access the ritual baths for the purpose of conversion under the principle of equality and freedom of religion, as enshrined in Basic Law on Human Dignity and Liberty.[113] In 2019, following a petition issued by the bereaved family of a fallen soldier before the Supreme Court, the General Staff Order was amended to allow fallen soldiers to receive full military honors in a secular or non-Orthodox ceremony.[114] Moreover, non-Orthodox minorities (and Jewish women) participation in public institutions has been fostered by allowing them to sit in religious councils.[115]

Bibliography

Ages, A., *The Diaspora Dimension,* (Dordrecht, Springer, 1973).

Ayoub, M., "Dhimmah in Qur'an and Hadith [with Commentary]", (1983) 5(2) *Arab Studies Quarterly* 172–191.

Baldin, S. (ed.), *Diritti tradizionali e religiosi in alcuni ordinamenti contemporanei* (Trieste, EUT, 2005).

Baldin, S., "Lo Stato nazione del popolo ebraico. Considerazioni sulla forma di Stato israeliano alla luce della legge fondamentale del 2018", (2018) 824, *Revista general de derecho publico comparado* 1–24.

Ben-Sasson, H.H. *et al.*, "Apostasy" in M. Berenbaum and F. Skolnik (eds.), *Encyclopaedia Judaica*, II., (Macmillan Reference, Detroit – USA, 2007), 269–277.

Berger, M.S., *Understanding Sharia in the West,* (2018) 6(2–3) *Journal of Law, Religion and State* 236–273.

113 *AAA 587/10, Conservative Movement v. Be'er Sheva Religious Council* [2016].

114 Originally, the Order provided for the choice between an Orthodox religious military funeral or a civilian funeral without military honors. Following the amendment of the Order, which allowed the funeral service to be consistent with the deceased lifestyle and beliefs, the Petitioner agreed to withdraw the petition. See *HCJ 3458/17, Hiddush – For Religious Freedom and Equality v. Israel Defense Forces* [2019].

115 According to *Jewish Religious Services Law, 25 L.S.I. 125, (1971)*, religious councils are local administrative bodies providing religious services under the supervision of the Rabbinate. From 1994 on, several judgments issued by the Supreme Court recognized Reformed and Conservative Jews' the right to sit in religious councils. A far-reaching decision on the matter was delivered by the Supreme Court in 1987, which ruled the appointment of a woman in the council of Yerucham. See H.C. 153/87, *Shakdiel v. Minister of Religious Affairs et al., PD, 42(2), [1987].*

De Blois, M., "Religious law versus secular law. The Example of the *get* Refusal in Dutch, English and Israeli Law', (2010) 6(2) June *Utrecht Law Review* 93–114.

Don-Yehiya, D., "The Resolution of Religious Conflicts in Israel", in A. Stuart Cohen, E. Don-Yehiya (eds.), *Conflict and Consensus in Jewish Political Life* (Ramat Gan, Bar-Ilan University Press, 1986).

Englard, I., *Religious Law in the Israel Legal System* (Israel, Hebrew University of Jerusalem, 1975).

Fournier, P., "Halacha, The Jewish State and the Canadian Agunah: Comparative Law at the intersection of Religious and Secular Orders", (2013) 44(65) *The Journal of Legal Pluralism and Unofficial Law* 165–204.

Gans, C., "Jewish and Democratic: Three Zionism and post-Zionism" in G. Sapir *et al.* (eds.), *Israeli Constitutional Law in the Making* (Oxford and Portland, Hart Publishing, 2013).

Garner, B.A. (ed.), *Black's Law Dictionary* (Chicago, St. Paul, MN – Thompson Reuters, 2001).

Harel, A., "Basic Law: Israel as the Nation State of the Jewish People", (2021) 49(2) *Nationalities Papers* 262–269.

Hashemi, K., *Religious Legal Traditions, International Human Rights Law and Muslim States* (Leiden – Boston, Martinus Nijhoff Publishers, 2008).

Hecht, N.S *et al.* (eds.), *An Introduction to the History and the Sources of Jewish Law* (Oxford, Oxford University Press, 1996).

Hirschl, R., *Comparative Matters: the renaissance of Comparative Constitutional Law* (Oxford, Oxford University Press, 2014).

Hirschl, R., *Constitutional Theocracy* (MA-London, England Harvard University Press, 2010).

Hofri-Winogrdow, A.S., "A Plurality of Discontent: Legal Pluralism, Religious Adjudication and the State", (2010–2011) 26 *Journal of Law and Religion* 101–133.

Kaplan, Y., "Enforcement of Divorce Judgments in Jewish Courts in Israel: the Interaction between Religious and Constitutional Law", (2012) 4 *Middle East Law and Governance* 1–68.

Karayanni, M., *A Multicultural Entrapment. Religion and State Among the Palestinian-Arabs in Israel* (Cambridge, Cambridge University Press, 2020).

Kaye, A., *The Invention of Jewish Theocracy. the Struggle for Legal Authority in Modern Israel* (New York, Oxford University Press, 2020).

Kravel-Tovi, M., "Jews by Choice? Orthodox Conversion, the Problem of Choice, and Jewish Religion and Politics in the Israeli State", (2019) 20(1) *Ethnography* 47–67.

Kymlicka, W., *Multicultural Odyssey. Navigating the New International Politics of Diversity* (New York, Oxford University Press, 2007).

Lifhshitz, H. and Sapir, G., "Jewish Religious Services Law – a Proposed Framework for Privatization Reform", (2006) 23 *Bar-Ilan Law Studies* 117–194 (in Hebrew).

Maoz, A., "The Application of Religious Law in a Multi-religion Nation State: the Israeli Model", in R. Bottoni *et al.* (eds.), *Religious Rules, State Law, and Normative Pluralism. a comparative Overview* (New York, Springer, 2016), 209–227.

Marko, J., "Ethnopolitics: the Challenge for Human and Minority Rights Protection", in C. Corradetti (ed.), *Philosophical Dimensions of Human Rights: Some Contemporary Views* (Dordrecht, Heidelberg, Springer, 2012), 265–291.

Menski, W., "The Uniform Civil Code Debate in Indian Law: New Development and Changing Agenda", (2008) 9(3) *German Law Journal* 211–250.

Natour, A., *Promoting Women's Rights in Islamic Law in a Non-Muslim State – Israel* (Lanham – Maryland, Lexington Books, 2021).

Navot, S., *The Constitution of Israel. a Contextual Analysis* (Oxford and Portland, Hart Publishing, 2014).

Neuberger, B., "Religion and State in Europe and Israel", (1999) 6(2) *Israel Affairs* 65–84.

Nichols, J.A., "Multi-Tiered Marriage: Ideas and Influences from New York and Louisiana to the International Community", (2007) 40(1) *Vanderbilt Journal of Transnational Law* 135–196.

Osman, A., "The Qur'an and the Hadith as Sources of Islamic law", in K.A El Fadl *et al.* (eds.), *Routledge Handbook of Islamic Law* (Abingdon, Routledge Handbooks Online, 2019).

F. Palermo, "Current and Future Challenges for International Minority Protection" in *European Yearbook of Minority Issues, vol. 10, 2011* (Leiden-Boston, Brill, 2013), 21–36.

Petty, A.R., "The Concept of "Religion" in the Supreme Court of Israel", (2014) 26 *Yale Journal of Law and the Humanities* 211–268.

Richmond, N. C., "Israel' s Law of Return: Analysis of Its Evolution and Present Application", (1993) 12(1) *Penn State International Law Review* 95–133.

Rinella, A., *La Sharia in Occidente. Giurisdizioni e diritto islamico: Regno Unito, Canada e Stati Uniti d'America* (Bologna, Il Mulino, 2021).

Rubinstein, A., "Law and Religion in Israel", (1967) 380 *Israel Law Review* 384–399.

Sapir, G., *The Israeli Constitution: from Evolution to Revolution* (New York, Oxford University Press, 2018).

Sapir, G. and Statman, D., *State and Religion in Israel. a philosophical-Legal Inquiry* (New York, Cambridge University Press, 2019).

Sassoon, D.M., "The Israel Legal System", (1968) 16(6) *The American Journal of Comparative Law* 405–415.

Sezgin, Y., "The Israeli Millet System: Examining Legal Pluralism through Lenses of Nation – Building and Human Rights", (2010) 43(3) *Israel Law Review* 631–654.

Sezgin, Y., *Human Rights under State-enforced Religious Family Laws in Israel, Egypt and India* (New York, Cambridge University Press, 2013).

Shahar, I., *Legal Pluralism in the Holy City: Competing Courts, Forum Shopping and Institutional Dynamics in Jerusalem* (London – New York, Routledge, 2016).

Shochetman, E., "The Halachic Status of the Courts of the State of Israel", (1991–1992) 12 *Techumin* 337 [in Hebrew].

Topidi, K., "Customary Law, Religion and Legal Pluralism in Israel: Islamic Law and Shari'a Courts in Constant Motion", (2019) 26 *Revista General de Derecho Pùblico Comparado* 1–19.

Yefet, K.C., "Israeli Family Law as Civil-religious Hybrid: a Cautionary Tale of Fatal Attraction", (2016) 1505 *University of Illinois Law Review* 1528–1533.

Zucker, N.L., *The Coming Crisis in Israel: Private Faith e Public Policy* (Cambridge, Mass., The MIT Press, 1973).

CHAPTER 8

Russian Orthodox Church and Migration in Russia: When Hell Is Paved with Good Intentions

Kiryl Kascian and Hanna Vasilevich

1 Orthodox Church in Russia's State Architecture

According to its Constitution, Russia is a multi-ethnic federal and secular state. This envisages the separation of the religious denominations from the state, their equality before the law, and the absence of an obligatory state-sponsored religion (Art. 14).[1] Recent constitutional amendments of 2020 introduced Art. 67.1. It refers to the "historically developed state unity" which is linked to the country's "thousand-year history" and "remembrance the ancestors who transferred [...] ideas and faith in God". It emphasizes the historical role of religion in the formation of Russia as a multi-ethnic state. At the same time, the concept "faith in God" is presented as an important element of Russia's national unity and thereby embedded in the relevant integration policies designed by the state.

Russia's religious landscape is quite diverse, albeit dominated by the Russian Orthodox Church (hereinafter: ROC). Russia's law on freedom of conscience and religious associations[2] confirms the secular nature of the state and acknowledges "Christianity, Islam, Buddhism, Judaism, and other religions" as "an integral part of the historical heritage of the peoples of Russia". At the same time, the law confirms Orthodoxy's special role in Russia's history, and "in the formation and development of its spirituality and culture". Thereby, the state ensures a *de facto* special status for the Russian Orthodox Church among other religious denominations.

---

1 Novyi tekst Konstitutsii RF s popravkami 2020 (New text of the RF Constitution with amendments) (2020). *The State Duma of the Federal Assembly of the Russian Federation*. July 3, 2010, available at: http://duma.gov.ru/news/48953/.

2 Federalnyi zakon ot 26 September 1997 No. 125-FZ "O svobode sovesti i o religioznykh obyedineniyakh" (Federal Law of 26 September 1997 No. 125-FZ "On freedom of conscience and religious associations"), as amended. *President of Russia*, available at: http://www.kremlin.ru/acts/bank/11523/page/1.

 | DOI:10.1163/9789004446816_010

After the collapse of the USSR, the Russian Orthodox Church experienced its revival accompanied by its growing impact on society, and participation in public debates and policy-drafting.[3] Yet, the Russian Orthodox Church cannot impose its views and solely design its policies towards the society at large and its specific segments, as the position of the state must be taken into account.[4] The actual impact of the ROC in Russia beyond the "churchified" segments of Russia's society, however, is that it is politically perceived as the "church of the majority" by default being placed as *primus inter pares* among Russia's "traditional religions".[5] It is frequently claimed that the proportion of ROC's adherents in Russia comprises up 80 percent because this approach merges the confessional affiliation of individuals with their ethnic and cultural identity.[6] Some opinion polls inform that, in 2021, 66 percent of Russian citizens identify themselves as Orthodox Christians in contrast to 75 percent in 2017.[7] However, the number of those who know specific Orthodox rites and important dates, or observe fasts is considerably lower.[8] Another public opinion poll shows that 42 percent of Russians believe that the ROC influences the country's politics; while 51 percent of respondents agree that the Church has a significant impact on Russia's social life.[9] Yet, in 2020, only 53 percent trusted the ROC as an institution, comparing to 70 percent in 2015 and 66 percent in 2019.[10] The same 2020 opinion poll revealed that only 39 percent trusted Vladimir Gundiayev (ROC's Patriarch Kirill), while 31 percent did not give credence to him.[11] The discrepancy of these figures explains why the debate about the actual number of Orthodox believers in the country is irrelevant for this analysis. At the same

3 T. Köllner, *Religion and Politics in Contemporary Russia Beyond the Binary of Power and Authority* (Abingdon, Routledge, 2021).

4 T. Bremer, *Cross and Kremlin: A Brief History of the Orthodox Church in Russia* (Grand Rapids, Eerdmans Publishing Co., 2013).

5 Verkhovskii, A., "The Russian Orthodox Church as the Church of the Majority", (2014) 52(5) *Russian Politics and Law* 50–72.

6 "Skolko veruyushchikh" (How many believers), SOVA Center, n.D., accessed June 15, 2021, https://web.archive.org/web/20220628055147/https://www.sova-center.ru/religion/discussions/how-many/about/.

7 "Velikiy post – 2021" (Great lent – 2021) (2021). *VCIOM – Russian Public Opinion Research Center*, March 15, 2021, accessed June 15, 2021, https://wciom.ru/analytical-reviews/analiticheskii-obzor/velikii-post-2021.

8 *Ibid.*

9 "O vliyanii RPC na raznye sfery zhizni strany" (On ROC's impact on different spheres of life of the country) (2020). *FOM – Public Opinion Foundation*, April 1, 2021, accessed July 15, 2021, https://fom.ru/TSennosti/14371.

10 *Ibid.*

11 *Ibid.*

time, this data confirms that the ROC plays an important role in Russia's politics and social life.

None of Russia's major political parties challenges the existing *status quo* of the country's major religious denominations. For instance, Gennadiy Zyuganov, the head of Russia's Communist Party,[12] repeatedly claimed that Jesus Christ was the first communist and compared the Sermon of the Mount with the Moral Code of the Builder of Communism.[13] As a result, the ROC's social and political influence significantly extends beyond the circle of its active adherents.

For years, Russia has been a subject of criticism concerning its less accommodative approach towards religious diversity. It typically resulted in complications with the official registration of the legal entities of the specific religious groups or de-legalization of their activities under the pretext of extremism. The first scenario can be illustrated by the situation of the Church of Scientology whose branches throughout the country were denied registration despite several favorable judgments of the European Court of Human Rights (hereinafter: ECtHR).[14] The second scenario relates to the situation of the organizational units of Jehovah's Witnesses. Based on Russia's Supreme Court judgment of 20 April 2017, their activities were declared extremist, resulting in the prohibition of their activities, liquidation of all their organizational units throughout the country, and confiscation of their property. While the Jehovah's Witnesses challenged these restrictive measures before the ECtHR, the decision of Russia's Supreme Court refers strictly to the legal entities representing this religious community and not to their religious doctrine. Additionally, the ECtHR as a tool to challenge domestic decisions of Russia's authorities may have limited effectiveness. In 2015, Russian legislators vested the country's Constitutional Court with powers to declare an international judgment as non-executable if it

12 This party is a successor of the Communist Party of the Russian Soviet Federative Socialist Republic, Russia's branch of the Communist Party of the Soviet Union (CPSU). Over decades, the CPSU designed and implemented the anti-religious policies in the Soviet Union targeted, *inter alia*, against the Orthodox Christianity.

13 "Russian party leader says Christ was first Communist" *TASS*, April 20, 2016, accessed June 15, 2021, https://tass.com/society/871310; "Jesus Was the First Communist, Russian Party Leader Says", *The Moscow Times*, September 2, 2021, accessed June 15, 2021, https://www.themoscowtimes.com/2021/09/02/jesus-was-the-first-communist-russian-party-leader-says-a74957.

14 See, for instance: ECtHR, *Church of Scientology Moscow v. Russia*, Appl. No. 18147/02, judgment (Grand Chamber), 24 September 2007; and ECtHR, *Church of Scientology of St. Petersburg and Others v. Russia*, Appl. No. 47191/06, judgment (Grand Chamber), 2 February 2015.

contradicts the norms of Russia's Constitution. In 2020, these provisions were incorporated in Articles 79 and 125 of the Constitution.

Although the Russian Orthodox Church does not directly shape the abovementioned state policies targeting the country's religious diversity, the ROC's position is very important in determining its restrictive context. At the ROC's official website, the Church of Scientology, the Jehovah's Witnesses, and several other denominations are usually designated as dangerous religious sects threatening Russian society. These statements can be interpreted as the Orthodox Church's official position and they are taken into account by Russia's policy-makers and judiciary. Moreover, they implicitly contribute to the formation of negative attitudes and prejudices in society towards these religious denominations.

Another important element of the Russian Orthodox Church is its transnational nature. The ROC's Statute establishes that its jurisdiction extends to the entire territory of the former USSR, except for Armenia and Georgia.[15] It stipulates that the Russian Orthodox Church "was continuing to identify with the space that is held in the Soviet times".[16] The ROC's transnationalism is supplemented by its Russo-centric ideology. It could be designated as a sort of Russian civilizational nationalism that brings together ethnocultural and religious aspects. The former perceives culture "by presumed confessional orientation," while the latter treats nationalism as "a definite messianic streak, based on the vision of a confrontation between "Orthodox Christian civilization" and Western secular civilization".[17]

Historically, the Russian Orthodox Church has acted as one of the most important social welfare organizations in Russia, having embraced the role of protector and caretaker for the most vulnerable members of the society.[18] It presupposes ROC's active engagement in the effective implementation of Russia's migration policies that go beyond the migrants' evangelization and provision of spiritual services according to their needs.

---

15 Article 3 of the Russian Orthodox Church's Statute provides that its jurisdiction shall extend to the persons of the Orthodox denomination residing in the ROC canonical territory specified as Russia, Ukraine, Belarus, Moldova, Azerbaijan, Kazakhstan, China, Kyrgyzstan, Latvia, Lithuania, Mongolia, Tajikistan, Turkmenistan, Uzbekistan, Estonia, Japan, as well as Orthodox Christians from other countries who voluntarily joined the ROC. "Statute of the Russian Orthodox Church", *Official Website of the Moscow Patriarchate*. December 2, 2017, accessed June 15, 2021, http://www.patriarchia.ru/db/text/133115.html.

16 T. Richters, *The Post-Soviet Russian Orthodox Church Politics, Culture and Greater Russia* (Abingdon, Routledge, 2013), at 87.

17 A. Verkhovskii, "The Russian Orthodox Church as the Church of the Majority" *supra*, at 57.

18 W. L. Daniel, *The Orthodox Church and Civil Society in Russia* (College Station: Texas A&M University Press, 2006), at 11.

Therefore, this chapter investigates the role of the Russian Orthodox Church in the implementation of Russia's migrant policies, taking into account the aforementioned role of ROC in the society, its transnational nature, and ideological postulates linked to Russian civilizational nationalism. The following parts of the chapter are designed accordingly. First, the main overview of Russia's migration policies is made with a focus on the cultural and linguistic elements. Subsequently, the interaction of the Russian Orthodox Church with the relevant state bodies and its own agendas are analyzed.

2 Russia's Migration Policies: Cultural and Linguistic Dimensions

Goss and Lindquist[19] demonstrate that the examination of the patterns of international migration should focus on "the articulation of agents with particular interests and playing specific roles within an institutional environment, drawing knowledgeably upon sets of rules in order to increase access to resources". This emphasizes the necessity of addressing the available institutional frameworks and the issues pertinent to the design of the sets of rules related to migration in Russia. In other words, in this section it is important to address what rules are set for migrants by the Russian authorities, and how linguistic, religious, and cultural elements are being embedded into these frameworks. It is also particularly important to designate the specific groups among its potential recipients.

Currently, Russia's migrant policies are shaped by the two conflicting approaches when the willingness to attract foreign labor clashes with the determination to control the migration flows as much as possible.[20] The former is determined by the overall demographic situation in the country and the increasing shortage of the labor force. The latter is embodied by the adoption of the strict measures that involve specific requirements that *per se* treat each migrant as a potential threat to the country. In 2017, Russian legislation was amended with the provisions specifying the procedure of citizenship deprivation for naturalized citizens convicted of extremist and terrorist crimes.[21] The recent amendments to the Law on Legal Status of Foreign Citizens in

19 J. Goss and B. Lindquist, "Conceptualizing International Labor Migration: a Structuration Perspective", (1995) 29(2) International Migration Review 317–351, at 345.

20 V. Malakhov *et al.*, *International Migration: the Political and Legal Dimension* [in Russian], (Moscow, RANEPA, 2020), available at: https://ssrn.com/abstract=3619089, at 35.

21 "Putin podpisal zakon o lishenii grazhdanstva osuzhdennykh za terrorizm i ekstremizm" (Putin signed a law on the deprivation of citizenship of those convicted of terrorism and extremism), *Sova Center*, July 31, 2017, accessed July 3, 2021, https://www.sova-center.ru/misuse/news/lawmaking/2017/07/d37585.

the Russian Federation and the Law on State Fingerprint Registration in the Russian Federation, signed by President Putin on 1 July 2021 can be seen as further set of restrictive measures.[22] They introduced compulsory fingerprint registration, photographing, and medical examination of labor migrants in Russia within 30 calendar days from the date of their entry into Russia for the foreigners who entered Russia visa-free and intend to stay in the country for more than 90 days a year.

In reality, the majority of the foreign labor force and the foreigners in general affected by this amendment, in particular, come from the countries of the former Soviet Union. Within the post-Soviet migration flows, Russia is typically the country that receives migrants.[23] The early 2000s were a turning point for the qualitative change of these migration flows. This period was marked by the significant decrease of the ethnic Russians as well as members of other ethnic groups who fluently spoke the Russian language and shared common Soviet experiences. Since the early 2000s, the migration flows have been dominated by the members of the groups of the southern republics of the Soviet Union, who belong to younger generations and are more distant to Russia's norms in terms of their cultural and religious background.[24]

In legal terms, Russia's legislation contains three important definitions. The first one is "foreign citizen" (Russian: *inostrannyi grazhdanin*) which is formulated as "a person who is not a Russian Federation citizen and who has the citizenship (allegiance) of a foreign state".[25] The second term is "speaker of the Russian language" (Russian: *nositel russkogo yazyka*). The members of this group are defined as "persons who speak Russian and use it on the daily basis in the family, household and cultural sphere, if these persons or their relatives in a direct ascending line permanently reside or had previously permanently

22 Federalnyi zakon ot 01.07.2021 №274-FZ "O vnesenii izmeneniy v Federalnyi zakon "O pravovom polozhenii inostrannykh grazhdan v Rossiyskoi Federatsii" i "Federalnyi zakon "O gosudarstvennoy daktiloskopicheskoi registratsii v Rossiyskoi Federatsii"" (Federal Law of 01.07.2021 No. 274-FZ "On amendments to the Federal Law "On the Legal Status of Foreign Citizens in the Russian Federation" and the Federal Law "On State Fingerprint Registration in the Russian Federation""). *Official Internet-Portal of Legal Information*, accessed July 3, 2021, http://publication.pravo.gov.ru/Document/View/0001202107010039.

23 V. Malakhov *et al.*, *International Migration: The Political and Legal Dimension*, *supra*, at 38.

24 M. Light, *Fragile Migration Rights Freedom of Movement in Post-Soviet Russia* (Abingdon, Routledge, 2016); R. Urinboyev, *Migration and Hybrid Political Regimes Navigating the Legal Landscape in Russia* (Oakland, University of California Press, 2021).

25 Federalnyi zakon ot 31 May 2002, No. 62-FZ "O grazhdanstve Rossiyskoi Federatsii" (Federal Law of 31.05.2002 No. 62-FZ "On Russian Federation Citizenship"), as amended. *Official Internet-Portal of Legal Information*, accessed July 3, 2021, http://pravo.gov.ru/proxy/ips/?docbody=&nd=102076357.

resided in the territory of the Russian Federation, or the territory of the Russian Empire or the USSR, within the State Border of the Russian Federation".[26] The law also provides concessions in obtaining this status for the citizens of Belarus and Ukraine who are fluent in Russian. Yet, the criteria established by the Russian legislation imply that the status of the "speaker of the Russian language" could be obtained by any foreigner irrespective of citizenship, religious affiliation, and ethnic background who currently permanently resides in Russia and has sufficient knowledge of the Russian language. The third term is "compatriots" (Russian: *sootechestvenniki*) designated as "the persons and their descendants who live outside the territory of the Russian Federation and belong, as a rule, to peoples historically living in the territory of the Russian Federation, as well as those who have made a free choice in favor of spiritual, cultural and legal ties with the Russian Federation, whose relatives in a straight ascending line previously lived in the territory of the Russian Federation".[27] According to the Law, the notion of "compatriot" could be extended nearly to every person who lived in the territory of the former Soviet Union. The main criteria for the classification as compatriots are, therefore, defined through the factors of "common language, history, cultural heritage, traditions, and customs".[28]

The concepts of "speaker of the Russian language" and "compatriot" are not identical and have different legal implications regarding the possibility to receive Russian citizenship in a fast-track procedure. There are two aspects to be addressed in this regard. First, these definitions designate specific groups among the foreigners with already established ties with Russia. The cultural and linguistic criteria specified above suggest the vision of the integration of the actual and potential migrants applied by the Russian authorities. Second, the reference to the "spiritual ties" with Russia in the case of compatriots might implicitly suggest the importance of the religious factor as one of the elements of the cultural embeddedness of the foreigners in the Russian lifestyle. In any case, these definitions demonstrate that the Russian authorities prioritize those migrants who share the same linguistic and cultural elements with the Russian society at large. Clearly, the general migration policies are aimed at

26 *Ibid.*

27 Federalnyi zakon ot 24 May 1999, No. 99-FZ "O gosudarstvennoy politike Rossiyskoi Federatsii v otnoshenii sootechestvennikov za rubezhom" (Federal Law of 24.05.1999 No. 99-FZ "On the state policy of the Russian Federation concerning the compatriots abroad"), as amended. *Official Internet-Portal of Legal Information*, accessed July 3, 2021, http://pravo.gov.ru/proxy/ips/?docbody=&firstDoc=1&lastDoc=1&nd=102059861.

28 *Ibid.*

the acquisition by the migrants of the knowledge of the Russian language and culture as the essential elements of their successful integration. Additionally, these general policies do not envisage the linguistic and cultural diversity of the non-Russian peoples historically living in the territory of the Russian Federation (i.e. Chuvashs, Chechens, Tatars, Udmurts, etc).

3 Russian Language as a Tool of Influence and Integration

As demonstrated above, the Russian language is one of the main criteria for Russia's authorities in measuring individual's cultural ties with Russia. In the USSR, the Russian language was the official language of the country and served as a medium for interethnic communication between different Soviet ethnic groups. Russian still performs the role of a *lingua franca* in the post-Soviet space, although in many post-Soviet countries the demand for the active knowledge of the Russian language has substantially decreased. Since the early 2000s, the Russian language became "a tool of identity-building aiming at the homogenisation of the population," being later supplemented by the focus on language promotion among foreign compatriots.[29] The adoption of a "[c]oncept of the state support and promotion of the Russian language abroad" on 3 November 2015 is an illustration of this trend. The concept was developed in pursuance of Russia's main policy priorities in the sphere of international cooperation, approved by the Russian president on 18 December 2010.[30] Thus, the Russian authorities perceive the language as a tool for retaining their presence and influence in the post-Soviet spaces, and as an element of Russia's foreign policy. The speakers of Russian, irrespective of their ethnicity, citizenship, and actual country of residence, are attributed to Russia's sphere of interest. The state also reserves for itself the right to protect its culture and identity which is automatically perceived as a Russian one.[31] An integral part of the

29 K. Zamyatin, "A Russian-speaking nation? The promotion of the Russian language and its significance for ongoing efforts at Russian nation-building" in P.A. Kraus *et al.* (eds.), *The Politics of Multilingualism Europeanisation, Globalisation and Linguistic Governance* (Amsterdam, John Benjamins, 2018), at 61.

30 H. Vasilevich, ""Russian World" and Compatriots' Policies: A View from the Other Side", (2020) III *Hungarian Journal of Minority Studies* 143–167.

31 "Koncepciya gosudarstvennoy podderzhki i prodvizheniya russkogo yazyka za rubezhom" (Concept of the state support and promotion of the Russian language abroad), President of Russia, accessed July 3, 2021, http://special.kremlin.ru/catalog/keywords/82/events/50644.

Russian culture, the Russian language is also defined as a tool for the creation of Russia's positive image abroad.

The support for Russian compatriots abroad is the other major topic of the activities of the Federal Agency for the Commonwealth of Independent States Affairs, Compatriots Living Abroad, and International Humanitarian Cooperation (*Rossotrudnichestvo*). The compatriots are therefore seen as carriers of Russian culture, values, and language and peculiar conductors of humanitarian ties and relations between Russia and foreign countries.[32] Therefore, the Russian language became an important instrument of the promotion of the so-called "Russian world," the concept that corresponds to a transnational "'naturally existing civilisational community' embodying a set of 'Russian' spiritual and moral values, and based on visions of a common history".[33] Russia's domestic policies aimed at the integration of the migrants into the Russian society were based on the same postulates, defined through the mastering of the Russian language and knowledge of the Russian culture. As Zamyatin notes,[34] "along with the Orthodox Christianity, language knowledge is considered as a stronger basis for categorisation than ethnicity, *inter alia*, in ascribing someone as belonging to the 'Russian World'". This suggests the active role assumed by the Russian Orthodox Church in the design of Russia's integration policies and the practical assistance to migrants to integrate in Russia.

4 Russian Orthodox Church as an Agent of Migrants' Integration

The approach of the transnational Russian Orthodox Church (ROC) largely supports the Kremlin's view regarding the "Russian world," also being consistent with Gellner's classic definition of nationalism with the understanding of culture primarily in confessional terms. As Vladimir Gundiayev specified in 2014, the "Russian world" has a civilizational dimension, being "a spiritual, cultural and value-centered dimension of the human person".[35] In his view, it is the religious dimension of the "Russian world" that is the source of the peacefulness

32 "Podderzhka sootechestvennikov za rubezhom" (Support of compatriots' living abroad), *Rossotrudnichestvo*, accessed July 3, 2021, https://web.archive.org/web/20210910162945/http://rs.gov.ru/ru/activities/5.

33 A. Cheskin and A. Kachuyevski, "The Russian-Speaking Populations in the Post-Soviet Space: Language, Politics and Identity", (2019) 71(1) *Europe-Asia Studies* 1–23, at 9.

34 K. Zamyatin, "A Russian-speaking nation? The promotion of the Russian language and its significance for ongoing efforts at Russian nation-building" *supra*, at 60.

35 "Svyateyshiy Patriarkh Kirill: Russkiy mir – osobaya tsivilizatsiya, kotoruyu neobkhodimo sberech" (His Holiness Patriarch Kirill: the Russian world is a special civilization that

of the people united by it.[36] He emphasized that people of different ethnicities could become a part thereof by embracing the cultural and spiritual component of the "Russian world" as their own.[37] In 2016, Gundiayev designated the "Russian world" as "a community of people who are connected not only by blood (albeit by blood too) but also, first of all, by values that originate from our tradition, from our common history, values that can be actualized at every moment of time".[38] He explicitly mentioned the role of the Russian language not only as a means of communication but also as a factor that shapes spiritual culture by transmitting traditions.[39] He emphasized the decisive role of the Russian language in the formation and preservation of the "Russian world," Russian identity, and culture beyond the challenges of globalization.[40]

This form of Russian civilizational nationalism with the understanding of culture primarily in confessional terms and inseparable from religion dominates the ROC's approach towards migrants in Russia. Despite its actual influence in the Russian society, the Russian Orthodox Church had for a long time refrained from purposeful work in this domain, lagging behind numerically smaller Protestant denominations and being limited to individual initiatives aimed at the missionary work among the Muslim migrant communities.[41] A qualitative change happened after 2013 when the Russian Orthodox Church concluded a cooperation agreement with the Federal Migration Service of Russia (hereinafter: FMS)[42] and adopted the "Principles and directions of work with migrants in the Russian Orthodox Church".[43] The cooperation agreement was signed by Gundiayev, on the ROC's behalf, and Konstantin Romodanovskiy,

---

must be preserved) (2014). *Official website of the Moscow Patriarchate*. September 8, 2014, accessed July 3, 2021, http://www.patriarchia.ru/db/text/3730705.html.

36 *Ibid.*

37 *Ibid.*

38 "Doklad Svyateyshego Patriarkha Kirilla na X Assamblee Fonda "Russkiy mir"" (Report of His Holiness Patriarch Kirill at the X Assembly of the Russkiy Mir Foundation) (2016). *Official website of the Moscow Patriarchate*, November 3, 2016, accessed July 3, 2021, http://www.patriarchia.ru/db/text/4658869.html.

39 *Ibid.*

40 *Ibid.*

41 R. Lunkin, "The Strategy of the Work of Religious Associations with Immigrants: from Social Adaptation to the Mission", (2019) 1 *Scientific and Analytical Herald of the Institute of Europe RAS* 77–83, at. 81.

42 "Soglashenie o vzaimodeystvii Russkoy Pravoslavnoy Tserkvi i Federalnoy migratsionnoy sluzhby Rossii" (Cooperation agreement between the Russian Orthodox Church and the Federal Migration Service of Russia) (2013), *Official website of the Moscow Patriarchate*, April 19, 2013, accessed July 3, 2021, http://www.patriarchia.ru/db/text/2917828.html.

43 "Printsipy i napravleniya raboty s migrantami v Russkoy Pravoslavnoy Tserkvi" (Principles and directions of work with migrants in the Russian Orthodox Church) (2014). *Official*

on behalf of the FMS in his capacity as its Head. The agreement was focused on the interaction of the ROC and FMS in compliance with the implementation of Russia's migration policy and took into account Russian traditional spiritual, cultural, historical, social, and legal values.

The main areas of the collaboration between the two entities, *inter alia*, included the organization of the Russian language courses for migrants,[44] ensuring the implementation of Russia's migration policies pertinent to the above-mentioned values that cover spiritual, cultural, historical, social, and legal domains, and the respect of Russia's native population. The FMS and the ROC got involved in the project entitled "Education: linguistic and cultural adaptation of migrants," aimed at the creation of an effective system of migrants' cultural and social adaptation in Russian society.[45] As a result of this project, a textbook on migrant integration was developed. Its analysis is provided below in this section of the chapter. The cooperation also envisaged the conclusion and extension of the scopes of the cooperation agreements between the ROC's and the FMS's territorial branches and coordination of their activities aimed at the accommodation of the migrants.[46] Further cooperation areas included prevention and overcoming of the inter-ethnic and interfaith conflict, development and implementation of the measures aimed at the prevention of xenophobia, mutual assistance in the prevention of illegal migration, and assistance to those foreign compatriots who expressed their willingness to settle in Russia.

---

website of the Moscow Patriarchate, November 20, 2014, accessed July 3, 2021, http://www.patriarchia.ru/db/text/460673.html. Accessed: 03-07-2021.

44 At the moment when the agreement was signed, there were 253 Russian language courses for migrants in Russia. 67 of them were organized free of charge with the assistance of the FMS territorial bodies, including 12 free Russian language courses were created based on the capacities of the Russian Orthodox Church's dioceses. "Podpisano Soglashenie o vzaimodeystvii Russkoy Pravoslavnoy Tserkvi i Federalnoy migratsionnoy sluzhby Rossii" (Cooperation agreement between the Russian Orthodox Church and the Federal Migration Service of Russia was signed) *Official website of the Moscow Patriarchate*, April 19, 2013, accessed July 3, 2021, http://www.patriarchia.ru/db/text/2917823.html.

45 The available information suggests that the Federal Migration Service of Russia assisted the Russian Orthodox Church in the selection of the regions participating in the project, the preparation of the materials on migration law for training manuals, and the organization of the courses. In other words, it was not the FMS, but the ROC that had a decisive vote on the contents and the essence of the materials developed under this project. *Ibid.*

46 At the moment when the agreement was signed, there had been 62 cooperation agreements in the sphere of migrants' integration concluded between the ROC's and the FMS's territorial units. Another nine had been about to be signed. *Ibid.*

The ROC's leadership perceived its engagement in the support and integration of the migrants not only as their Christian duty but also as a tool to prevent criminality among migrant communities, "including the formation of the criminal ethnic groups".[47] ROC's Patriarch explicitly stated that the lack of understanding of the local culture, language and traditions could become the reasons for the domestic conflicts. He also clearly linked the concerns expressed by the Russian society towards the raise of the actual number of migrants arriving in Russia and the growing number of conflicts involving migrant communities.[48]

This concern is clearly visible in Article 3 of the cooperation agreement where migrants are presented as a threat to Russian society. The Article envisages measures aimed at the provision of Russia's population with objective information about the specifics of migrants' psychology, their motivations, and problems, including those arising from their adaptation to the new conditions and general integration into the Russian society.[49]

Gundiayev's position is very much consistent with the FMS's general strategy. According to Romodanovskiy's view, the documents focused on migrants' integration and adaptation should include not only legal but also a spiritual basis.[50] Moreover, Romodanovskiy underlined that the patience of the Russian people (understood both in civic and ethnic terms) has its limits.[51] The targeted work with the migrants is focused on attracting those who can actually contribute to or are demanded by the Russian economy and society. Migration is also seen as a temporary solution to address the actual shortage of the labor force before this problem is solved. Thus, both the FMS and the ROC treat the migrants merely as a tool for Russia's economic development that should fit Russian culture and traditions (and the ROC perceives the religious component as a significant part thereof). In their view, the migrants should not create conflicts; neither they should remain in the country permanently. Thus, their integration can be merely seen as a mechanism predominantly aimed at comforting the needs of Russia's natives. The cognizance of the actual needs of the migrants remains secondary in this scheme.

47 *Ibid.*

48 *Ibid.*

49 "Cooperation Agreement between the Russian Orthodox Church and the Federal Migration Service of Russia" *supra.*

50 *Ibid.*

51 *Ibid.*

The only category which is the exception from this rule is the Russian compatriots who are expected to settle in Russian permanently. The cooperation between the ROC and the FMS aimed at the integration of the returning compatriots is incorporated in their cooperation agreement, though without clearly specified strategies and activities. Still, the Russian returning compatriots did not need to learn the Russian language and the essence of the Russian culture and traditions as such. The most important for them is to grasp the current trends in Russian society and the patterns of its development. Nevertheless, there have not been any special program, strategy, or methodological recommendations offered as a part of this cooperation scheme. Thus, the general approach of the ROC and the FMS towards both returning compatriots and labor migrants is based on the two premises. The first one involves the development of their "legal awareness," while the second one encompasses the implementation of "measures to promote their law-abiding behavior" in Russia, as Article 3 of the cooperation agreement stipulates.[52]

From the formal point of view, the Orthodox Church's activities are primarily focused on cultural issues which consist of various types of educational activities aimed at the inclusion of the newcomers into Russia's cultural context.[53] These endeavors comprise studies of the Russian language, culture, and legal foundations. At the same time, the ROC's missionary activities among the migrants remain secondary. Yet, the regional structures of the Russian Orthodox Church in Moscow organized the translation of leaflets "The Eternal God Calls You to Him" and some other catechism materials into the Uzbek, Tajik and Kyrgyz languages, seeing the native languages of the migrants as an important element for preaching among them.[54] Priest Dionisiy Grishkov, the head of the "Home Nearby," justified this approach, *inter alia*, by the fact that all peoples of Central Asia had their Christian histories, and "even if they lacked thereof, the Church has to take care of the implementation of the commandment to teach all nations".[55]

52 "Cooperation Agreement between the Russian Orthodox Church and the Federal Migration Service of Russia" *supra*.

53 R. Lunkin, "The Strategy of the Work of Religious Associations with Immigrants: from Social Adaptation to the Mission" *supra*, at 82.

54 "Zavershen perevod prosvetitelskikh listkov "Vechnyi Bog zovet vas k sebe" na uzbekskiy, tadzhikskiy i kirgizskiy yazyki" (Translation of educational leaflets "The Eternal God is calling you to him" into Uzbek, Tajik and Kyrgyz languages was completed), *Moscow City Eparchy of the Russian Orthodox Church*, September 27, 2018, accessed July 3, 2021, http://moseparh.ru/zavershen-perevod-prosvetitelskix-listkov-vechnyj-bog-zovet-vas-k-sebe.html.

55 "Liturgiya dlya trudovykh migrantov: Ne naydya sebya v islame, urozhentsy Sredney Azii zapolnyayut dukhovnuyu pustotu pravoslaviyem" (Liturgy for labor migrants: Not finding

However, the cooperation agreement between the ROC and the FMS creates an impression as if it was focused merely on the adult migrants who leave their families in their home countries. A more targeted ROC's program focused on the children of the labor migrants was launched only in 2018 and beyond the scope of the activities established in the agreement. One of the most profound examples of the ROC's attempts to work with migrant children dates back to 2018 when a Sunday school at the Church of Saint Euphrosyne of Moscow was established in the Moscow district of Kotlovka. In the beginning, this initiative accepted 16 children[56] and became the first phase of the activities of the charitable foundation "Home Nearby" (Russian: *Riadom dom*) aimed at working with migrants.[57] It became the first Russian language school for the children of migrants that provides education free of charge. At this school, the professional teachers, speech therapists, and volunteers work to prepare the pre-school children for primary school and help school children with the curriculum and with the main focus on teaching the Russian language. By the end of the academic year 2018–2019, the group had grown to 50 children.[58] Initially, the classes took place once a week on Sundays, but as of 2021, the classes are organized three times a week for six groups and in six tracks.[59] Grishkov designates this project as a systematic activity of teaching the children which ensures free and accessible tutoring at a professional level.[60] However, the number of migrants covered by these endeavors remains very marginal comparing to the actual figures of the labor migrants coming to Russia.

The second phase of the "Home Nearby" activities aimed at helping migrants was launched in 2019 when a medical office was opened. Initially,

---

themselves in Islam, the natives of Central Asia fill the spiritual void with Orthodoxy), *Nezavisimaya Gazeta*, July 18, 2018, accessed July 3, 2021, https://www.ng.ru/ng_religii/2018-07-18/13_446_liturgy.html.

56 "V Sinodalnom otdele po blagotvoritelnosti obsudili voprosy okazaniya sotsialnoy i meditsinskoy pomoshchi migrantam" (Synodal Charity Department discussed issues of providing social and medical assistance to migrants), *Official website of the Moscow Patriarchate*, July 31, 2019, accessed July 3, 2021, http://www.patriarchia.ru/db/text/5480184.html.

57 "V Moskve sostoyalsya kruglyy stol o tserkovnoy pomoshchi migrantam" (A round table on church assistance to migrants was held in Moscow) *Synodal Department for Church Charity and Social Service of the Russian Orthodox Church*, February 4, 2021, accessed July 3, 2021, http://www.diaconia.ru/v-moskve-sostoyalsya-kruglyj-stol-o-cerkovnoj-pomoshhi-migrantam.

58 "Synodal Charity Department discussed issues of providing social and medical assistance to migrants" *supra*.

59 "A round table on church assistance to migrants was held in Moscow" *supra*.

60 *Ibid.*

it was located at the Church Hospital of Saint Alexis of Moscow. The office provided the migrants with the consultations with a general practitioner, who could subsequently referred them to the city hospital, where certain medical services provided to the migrants could be covered by the "Home Nearby" foundation.[61] As Grishkov emphasized, in 2020, the foundation received support from the Federal Agency for Nationality Affairs which provided more sustainability to the project. Specifically, it ensured the possibility to pay for several expensive high-tech surgeries for migrants and enabled the launch of the scheduled medical operations regularly, i.e. three to four operations per month.[62] Grishkov also designated the third phase of the project launched in 2020 during the Covid-19 pandemic. It included systematic humanitarian aid provided to the migrants in the form of a regular supply of food. Started as weekly food distributions, it evolved into the provision of four to five migrant families with food on a regular basis. In fact, the endeavors of the "Home Nearby" foundation are an evident example of good practices implemented by the ROC within its cooperation with the FMS in the sphere of migrants' integration. However, this example does not change the ROC's general framework focus towards the work with migrants. Instead, it reveals the existing gaps of the ROC's strategies by showing the specific directions of the potential areas where a more targeted approach towards migrants could be applied.

The current framework focus of the Russian Orthodox Church could be illustrated by the textbook "Russian Language, History and Fundamentals of Russian Law." It was prepared and published in 2014 within the project "Education: linguistic and cultural adaptation of migrants," being a result of cooperation of the ROC and the Russian Orthodox University and supported by the presidential grant. It was Archpriest Vsevolod Chaplin, the then Chairman of the Synodal Department for the Cooperation of Church and Society and Co-Chairman of the Joint Commission of the ROC and the FMS, who became editor of the textbook.

According to Maxim Parshin who chaired this project, the textbook is a manual that, among other things, explains to migrants the rules of behavior in public places, relations between men and women, and Russian traditions. The textbook aims at helping migrants to understand the Russian culture and avoid miscommunication with the native peoples of Russia and, thus, prevent potential inter-ethnic conflicts.[63] Oddly enough, the textbook's main message

61 *Ibid.*

62 *Ibid.*

63 "RPTs podgotovila uchebnik dlya migrantov" (ROC prepared a textbook for migrants),*Izvestiya*, December 11, 2014, accessed July 3, 2021, https://iz.ru/news/580608.

for migrants aimed at conflict prevention is to be invisible and non-active, like "do not talk loudly, do not wave your hands or push".[64] If a conflict situation occurs, migrants are advised "not to threaten or use force, [and to] resolve the conflict calmly through dialogue" because "otherwise people will look at you as an enemy, with whom one should not talk, but fight".[65] To differentiate between the good and the evil, the textbook refers to Christian values as the core of the Russian culture. Thus, all the Russian traditions, ways of behavior, and daily routines are described from the perspective of Russian Orthodox Christianity. The textbook's section devoted to religion is structured to show the similarities between Christianity and Islam, slowly switching towards the implicit promotion of Orthodoxy. The four traditional religions in Russia are mentioned shortly and without details. The linkage between the post-Soviet Central Asian states and the Russian Orthodox Church is made through a persistent reminder about the presence of its church houses in Uzbekistan, Tajikistan, Turkmenistan, and Kyrgyzstan. Furthermore, the attitude towards the work and the labor ethics are shown exclusively from the religious perspective. For instance, the textbook claims that "[i]n the Russian culture, work is about serving God and the others" or "[o]ur faith in God and our love for the others – for our families that we feed, for those who work with us and for the society as a whole – is shown by our conscientious, hard work".[66]

The above promotion of knowledge about Russian culture from the perspective of the Russian Orthodox Church suggests that migrants' specific needs are not taken into account and the integration into the Russian culture merely implies assimilation. Furthermore, the book contains a significant discrepancy between the level of the Russian language which can be learned from its linguistic part and that of the legal part. The former teaches the migrants quite simple phrases necessary for everyday use. The latter is written in a quite difficult language without simple clarifications necessary for the people without sufficient fluency in Russian and legal background. It suggests that the parts of the textbook written by different people were insufficiently accommodated and adapted to the migrants' needs.

64 V. Chaplin (ed.), *Russian language, history, and foundations of legislation. An educational manual for labor migrants and teachers, supra*, at 167.

65 *Ibid.*

66 *Ibid.*, at 176.

5 Conclusion

The Russian Orthodox Church has significantly increased its role in Russian society after the collapse of the USSR, being an important player in shaping policies pursued towards different societal segments in Russia. This entity pursues its own agendas which constitute a sort of Russian civilizational nationalism and bring together ethnocultural and religious aspects. Despite the secular nature of Russia as a state, the ROC has maintained close cooperation with the state in the domain of integration of the labor migrants and returned compatriots, promoting the Christian values, and, in many cases, ignoring the multi-confessional character of the society in Russia.

Until recently, however, the ROC lacked a consistent policy aimed at the integration of migrants. Since the early 2010s, it shifted towards a more focused approach towards working with migrants. The analysis of the textbook "Russian Language, History and Fundamentals of Russian Law" provides necessary evidence about the ROC's current framework focus towards migrants. It demonstrates the ROC's ideological perception pertinent to the behavior norms and promotes obedience towards the existing cultural order. It also ignores the ethnic and confessional diversity of Russia's society and the possibility for the migrants to preserve their identity and traditions. The contents of the textbook also demonstrate that the ROC's strategies fail to formulate and implement the concept of effective integration of the migrants which obviously goes beyond the knowledge of the Russian language and the Christian values shaped by the Russian Orthodox Church.

The overall assessment of the ROC's work with migrants suggests that the focus is trained on the adult migrant laborers, while work with women and children is significantly overlooked. Apart from the language training, there are other domains, like medical treatment of the migrants, in which different structures of the ROC participate. However, these initiatives are merely local and cover only a small number of migrants. They are typically performed by charities and do not always have a structured approach.

To sum up, the Russian Orthodox Church's endeavors related to the support of the migrants increase the visibility of the church's involvement in the integration processes, albeit in a very limited way due to the ROC's focus on the promotion of their own agendas. The analysis of its strategies implies that the ROC's approach towards migrants is based on the idea of conflict prevention, whereas the best strategy suggested to migrants is their assimilation to the Russian cultural and linguistic space.

Bibliography

Bremer, T., *Cross and Kremlin: a Brief History of the Orthodox Church in Russia* (Grand Rapids, Eerdmans Publishing Co., 2013).

Chaplin, V.A. (ed.), *Russian Language, History, and Foundations of Legislation. An Educational Manual for Labor Migrants and Teachers* [in Russian] (Rostov-on-Don, Foundation, 2014).

Cheskin, A. and A. Kachuyevski "The Russian-Speaking Populations in the Post-Soviet Space: Language, Politics and Identity", (2019) 71(1) *Europe-Asia Studies* 1–23.

Daniel, W. L., *The Orthodox Church and Civil Society in Russia* (College Station, Texas A&M University Press, 2006).

Goss, J. and B. Lindquist, "Conceptualizing International Labor Migration: a Structuration Perspective", (1995) 29(2) *International Migration Review* 317–351.

Köllner, T., *Religion and Politics in Contemporary Russia Beyond the Binary of Power and Authority* (Abingdon, Routledge, 2021).

Light, M., *Fragile Migration Rights Freedom of Movement in Post-Soviet Russia* (Abingdon, Routledge, 2016).

Lunkin, R., "The Strategy of the Work of Religious Associations with Immigrants: from Social Adaptation to the Mission" [in Russian], (2019) 1 *Scientific and Analytical Herald of the Institute of Europe* RAS 77–83.

Malakhov, V., *et al.*, *International Migration: the Political and Legal Dimension* [in Russian] (Moscow, RANEPA, 2020), available at: https://ssrn.com/abstract=3619089.

Richters, K., *The Post-Soviet Russian Orthodox Church Politics, Culture and Greater Russia* (Abingdon, Routledge, 2013).

Urinboyev, R., *Migration and Hybrid Political Regimes Navigating the Legal Landscape in Russia* (Oakland, University of California Press, 2021).

Vasilevich, H., ""Russian World" and Compatriots' Policies: a View from the Other Side", (2020) III *Hungarian Journal of Minority Studies* 143–167.

Verkhovskii, A., "The Russian Orthodox Church as the Church of the Majority", (2014) 52(5) *Russian Politics and Law* 50–72.

Zamyatin, K., "A Russian-speaking Nation? the Promotion of the Russian Language and Its Significance for Ongoing Efforts at Russian Nation-building" in P.A. Kraus *et al* (eds.), *The Politics of Multilingualism Europeanisation, Globalisation and Linguistic Governance* (Amsterdam, John Benjamins, 2018).

CHAPTER 9

Conclusions

Silvio Ferrari

The Issues at Stake. This book on the accommodation of religious diversity is driven by a question that may not be novel but that has not yet been adequately addressed, particularly in light of recent migration trends that have created new religious minorities and claims. As posed by Roberta Medda-Windischer, Kerstin Wonisch and Alexandra Cosima Budabin, the fundamental question facing contemporary pluralist societies is "how to reconcile the demands of religious and cultural diversity alongside political unity, that is, how to create a political community that is cohesive, stable, and satisfies the legitimate aspirations of minorities".[1] This reconciliation of disparate claims demands State responses that seek to 'square the circle' and thereby rewrite the meanings and boundaries of religion and politics.

The contributions collected in this volume show that the time for exhaustive and definitive answers has not yet come. We are still in the midst of an earlier stage, that of reflecting on current experiences in order to draw inputs that can help us formulate these answers. The main asset of this book consists in the presentation of very different case-studies that reach across geographical regions from Europe to the Middle East through various methodological approaches. These case-studies discuss and assess policies and measures for accommodating minority claims and building cohesion to work towards addressing the question raised by the three editors of the volume. Needless to add that I, too, do not possess these answers and must be content to ask questions and raise doubts: but sometimes questions and doubts help to deepen reflection.

The variety of contributions collected in this volume does not prevent the identifying of some thematic knots that in different forms underlie many of them. I will point to a couple of these themes, chosen from those that are most controversial, for thinking about religious accommodations in light of increasing diversity.

1 See introduction chapter by R. Medda-Windischer, K. Wonisch, and A.C. Budabin in this volume, at 1.

 | DOI:10.1163/9789004446816_011

Straight line or triangle? Many authors in this volume underline the need to broaden perspectives in order to better understand the implications of legal pluralism for the management of religious diversity. Elham Manea summarizes a key concern in the field: "At the heart of the discourses taking place currently on legal pluralism lies the question of how to balance equality and difference".[2] Looking at the problem from this angle puts us on the side of the law maker, who must find the balance between equality and diversity to avoid, on the one hand, imposing the straitjacket of equality on the variety of real life and, on the other hand, embracing this variety to the point of irreparably fragmenting the legal order. However, if we look at the issue from the point of view of the individuals and groups that constitute a society, a perspective presented in many of the chapters here, the problem becomes more complex. Instead of a straight line at the two ends of which stand equality and diversity, the problem takes the form of a triangle at the vertices of which stand equality, diversity, and freedom.

Within the horizon traced by legal pluralism, the State has the task to provide for different ways of regulating the same legal relationship, but only the individual has the right to choose the one that best corresponds to his or her beliefs. The inclusion of freedom of individuals and groups in the dialogue between equality and diversity makes the picture more complicated, raising new questions and offering new inputs for the sustainable management of legal pluralism. However, only a balanced combination of these three components can lead us toward an integrated society, the goal of squaring the circle as set out by the editors in their opening pages.[3]

The freedom to choose between equality and diversity. The challenge of fostering political communities that recognize religious minority rights is often represented as a pendulum swinging between equality (the politics of sameness) and diversity (the politics of difference). For the former, we find supporters of the former position advocating a strategy aimed at ensuring freedom of religion or belief for all on the same footing.[4] To assure equality, it is understood that general rules aimed at ensuring individual and collective religious freedom, allowing that they are correctly implemented, are sufficient

2 See Chapter 3 by E. Manea in this volume, at 36.

3 As noted by the editors of this volume in their introduction, at 4. An integrated society is "based on the recognition of dignity in the various lifestyle choices and traditions and in the context of equitable access to rights as well as on fair and non-discriminatory sharing of resources, goods and services".

4 L. Binderup, "Liberal Equality – from Minority Rights to the Limits of Tolerance. In The Rights and Plights of Religious Minorities", (2007) 4(2) *Res Cogitans* 95–109.

to protect minorities from discrimination and enable them to maintain and develop their religious identity. Instead, the advocates of the latter position are in favor of special legal measures to protect the identity of and guarantee non-discrimination against minority religions.[5] In the absence of specific measures to remedy the situation of inferiority and vulnerability in which minorities are almost always placed, such objectives will be unattainable. In their view, it is more a matter of the structural deficiency of a system based on the principle of "the same freedom of religion or belief for all" than of the correct implementation of its rules.

Another way to understand the space between the freedom to choose equality and diversity is to compare systems based on legal uniformity or legal pluralism.[6] Accommodations of religious minority rights are more likely to encounter problems in a legal order founded on the principle of a uniform law that applies to all citizens. Moreover, a system based on legal pluralism may be more open to accepting different rights and obligations for members of majority or minority religious groups.[7]

The debate around the individual freedom to choose between equality and diversity emerges in different forms in the first two chapters of this book, which analyze the effects of legal pluralism in Greece on diversity management. The chapters are devoted to the legal status of the Muslim minority in Thrace after Law 4511/2018 and the decision of the European Court of Human Rights (ECtHR) in the *Molla Sali v. Greece* case. This was a landmark case that concerned the application of Islamic inheritance law with the consequent reduction of the share due to female heirs. The question is whether the case offers helpful inputs to manage religious diversity in Europe and provides guidelines to build a sound framework for promoting minority and human rights, particularly in light of new religious communities that emerge from migration flows.

Kyriaki Topidi explains that the case took up the question of "how to accommodate within liberal legal contexts laws of a non-liberal character".[8] The legal pluralist perspective takes into account the co-production of norms that are promoted by different actors, producing theoretical and empirical challenges that contend with State sovereignty, minority protection, and individual rights.

5 J.A. Van der Ven, "Religious Rights for Minorities in a Policy of Recognition", (2008) 3 *Religion and Human Rights* 155–183.

6 S. Ferrari, K. Wonisch and R. Medda-Windischer, "Tying the Knot: A Holistic Approach to the Enhancement of Religious Minority Rights and Freedom of Religion", (2021) 12 *Religions* 1–17.

7 T. Modood and T. Sealy. "Freedom of Religion and the Accommodation of Religious Diversity: Multiculturalising Secularism", (2021) 12 *Religions* 1–14.

8 See Chapter 1 by K. Topidi in this volume, at 28.

Commenting on the decision of the ECtHR, she emphasizes the weight given to the freedom of each individual: the recourse to the jurisdiction of religious bodies is legitimate only if it is the result of a free and conscious individual choice. The Court declared that the "right to self-identification [...] must be respected both by the other members of the minority and by the State itself".[9] Topidi sees this rule on the right to self-identification as a member of a religious minority as being in line with the UN Declaration on the Rights of Persons Belonging to National or Ethnic, Religious and Linguistic Minorities. Overall, Topidi argues that the case represented a (re)-pluralization of state law that reflects increasing legal pluralism. She notes that, in Greece, the size of 'New Islam' has now overtaken that of the historic Muslim communities, a situation demanding solutions to diversity management such as interreligious dialogue that may even require a formalized public engagement framework.

Picking up the thread of the impact of new religious minorities, Christos Tsevas examines the *Molla Sali* judgment in light of the mixed migration flows into Greece and Europe. He argues for an interactive approach to different normative systems at the national, European, and international levels that would include both traditional and modern instruments. Tsevas also highlights the other pillar on which the ECtHR decision on *Molla Sali* rests: non-discrimination. On the basis of its previous case law, the ECtHR ruled that "freedom of religion does not require the contracting states to create a particular legal framework in order to grant religious communities a special status entailing specific privileges. Nevertheless, a State which has created such status must ensure that the criteria established for a group's entitlement to it are applied in a non-discriminatory manner".[10]

The balancing of these two elements – freedom of choice and non-discrimination – requires further considerations.

First, the primacy of individual freedom: when, in the same geographical space defined by the boundaries of a nation State, more than one legal order coexists, the individual enjoys absolute freedom to make his/her choice between the different available options, irrespective of the religion in which he/she has been born or the religion he/she professes at the time of the choice. A Jew may, if he/she so wishes, celebrate a marriage according to Jewish law and this marriage, under certain conditions, will also have value for the State; but the fact that bride and groom are Jewish should not prevent them, if they so wish, from celebrating a civil marriage. If a State decides to provide

9 *Ibid.*, at 29.

10 See Chapter 2 by C. Tsevas in this volume, at 141.

public school students with the option of choosing between different dietary regimes – kosher, halal, vegetarian, etc. – in school canteens, each student should be able to opt for his or her preferred regime. No one should demand that they show a certificate to prove their affiliation to a religious group in order to gain access to specific foods.

Second, as discussed in the volume, the ECrtHR decision in the *Molla Sali v. Greece* case clearly states that the principle of non-discrimination is the limit to the State's recognition of legal pluralism. This conclusion is usually taken for granted, but if individual freedom is given due weight, additional questions arise. The ECrtHR decision does not consider whether there is a difference between individuals who are *deprived* of a right against their will and thus discriminated against and others who *renounce* that right and, as a result of this choice, are in the same objective (but not subjective) legal situation as the former. Does the principle of non-discrimination also apply to an individual who, by a free and conscious decision, renounces his or her own right, thereby placing himself or herself in a legal position which is detrimental when compared to that of other citizens? And if this question is answered in the affirmative, does not the very essence of legal pluralism, which consists of the right of every person to choose among different possibilities of regulating a legal relationship, end up being thwarted? The answer usually given to the latter question is that legal pluralism cannot be without limits and that there are inalienable rights, which the person who holds them cannot renounce. But this category of rights should be handled with caution since it implies a restriction of individual freedom.[11]

As the discussions in this book demonstrate, the issue of balancing the freedom of choice and non-discrimination has a longer history, with legacies from colonial and imperial pasts. However, concern for the Muslim question that was once a geopolitical affair is now also an internal concern that strikes at the stability and cohesion of European society.[12] The dilemma of balancing freedom of choice and non-discrimination was very much present in 2010 in France at the time of the introduction of the law that prohibited walking in public spaces with a covered face, commonly referred to as the anti-burqa law.[13] Faced with both the objection of some Muslim women who claimed that

11 Giorgio Maniaci argues that "an individual's freedom can be restricted without needing to state: "You must not do X" or "It is forbidden to do X", but instead assigning him or her a right. It is enough to make this right inalienable". G. Maniaci, "La dittatura dei diritti indisponibili", (2014) 14(14) *Diritto & Questioni Pubbliche* 669–710, at 669.

12 E. Pace, "Religious Minorities in Europe: A Memory Mutates", (2021) 12 *Religions* 1–13.

13 See A. Ferrari and S. Pastorelli (eds.), *The Burqa Affair Across Europe: Between Public and Private Space* (London and New York, Routledge, 2016).

they wanted to wear the burqa and the impossibility of declaring that their decision was the result of an imposition, the French Council of State declared that women's self-determination is irrelevant. The Council of State ruled that even in the case where the decision to wear the burqa was made freely and consciously, these women were in an objective "situation of exclusion and inferiority that is clearly incompatible with the constitutional principles of freedom and equality".[14] This conclusion is tantamount to saying that Muslim women must be protected from themselves, a very contentious statement which some might consider dangerous: do not Catholic nuns in a cloistered convent (or similar figures found in other religions) place themselves in a situation of objective exclusion or inferiority when they give up their freedom of movement, communication, and dress?

However, the *Molla Sali* case is different since the application of Islamic law had been carried out against the woman's will. Still, how should we deal with the possible scenario of a Muslim woman who asks for Islamic law to be applied to the determination of her inheritance shares knowing full well that in doing so her share will be less than what she would be given if State law had been applied, nevertheless, believing that, in the words of the Latin aphorism *magis oportet oboedire Deo quam hominibus* (we ought to obey God rather than man)? Should the State authorities merely ascertain that the woman's decision is free, informed and conscious, or should they prevent *tout court* that the woman's request be granted?

These questions are also the focus of Elham Manea's contribution on legal pluralism in the United Kingdom and the application of Islamic law. From a gender and human rights perspective, she shows how women in closed communities within the State face particular challenges in accessing the British legal system. The common thread of this contribution is the need to protect women, and Muslim women in particular: many of whom have unregistered religious marriages and therefore cannot enjoy the protection provided by State law to married women as these marriages are legally nonexistent. Manea explains how the United Kingdom is considering measures that would make "civil marriage before or during a religious marriage mandatory".[15] Imams, "who fail to ensure the civil registration, will face legal consequences".[16] These proposed measures not only address obstacles to integration for minority communities but also recognize how this soft legal pluralism may disproportionately affect women and girls.

---

14 French Council of State, Decision no. 2010-613, 7 October 2010, in *Journal Officiel*.

15 See Chapter 3 by E. Manea in this volume, at 71.

16 *Ibid.*, at 71.

Here is another situation that raises the question of whether Muslim women should be protected or be placed in a position to consciously and freely make the choices they see fit for their lives, including those choices that are not shared by the majority of a country's population? In other words, is the task of the State to act on behalf of Muslim women in making these choices, or to ensure that these choices are made freely, consciously, and informedly? Manea points out many of the women's rights groups, including groups and individuals with Muslim heritage, that work to raise awareness to problems in the soft parallel legal system that exists in Britain.[17] There remain many social constraints that make it difficult for Muslim women to make these kinds of choices, but I remain convinced that in the long run the solution lies not in their protection but in their empowerment through processes of cultural, social and economic promotion that are certainly long-term but just as surely more effective than legislative interventions.

Freedom of choice and secular default option. Various chapters in the volume take up secularism as a category through which religious accommodations are debated. Westreich and Westreich's chapter is devoted to Israeli family law, a sphere where religious courts and laws interact with secular civil courts and laws. The two authors point out that "religious law and religious courts are an intensive presence in legal family matters" although "their influence is not absolute".[18] There is an ongoing process aimed at "limiting the jurisdiction of rabbinical courts, limiting the scope of Jewish law as applied in certain family matters, and integrating liberal aspects to the interpretation of Jewish religious law by secular civil courts".[19] However, these limited transformations of Israeli family law do not affect the exclusive jurisdiction of the rabbinical courts which "is imposed by law and cannot be changed at the will of the parties. This is the case in matters of marriage and divorce, in which Jewish religious law applies".[20] This finding leads to the identification of a second element that individual freedom introduces in the search for the correct balance between equality and diversity that forms the basis of sustainable legal pluralism: the need for a secular alternative to the religious choices allowed by the legal system. As a response to the legal pluralism of Israel, there is widespread practice of 'forum-shopping' between religious and secular courts, as Parilli explains in her chapter. This has been especially important for women in matters of family law who seek "to bypass the patriarchal religious codes applied by religious

17 *Ibid.*, at 67.

18 See Chapter 4 by E. Westreich and A. Westreich in this volume, at 154.

19 *Ibid.*, at 172.

20 *Ibid.*, at 153.

tribunals".[21] Parilli reveals additional shortcomings of the absence of civil marriage in Israel as there are immigrants who may acquire citizenship under the secular Law of Return but whose 'Jewishness' is contested by religious authorities; these individuals may be unable to marry.[22]

Without the secular default option of a civil marriage (which as noted earlier should be open to all citizens, Jews included), the Israeli system of legal pluralism remains inescapably flawed. This point has been clearly made by the United Nations Human Rights Committee when examining the legal systems of countries as diverse as Israel, Egypt or Indonesia, whose citizens do not have the right to celebrate a civil marriage. They can only choose between the different forms of celebration (and regulation) of marriage provided by the religions recognized in the country (unless they resort to dubious strategies such as the recognition at home of a civil marriage celebrated abroad or the establishment of a de facto marriage). Failure to allow a civil marriage celebration, concluded the UN Human Rights Committee, entails a violation of article 19 of the International Covenant on Civil and Political Rights which upholds "the right to freedom of thought, conscience and religion implies that the legislation of each State should provide for the possibility of both religious and civil marriages".[23] The same point was made by the United Nations Special Rapporteur on Freedom of Religion and Belief, Asma Jahangir. In her 2009 report following a country visit to Israel, she stressed the discriminatory aspect inherent in not providing the possibility of celebrating a civil marriage that would be recognized by the State: "The Special Rapporteur would like to emphasize that freedom of religion or belief also includes theistic, non-theistic and atheistic beliefs as well as the right not to profess any religion or belief. In order to prevent any discrimination based on religion or belief, the State should provide a civil alternative for those who are currently ineligible for marriage in Israel".[24] The Israeli example reveals the role of international institutions in addressing weaknesses of national frameworks that fail to protect not only religious minorities but also non-religious groups.

---

21 See Chapter 5 by A. Parrilli in this volume, at 187.

22 *Ibid.*, at 192.

23 UN Human Rights Committee (HRC), CCPR General Comment No. 19: Article 23 (The Family) Protection of the Family, the Right to Marriage and Equality of the Spouses, 27 July 1990, n. 4, available at: https://www.refworld.org/docid/45139bd74.html [accessed 24 January 2020] n. 4. U.N. DOC. HRI/GEN/1/Rev.1 at 28 (1994).

24 A. Jahangir, *Report of the Special Rapporteur on freedom of religion or belief*, Addendum – Mission to Israel and the Occupied Palestinian Territory, 12 January 2009, n. 46 (A/HRC/10/8/Add.2). See also H. Bielefeldt, *Report of the Special Rapporteur on freedom of religion or belief*, Addendum – Mission to Jordan, 27 January 2014, n. 72 e 74 (A/HRC/25/58/Add.2).

Freedom of choice and agreements between States and religious minorities. The last three contributions touch on the issue of the freedom to choose between equality and diversity in a more indirect but equally significant way. They concern two countries, Italy and Russia, that have different religious and cultural backgrounds but are linked by the presence of an old and relatively strong majority church. The dominance of the Russian Orthodox Church, as Kascian and Vasilevich argue, has led to its influence in the implementation in Russia's migrant policies, specifically in assisting with cultural and social adaptation. This prominent work with migrants includes the preparation of integration materials that center "Christian values as the core of the Russian culture".[25] It is not always easy to reconcile this fact with the respect for the different religious identities of migrants.

The chapters devoted to Italy written by Francesco Alicino and Alessandro Ferrari deal with an issue that also arises in many other countries: managing the diversifying of the religious landscape. Religious pluralism has been "caused not only by the proliferation of different confessions" but also by the "increased presence of three new categories: unaffiliated believers; believers who, although they remain faithful to their denominational religion, adopt forms of personal spirituality; and nonreligious people who assert patent claims against the public role of religions".[26] Indeed, many European countries find it difficult to include the 'new religious minorities' and their organizations, particularly, but not exclusively, those emerging from migration flows from Muslim-majority countries in their national legal systems.[27]

Recognition of religious organizations is a thorny and prominent topic in the regulation of relations between States and religions, attracting the attention of scholars and international organizations.[28] There is agreement that the protection that international law grants religious organizations does not depend on whether they have been recognized by the State and thereby enjoy legal personality. Thus, according to international and human rights law, unrecognized and unregistered religious organizations are entitled to the same rights of liberty, autonomy, and self-administration as those enjoyed by those

25 See Chapter 8 by K. Kascian and H. Vasilevich in this volume, at 219.

26 See Chapter 6 by F. Alicino in this volume, at 78.

27 J. Marko, M- Lakitsch, F.Winter, and K.Wonisch (eds.), *Religious Diversity, State, and Law. National, Transnational and International Challenges* (Leiden, Brill-Nijhoff, 2022).

28 OSCE-ODIHR, *Guidelines on the Legal Personality of Religious or Belief Communities* (Warsaw, OSCE-ODIHR, 2014).

which are recognized and registered.[29] Further, the principles underlying the freedom of religion and association include the right of every religious organization to obtain legal personality. States should therefore ensure that access to legal personality should not be more difficult for religious or belief organizations than for other categories of groups or communities.[30] However, domestic legislation does not always respect, and often even openly contradicts, these standards.

Yet, international law leaves States free to establish their own system of relationships with religious organizations. In Italy, as in Portugal, Spain, Hungary, Croatia and other countries, the conclusion of agreements between State and religious organizations is the main legal instrument through which religious organizations participate in the definition of their legal status. These agreements have been effective in securing a number of rights for traditional religious minorities but are less effective in relation to minority communities – the Muslim, Protestant evangelical, and humanistic ones in particular – that have developed in recent decades due to migration. This is due to the fact that entering into agreements requires "a relatively comprehensive religious institution capable of representing a denomination at the national level",[31] a centralizing structure that many of the 'new religious minorities' do not have (and in some cases do not even want to create). Alicino therefore concludes that the system of agreements appears functional "to traditional Judeo-Christian denominations", but much less so "for other minority groups, other than the traditional ones".[32] This lack of capacity to include religions outside of the Judeo-Christian tradition in the legal system surfaces a serious challenge going forward for States dealing with increasing pluralism in Europe stemming from migration flows. A good example of these challenges is offered in Ferrari's chapter, which points out how, in order to gain a legal status, "Muslim associations see no other way of bridging the gap between themselves and (generically) private associations than to 'camouflage' their religious identity".[33] This path risks further exclusion of Muslims in particular from the public sphere and may reinforce their marginalization. In addition, the Italian case demonstrates

29 UN Human Rights Committee, *CCPR General Comment No. 22: Article 18 (Freedom of Thought, Conscience or Religion)*. (1993) CCPR/C/21/Rev.1/Add.4. Available online: https://www.refworld.org/docid/453883fb22.html.

30 OSCE-ODIHR, *Guidelines on the Legal Personality of Religious or Belief Communities*, at 19.

31 See Chapter 6 by F. Alicino in this volume, at 85.

32 *Ibid.*, at 86.

33 See Chapter 7 by A. Ferrari in this volume, at 117–118.

how States operate with a wide margin of discretion in defining the system of recognition or registration that best suits their traditions and needs.[34]

What to do, then? I would point out, first of all, that the legal problems posed by the 'new religious minorities' are by no means a new phenomenon. The social transformations prompted by interactions between 'new' and 'old' religious minorities have a long history, particularly in Europe.[35] The various Jewish communities were as jealous of their independence as are, today, the Muslim or Protestant evangelical communities. However, this tradition of independence did not prevent them from creating unions, federations or other bodies capable of concluding agreements with the state. The problems posed by the 'new religious minorities' related to food rules, festive days of rest, and religious symbols were faced and, in many cases, resolved long before recent migration flows caused Muslim and Protestant evangelical communities to grow in many European countries. Also, the claims of atheistic groups go back at least two centuries. These historical examples offer some hints on the way forward in squaring the circle in order to accommodate religious needs and build stable societies.

At least in part, therefore, it is a matter of time. Yet, this call for patience does not detract from the need to adapt the agreement system to new exigencies, which involves limiting the discretionary power enjoyed by public authorities in deciding whether and when to enter into agreements, extending them to atheistic groups, and seeking a better "balance between universal principles of liberal constitutionalism and ethnic-cultural-religious differences".[36] The other path, which is not an alternative to the first, is the one indicated by Ferrari drawing from the example of the management of the 'Muslim Question' in Italy. In the concluding part of his chapter, he suggests that these reforms be accompanied by legislative interventions that broaden the base of rights recognised to the religious communities that cannot or do not want to enter into agreements with the state.

This last suggestion deserves careful consideration. The right to be different requires, in order to be sustainable, that the right to be equal is guaranteed, that is, that there is a broad and solid platform of rights that are assured to all religious groups, large and small, old and new. This is precisely what is lacking in countries such as Italy, where the conclusion of agreements between the State and some religious minorities has shortened the distance between them

34 S. Ferrari, K.Wonisch, and R.Medda-Windischer, "Tying the Knot" *supra.*

35 M. Ventura (ed.), *The legal status of old and new religious minorities in the European Union* (Granada, Comares, 2021).

36 See Chapter 6 by F. Alicino in this volume, at 104.

and the majority church but has at the same time widened the gulf separating them from all other minorities left without an agreement.

This book has arrived in a moment of greater urgency surrounding the question of managing religious diversity in light of migration. Data provided by the *Atlas of religious or belief minorities*, a mapping tool of rights enjoyed by religious minorities, confirm that this is the new fault line that has been created among religious minorities in EU countries.[37] Among the findings from Atlas, it emerges that "Christian minorities generally enjoy more rights than non-Christian minorities" and that there is no EU country where religious minorities enjoy the same rights as the country's majority religion. If these gaps are not bridged, the risk of dangerous friction becomes high. To this end, it is incumbent on States to eliminate any differences in the treatment of majority and minority religions as well as to avoid a selective approach to minority issues that may favor the protection and promotion of the rights of some religious groups over others.

As the chapters in this volume make clear, the reconciliation of the demands of religious diversity and equal rights remains an unsettled and contentious process that has entered a new phase in light of recent migration flows. The empirical approach of the contributions of this book reveals the many actors and factors at play that shape the conditions for the careful deliberations, negotiations, and agreements that are needed to foster a sense of common belonging, unity, and respect for diversity. Further research can continue to address this salient challenge for societies and unpack these processes of engagement. In doing so, a greater balance between diversity and equality can be achieved.

Bibliography

Bielefeldt, H., *Report of the Special Rapporteur on Freedom of Religion or Belief*, Addendum – Mission to Jordan, 27 January 2014, n. 72 e 74 (A/HRC/25/58/Add.2).

Binderup, L., "Liberal Equality – from Minority Rights to the Limits of Tolerance. in the Rights and Plights of Religious Minorities", (2007) 4(2) *Res Cogitans* 95–109.

Ferrari, S., Wonisch, K., and Medda-Windischer, R. "Tying the Knot: a Holistic Approach to the Enhancement of Religious Minority Rights and Freedom of Religion", (2021) 12 *Religions* 1–17.

37 Atlas of Religious or Belief Minority Rights, accessed 13 September 2023, http://www.atlasminorityrights.eu.

Ferrari, A. and S. Pastorelli (eds.), *The Burqa Affair Across Europe: Between Public and Private Space* (London and New York, Routledge, 2016).

French Council of State, Decision no. 2010-613, 7 October 2010, in *Journal Officiel*.

Jahangir, A., *Report of the Special Rapporteur on freedom of religion or belief*, Addendum – Mission to Israel and the Occupied Palestinian Territory, 12 January 2009, n. 46 (A/HRC/10/8/Add.2).

Maniaci, G., "La dittatura dei diritti indisponibili", (2014) 14(14) *Diritto & Questioni Pubbliche* 669–710.

Marko J., Lakitsch M., Winter F., and Wonisch K. (eds.), *Religious Diversity, State, and Law. National, Transnational and International Challenges* (Leiden, Brill-Nijhoff, 2022).

Modood, T., and T. Sealy. "Freedom of Religion and the Accommodation of Religious Diversity: Multiculturalising Secularism", (2021) 12 *Religions* 1–14.

OSCE-ODIHR, *Guidelines on the Legal Personality of Religious or Belief Communities* (Warsaw: OSCE-ODIHR, 2014).

Pace, E., "Religious Minorities in Europe: a Memory Mutates", (2021) 12 *Religions* 1–13.

UN Human Rights Committee, *CCPR General Comment No. 22: Article 18 (Freedom of Thought, Conscience or Religion)*, (1993) CCPR/C/21/Rev.1/Add.4, available at: https://www.refworld.org/docid/453883fb22.html.

Van der Ven, J. A., "Religious Rights for Minorities in a Policy of Recognition", (2008) 3 *Religion and Human Rights* 155–183.

Ventura, M. (ed.), *The Legal Status of Old and New Religious Minorities in the European Union* (Granada, Comares, 2021).

Index

www.ingramcontent.com/pod-product-compliance
Lightning Source LLC
LaVergne TN
LVHW020635300926
849161LV00004B/713